Ultimate Trout Fishing
in the Pacific Northwest

Ultimate
Trout Fishing
in the Pacific Northwest

Larry E. Stefanyk,
with various contributors

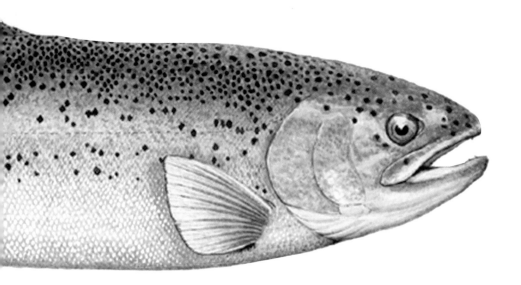

Harbour Publishing

Harbour Publishing Co. Ltd.

P.O. Box 219, Madeira Park, BC, V0N 2H0

www.harbourpublishing.com

Edited by Dr. Adipose Huxley and Scott Steedman
Cover photograph of a jumping steelhead on the Dean River, BC, by Keith Douglas, All Canada Photos.
Text design by Roger Handling
Cover design by Anna Comfort
Indexed by Marysia McGilvray
Printed and bound in Canada

Caution: Every effort has been made to ensure the reader's awareness of the hazards and level of expertise
involved in the activities in this book, but your own safety is ultimately up to you. The authors and publisher
take no responsibility for loss or injury incurred by anyone using this book.

 Canada Council   Conseil des Arts
for the Arts   du Canada

 BRITISH COLUMBIA
ARTS COUNCIL
An agency of the Province of British Columbia

Harbour Publishing acknowledges financial support from the Government of Canada through the
Canada Book Fund and the Canada Council for the Arts, and from the Province of British Columbia
through the BC Arts Council and the Book Publishing Tax Credit.

Library and Archives Canada Cataloguing in Publication

Stefanyk, Larry E.

       Ultimate Trout fishing in the Pacific Northwest / by Larry E. Stefanyk.

Includes index.

ISBN 978-1-55017-548-6

       1. Trout fishing—Northwest, Pacific. I. Title.

SH688.N74S74 2011   799.17'5709795   C2011-900562-X

To my best friend, who has supported me in all of my endeavors for years: my lovely wife, Janice.

Contents

Introduction

I first met Larry E. Stefanyk at *BC Outdoors* and *BC Sports Fishing* magazines. I was editor. He was in sales. Both of us were into fishing.

The office of the magazine was in downtown Vancouver, on Beatty Street. Our residences, however, remained on Vancouver Island. Lawrence (as I call him, much to his chagrin) lived in Parksville with his lovely wife Janice and I lived in Campbell River. That awkward commuting arrangement was good for one thing—long talks on the ferry from the mainland to the island, and back again.

Lawrence was mad about fishing. So mad in fact that I thought Janice might be equally as mad, although with a different application of the word. I soon found out that they both loved fishing and anything to do with fishing. The only thing she got mad about with Lawrence's fishing was when he went without her.

It wasn't long before Lawrence picked up on a niche that needed filling. He became the founder and publisher of *Island Fisherman* magazine, which he now publishes out of Campbell River seven times a year with a healthy distribution and an ardent following of readers. I soon returned as Publisher and Editor of the Campbell River *Courier-Islander* newspaper, something I have done lovingly, off and on, for over twenty years.

Lawrence fishing Spider Lake on Vancouver Island.

During that time at *BC Outdoors*, we were both greatly influenced by the late Bob Jones. His books, magazines and other published titles, both as editor and writer, and his incredible capacity for good single malt, left us in awe. We both owe him a debt we can't repay. Except, of course, with a book like this.

Bob would have loved it. He would have picked out small details we may have missed here and there. He would have suggested a sharper pen for both editor and writer. He would have growled about the layout, barked about deadlines and complained about style points. But he also would have come upon sections of the book and, while tugging his famous white beard, said, "Mmmmm, that's interesting. I didn't know that."

I think that's what Lawrence wanted and I think that's what Lawrence has achieved. In this book I am sure you too will stop and say, "Mmmmm, that's interesting. I didn't know that."

And if it helps you catch an extra trout or two, I think that would please Lawrence even more.

Dr. Adipose Huxley
November 7, 2010

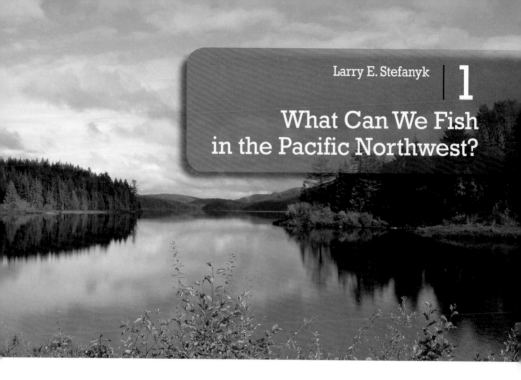

Larry E. Stefanyk | 1

What Can We Fish in the Pacific Northwest?

British Columbia contains more than 12,000 miles (20,000 km) of coastlines, 25,000 lakes and tens of thousands of miles of rivers and streams, which are home to more than eighty species of freshwater or sea-run wild native fish, and many of which support an impressive array of recreation angling opportunities for which the province is world-renowned.

Apple Point on Brewster Lake near Campbell River, BC.

Our freshwaters are also home to non-native fish species that have been introduced across the province to create new and augment existing fisheries.

Whatever method you use to fish, you can fish here and have spectacular results. Depending, of course, on regulations.

Fly-fishing, spin fishing, single-action casting or bait fishing—it's all here.

Small rainbow trout caught on a black knat fly.

Species include:

TROUT	CHAR
Brown	Dolly Varden
Rainbow	**SALMON**
Steelhead	Kokanee
Brook	Coho
Bull	Pink
Lake	Chinook
Coastal Cutthroat	Chum
Westslope Cutthroat	Sockeye

The main keys are: identify your species, identify your methods, make sure they are within regulations and, finally, enjoy.

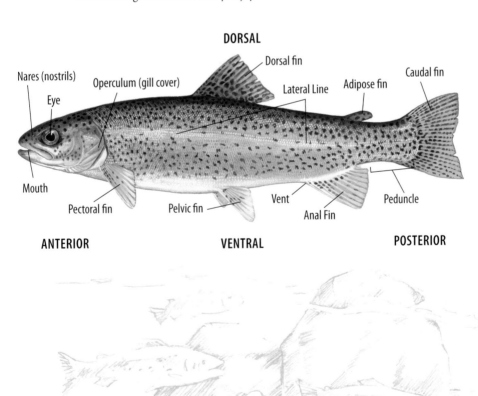

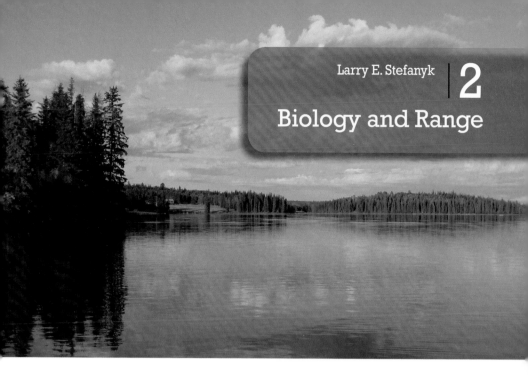

2A: Rainbow and Steelhead Trout

Rainbow Trout

Small black spots mostly restricted to above the lateral line

Radiating rows of spots on tail

No teeth in throat at back of tongue

Kingdom: Animalia
Phylum: Chordata
Lass: Actinopterygii
Order: Salmoniformes
Family: Salmonidae

Genus: *Oncorhynchus*
Species: *O. mykiss*
Common names: Kamloops trout, Gerrard trout, coast rainbow trout, redband trout, redsides, Pacific trout, steelhead, silver trout

These highly regarded freshwater game fish are indigenous to the Pacific slopes, from California to Alaska. This trout is a species of salmonids native to tributaries of the Pacific Ocean in North America. The oceangoing (anadromous) forms (including those that return for spawning) are known as steelhead.

Rainbow trout is a species of North America salmonids native to tributaries of the Pacific Ocean.

The species was originally named by Johann Julius Walbaum in 1792, based on type specimens from the Kamchatka Peninsula. Dr. Meredith Richardson named a specimen of this species *Salmo gairdneri* in 1836, after a naturalist in the employ of the Hudson's Bay Company, and in 1855, W.P. Gibbons found a population and named it *Salmo iridia*, later corrected to *Salmo irideus*; however, these names became deprecated once it was determined that Walbaum's type description was conspecific and therefore had precedence (see e.g., Behnke, 1966). More recently, DNA studies showed that rainbow trout are genetically closer to Pacific salmon (*Onchorhynchus* species) than to brown trout (*Salmo trutta*) or Atlantic salmon (*Salmo salar*), so the genus was changed.

Unlike the species' former epithet *iridia* (Latin for "rainbow"), the specific epithet *mykiss* derives from the Kamchatkan place name Mykizha; all of Walbaum's species names were based on Kamchatkan names.

In British Columbia rainbows can vary greatly in appearance, depending on their watershed. Color varies according to size and habitat; the back and upper sides may be bluish or greenish, the sides and belly

Rainbow trout showing different watershed colors.

silvery in some fish or yellowish-green in certain young found in streams or rivers. They may be heavily spotted on the back, sides, dorsal fin, caudal fin and sometimes the base of the anal fin. The adipose fin can have spots that often form a black border around the edges. The dorsal, anal and pelvic fins often have white or orange on the leading edge. Their color is silvery overall, often with a pinkish to reddish band along the lateral line. The tail is slightly forked, but more forked in juveniles. During spawning, bodies darken to a smoky-gray hue.

Rainbows occupy many different types of ecosystems, including large and small lakes and rivers and streams. More *silvery* colors are the norm for lake residents and are usually found in deeper, colder water, from 55 to 65°F (12 to 18°C), with adequate shallows and vegetation for good food production. Rainbows enjoy a varied diet, readily engulfing worms and all types of terrestrial and aquatic insects, fish eggs and even small birds and mammals. They vary considerably in size, depending mainly on their life history and food base. Resident trout in rivers tend to be smaller than trout that feed in richer lakes; a 12-inch (30-cm) fish is a good catch. Some of the larger-lake rainbows can range from 5 to 10 lb (2.3 to 4.5 kg). Most stream- and river-dwelling rainbows acquire their nutrition from insects and are therefore a perfect target for fly fishers, as they inhabit riffles, pools, areas below waterfalls, undercut banks and brush and current breaks behind boulders—all habitats that provide their two essentials, food and cover.

Salmon Lake on the Douglas Lake Ranch near Kamloops, BC.

Male rainbow trout showing pink cheeks and reddish strip.

Lake anglers often find excellent dry fly action, but at times must resort to deeply sunken nymph patterns; lures are normally trolled rather than cast. Larger lakes that are known to harbor big fish usually call for hefty rods and reels reminiscent of salmon gear. To anglers, the definitive characteristics of rainbows, particularly the males, are the pink "cheeks" and the prominent pink-to-reddish stripe on the sides. Rainbows that eat fish can reach a larger size, like the legendary Gerrard strain of Kamloops, a trout native to the Kootenays, where reports of fish as large as 56 pounds (25 kg; Jewel Lake, near Greenwood, 1913) appear authentic.

The temperature tolerance of rainbow trout is from 32 to over 80°F (below 0 to 26°C), with the preferred level below 70°F (21°C). In lakes, rainbows may be found near the surface, but as the upper layers warm, they tend to seek a level between 56.5 and 60°F (13 to 15.5°C). Lake rainbows enter streams to spawn in spring. Lakes without streams, however, rarely support sustainable populations of these trout. Vancouver Island populations of rainbow trout spawn from January to June and later in some cold-water lakes at high elevations. In the wild, they can be divided practically rather than scientifically into coastal, migratory and freshwater pure strains. Unlike other trout, rainbows are a mixture of different lineages and behaviors with a tendency to crossbreed when they can. Spawning time differs widely among strains and races, with barely any part of the year not being a spawning time for resident rainbows.

Bait is a very popular choice of fishermen everywhere as rainbows find worms almost irresistible. They can also be enticed with roe and even a few less-than-natural baits such as cheese, miniature marshmallows or corn kernels. You may use freshwater invertebrates (e.g., aquatic insects and crayfish) in streams as bait unless a bait ban applies. But when fishing in a lake, you may not possess or use for bait any aquatic invertebrate; this includes the aquatic stage of any insect, such as dragonfly nymphs or caddis fly larvae. Rainbow trout are also drawn to spinners, plugs and spoons in a variety of sizes and colors and will readily take a wide variety of wet and dry flies. Basically, flies are either attractors that appeal to the trout's aggressive reflexes or imitators that mimic natural prey.

Freshwater Fisheries Society of BC

gofishbc.com

Freshwater Fisheries Society crew preparing to stock another lake.

The Hatchery Program in British Columbia

Trout have been cultured in British Columbia for about a hundred years and are now managed by the Freshwater Fisheries Society of BC (FFSBC), whose mandate is "to conserve, restore and enhance the freshwater fish resources of British Columbia for the benefit of the public." The FFSBC is striving to implement stocking programs that support this mandate and has developed specific strains of rainbow trout for stocking programs. The FFSBC stocks five fish species or subspecies for recreational angling purposes in BC lakes; these include rainbow trout/steelhead, coastal cutthroat trout, westslope cutthroat trout, kokanee and eastern brook trout. The majority of lake stocking is with rainbow trout, and the FFSBC has developed a number of special strains of rainbow trout depending on lake environment and/or desired fishery.

Some 6,327,961 trout were released in 783 water bodies in British Columbia in 2010 and as many as 1,300 lakes have been stocked with rainbows over the last few years. Some of the lakes in British Columbia have been stocked with strains based strictly on wild populations; the Blackwater River rainbow trout, Pennask Lake rainbow trout and Tzenzaicut Lake rainbow trout are naturalized "native" populations. The other stocked trout is the Fraser Valley domesticated rainbow trout.

Pennask Lake Rainbow Trout

They are mid-water foragers that feed primarily on benthic organisms such as chironomid pupae and are most active at dusk and in the dark, as they prefer deep, open water. They are lightly spotted on the body and are generally small at maturity. When hooked they are good jumpers and have a reputation for being very aggressive.

Pennask Lake rainbow trout can be very aggressive.

Blackwater River Rainbow Trout

They are shoal foragers preferring to feed in shallow water and are active during the day. They prefer larger prey such as dragonfly nymphs, snails, leeches and small non-salmonidae fish. They are highly piscivorous (relying mainly on fish for food) at maturity and are fast-growing and more heavily spotted than the Pennask strain. Because they are aggressive, shallow-water foragers, anglers find them easier to target. This attribute and their fast growth make them highly sought after.

Blackwater River rainbow trout are shallow-water foragers.

Tzenzaicut Lake Rainbow Trout

These trout prefer to forage in open water, like the Pennask strain, but tend to be far more piscivorous, preying on juvenile non-salmonidae fish, and are most active at dusk. They thrive in cold water in low-productivity systems containing a wide range of non-salmonidae fish species. At maturity they may have yellow-tinged sides,

Ten-pound (4.5 kg) Tzenzaicut rainbow trout caught at Watch Lake by Angelo Piazzon using an olive leech pattern. Janice M. Stefanyk photo.

concentrated ventrally, quite similar to cutthroat trout. Mature adults take on a very dark red and yellow color. When hooked the fish is known to be a strong fighter that exhibits exceptional leaping abilities and recovers well upon being released.

This Gerrard rainbow was caught in December with Kootenay Kingfisher Charters at Arrow Lakes using a bucktail fly.

Fraser Valley domesticated rainbow trout grow fast and can achieve a relatively large size.

Stock reports designate triploid trout as 3N: an all-female non-reproductive population.

Gerrard Rainbow Trout

Gerrard rainbow are also piscivorous by nature, feeding primarily on kokanee salmon. They will follow the kokanee migration into lakes, feeding in cold, deep, open waters during the summer months and closer to the surface during the winter. A large strain, they reach 20 lb (9 kg) for the males and 15 lb (7 kg) for the females, and a 35.5-lb (16.2-kg) individual has been taken.

Fraser Valley Domesticated Rainbow Trout

These trout start by eating artificial food and once released will adopt a wild diet of various invertebrates. They grow fast and achieve a relatively large size when stocked in productive lakes. They are heavily spotted on tail and body, above and below the lateral line and on the caudal fin. Not normally jumpers, they will still put up a good fight.

The stock reports are available at www.gofishbc. com.

The symbols in the report for species are: RB-Rainbow trout; CT-Cutthroat trout (land locked); ACT-Anadromous cutthroat trout (sea-run); ST-Steelhead; EBT-Eastern Brook; KO-Kokanne and WCT-Westslope cutthroat.

The symbols AF3N and 3N stand for an all-female population. This is done by testosterone derivatives to halt ovary development and produce normal testes. The benefits of an all-female stock include slower maturation, which leaves more time for the fishery and to grow larger fish. As there are no males, it is a non-reproductive population.

FFSBC has developed a special treatment to enhance the angling experience: triploidization and the creation of all-female stock. This is done by applying hydrostatic pressure shocking or hot water to the eggs shortly after fertilization. This technique results in the retention of the second polar body (normally extruded shortly after fertilization), creating three sets of chromosomes instead of the usual two. The result is sterility in both males and females. This increases size, because the energy that fish usually divert into reproduction goes instead into body growth.

Steelhead Trout

Kingdom: Animalia
Phylum: Chordata
Lass: Actinopterygii
Order: Salmoniformes
Family: Salmonidae
Genus: *Oncorhynchus*

Species: *O. mykiss*
Common names: Steelhead trout, coastal rainbow trout, salmon trout, hardhead, metalhead, halfpounder. Historically called steelhead-salmon.

This rainbow trout (*Oncorhynchus mykiss*) is a species of salmonid native to tributaries of the Pacific Ocean. The steelhead is a sea-run rainbow trout.

Historically called steelhead-salmon or salmon-trout, this sea-run form of the rainbow trout has the same general appearance, especially when young. The body shape is more streamlined and torpedo-like than the resident rainbow. When fresh from the sea, steelhead are usually a very bright silver. As they approach spawning, a pink to red lateral line appears over the gill cover; then the fish gradually darken to a dull gray.

Steelhead-salmon, or salmon-trout, is a sea-run form of the rainbow trout and has the same general appearance.

Steelhead trout occur along the entire coast of the Pacific Northwest. There are two distinct races, winter steelhead and summer steelhead, so named because of the season in which they enter their home streams to spawn. Winter steelhead enter freshwater in the fall and winter, summer-run steelhead enter in the spring and summer. The two runs are quite separate, as the fish differ in their state of maturation. Winter-run steelhead are almost fully mature when they enter freshwater and spawn shortly thereafter. In contrast, the summer-run fish are immature when they enter the rivers and spend up to eight months in freshwater before they spawn.

Different runs of steelhead as well as resident rainbow can occur in the same river. Adult steelheads spawn in gravel areas in the main rivers and tributaries and may return to spawn a second

In late June the summer-run steelhead makes its way into the rivers enlarged by runoff that the fish call home.
Rory Glennie photo

or even third time. The time spent in their home streams or rivers varies from one to five years, depending on stream temperature and food. Juvenile steelhead transform into smolts in the spring or early summer and then migrate to the sea. The smolts wait until they are two to four years old before they migrate to salt water. Once in the ocean they appear to move directly offshore. They return to freshwater after two to four years at sea on their initial spawning migration. They ascend their natal streams and hold (for up to six months) in deep pools containing an abundance of cover before spawning. Young steelhead eat invertebrates, crustaceans, insects and salmon eggs when available. At sea they feed primarily on fish, squid and scuds.

Summer steelhead have been known to feed when they enter their natal river or stream and can be induced to strike a lure or fly. When they move into streams

and rivers to spawn, their feeding slows but does not stop altogether; they will engulf drifting eggs, small fishes and a variety of aquatic insects. Winter steelhead feed rarely, but will ingest an object if it drifts past them. Of particular interest to anglers is the behavior of the steelhead once it enters streams and rivers on its way to the spawning grounds. In the stream environment, it behaves just like the native, stream-dwelling rainbow: it retires to riffles, pools, waterfalls, undercut banks and brush, boulders and other habitats that provide current breaks or cover.

Jay Mohl with a beautiful steelhead trout.

Usually the most critical factors to success are temperature and precipitation. Heavy fall and winter rains cause rivers to swell, bringing in many fresh, aggressive fish. Most anglers develop a feel for when the fish will start biting. Rain brings in the fish but usually they won't hit well when the rivers are too high and roily. When the rivers start to clear, the fishing peaks. A good knowledge of the rivers in your area will enable you to pick and choose the best spots. Some rivers clear up quickly, while others may take several days after a big storm. The timing of steelhead runs is more or less consistent from year to year, with some variations resulting from water levels. Many steelheaders fish the peaks of runs in various rivers, moving around to hit the strongest runs such as those in the Stamp, Gold and Cowichan rivers.

Gear for steelhead is necessarily heavier than for native rainbows. Migratory fish are quite a bit bigger in size and therefore require longer rods with much more backbone. West Coast anglers use dink floats, bottom-bouncing, back-trolling plugs or fly-fishing. Bait anglers use a variety of fresh, prepared or imitation roe in the single egg or roe bag form, depending on the conditions and regulations. Big river anglers will often fish out of river or jet boats, using a variety of floats with yarn flies and other roe imitations, plugs or spoons.

Few steelhead live longer than nine years. At that age they can weigh up to 44 lb (20 kg); the record size is 48 inches (120 cm) and 51.9 lb (23.6 kg).

Note: Be aware of bait bans in different river systems.

If you intend to fish for steelhead anywhere in BC (whether you intend to keep or release your catch) your license must have a Conservation Surcharge Stamp for steelhead. All wild steelhead must be released. The annual province-wide quota for hatchery steelhead is 10, and you must immediately record your retention of your hatchery steelhead on your basic angling license.

2B: Cutthroat Trout (sea-run and resident)

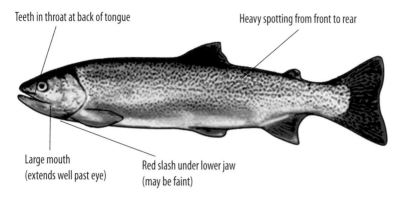

Teeth in throat at back of tongue

Heavy spotting from front to rear

Large mouth
(extends well past eye)

Red slash under lower jaw
(may be faint)

Kingdom: Animalia
Phylum: Chordata
Class: Actinopterygii
Order: Salmoniformes
Family: Salmonidae
Genus: *Oncorhynchus*

Species: *O. clarkii* (named after Captain William Clark of the Lewis and Clark expedition)
Common names: Red-throated trout, sea trout, yellowbellies, cutties, cutts, harvest trout

There are two basic life-history types, sea-run and freshwater-resident. Sea-runs are native to western North America and live primarily in the Pacific Ocean. As adults they return to freshwater in the late summer and early fall and head up the streams and rivers before the pink salmon migrate up the same systems. There they feed on salmon eggs and prepare to spawn. Freshwater residents live in lakes, streams or rivers throughout their lives and are known as non-migratory.

You can see why cutthroat are commonly called red-throated trout.

Cutthroat trout have irregular black spots evenly distributed on the front and back half of their body and differ from all other trout by having many spots all over the sides of the body, on the head and often on the belly and fins. Their coloration can range from golden to gray to dark green on their backs, olive-green on their sides and

silvery below, depending on subspecies and habitat. All populations have a distinctive red or orange slash along the inner edge of each half of the lower jaw, hence the common name, cutthroat trout. Unlike rainbow trout, cutthroat have small teeth at the base of their tongues. Sea-run (anadromous) fish may reach weights of 8 lb (3.6 kg) with an average length of 18 inches (45 cm), but those fish that remain permanently in freshwater may reach a weight of 15 lb (7 kg) and a length of 28 inches (70 cm); the average would be 16 inches (40 cm) and 2 lb (1 kg). As adults, different populations and subspecies of cutthroat can range from 6 to 30 inches (15 to 75 cm) in length, making size an ineffective indicator as to species.

This sea-run cutthroat trout may reach a weight of 8 lb (3.6 kg), but those fish that remain permanently in freshwater can be considerably larger. Frank Dalziel photo

Sea-run or coastal cutthroat can be found along the entire BC coast, including most coastal islands with suitable habitat and in practically all streams and lakes in the region. They rarely penetrate more than about than 100 miles (160 km) inland but enter virtually all of BC's rivers and streams to spawn in the Fraser River system up to Hope.

On the central and northern coast, cutthroat sometimes occur well inland. They prefer small, cool, clean, gravelly, lowland streams with relatively low gradients; some fish spawn in side channels if available. Sea-run populations spend from one to four

Cutthroat prefer inland lowland streams that are small, cool, clean and gravelly with relatively low gradients.

Opportunities for cutts are available in a larger number of lakes in the Pacific Northwest.

summers in freshwater before migrating to the sea. Studies have shown that cutthroat are primarily found in the smaller streams while larger streams are predominantly inhabited by steelhead trout and pink salmon. Where both species occur, cutthroat predominate in smaller tributaries and headwater reaches while steelhead occupy the lower reaches of the main stream.

Regardless of their age when they enter the sea, cutthroat return each fall to overwinter in freshwater. They have been found to return to the sea before the pink fry head back to the estuaries, where sea-run cutthroat are waiting for a meal. Unlike steelhead and other Pacific salmon, sea-runs do not make lengthy migrations out to sea. Generally speaking, they will remain in or near estuarine waters, usually within 5 to 10 miles (8 to 16 km) of their natal stream. Some cutthroat, however, have been shown to move as far as 70 miles (110 km) into the open ocean.

All coastal cutthroat are carnivorous. In estuaries or near shore, they move in and out with the tides as they forage on aphipods, isopods, shrimp and marine fishes including northern anchovy, kelp greenling, cabezon, rockfish and occasionally young salmonids. The non-migratory stream or lake residents feed on insect larvae and nymphs of aquatic insects and will take insects from the surface. Cutthroat become more piscivorous as they grow. Their diet often includes salmon fry, sticklebacks and sculpins. In larger lakes that support sockeye salmon, cutthroats prey on juvenile salmon. During salmon spawning season they will eat loose eggs. They can live to a maximum age of ten years but few actually survive long enough to spawn more than twice.

Cutthroat trout spawning apparently takes place in the spring three to five weeks after ice breakup and occurs in small gravelly streams. Some fish spend as many as four years in creeks before migrating to a lake. They are common in large lakes and

in small deep lakes and use all depths of the water table. If they share the system with rainbows they are usually found near cover. In lowland lakes on Vancouver Island and elsewhere along the BC coat, cutthroat are more common than rainbows and usually grow to a larger size. A lot of these systems also contain Dolly Varden, which shift into deeper water in the presence of cutthroat. Such cutthroat are usually about 12 inches (30 cm) long and weigh about 1 lb (500 g), but can grow to be as heavy as 10 lbs (4.5 kg) in some lakes. Cutthroat are hard fighters; they can be large, but usually do not leap and thrash as much as rainbows do. They will strike a wide selection of lures and flies.

The limits for cutthroat trout in tidal waters are as follows:

The prize we are all after: a beautiful cutthroat trout.

South of a line due west from Cape Caution (areas 11 to 29); wild trout: catch and release only. Hatchery trout: 2, none of which may be less than 12 inches (30 cm). North of a line due west from Cape Caution (areas 1 to 10); hatchery and wild trout: 2, only one of which may be greater than 20 inches (50 cm). None may be less than 30 cm.

This information can be found in the Finfish limits table under Trout:

http://www.pac.dfo-mpo.gc.ca/fm-gp/rec/species-especes/fintable-tableaupoisson-eng.htm

http://www.pac.dfo-mpo.gc.ca/fm-gp/rec/species-especes/trout-truite-eng.htm

A 12-inch (30-cm), stream-fooled cutthroat.

2C: Westslope Cutthroat Trout

Teeth in throat at back of tongue

Spots more numerous on posterior half of body

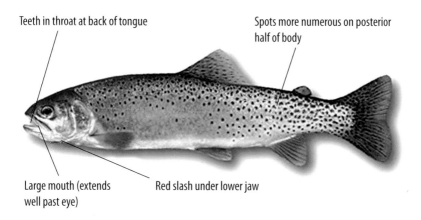

Large mouth (extends well past eye)

Red slash under lower jaw

Kingdom: Animalia	**Family:** Salmonidae
Phylum: Chordata	**Genus:** *Oncorhynchus*
Class: Actinopterygii	**Species:** *O. clarkii lewisi*
Order: Salmoniformes	**Common name:** Cutties

Westslope cutthroat are found along the western slope of the Rocky Mountains in the southeastern portion of the province. They can be found in the upper Kootenay and Pend d'Oreille river systems and their tributaries. They are also present in the Flathead River drainage system in the southeast corner of the province and in the upper Columbia River tributaries, upstream of Kinbasket Reservoir. A few isolated populations also exist in the Kootenays and the Okanagan Valley.

Westslope trout spawn throughout May and June. Photo Kelly Laatsch

On westslope cutthroat, the spots below the lateral line are concentrated on the back half of the body and are almost absent on the front half. In contrast, on coastal cutthroat trout, the irregular black spots below the lateral line are evenly distributed on the front and back halves of the body. All populations have a distinctive red or orange slash along the inner edge of each half of the lower jaw. One of the more striking differences between coastal and westslope cutthroat is their diet. The coastal strain is highly piscivorous while westslope are primarily insectivores, feeding on dipterans and mayflies; as they mature they add caddis fly nymphs and other insects like grasshoppers in August and September. Adults may have one of three different lifestyles: migrating between lakes and streams, fluvial migrating between main rivers and smaller streams, or remaining in either rivers or streams. These fish spawn in the spring (May through June) about three to five weeks after the ice breaks up. Eggs are laid and fertilized in a "redd," a gravel nest built by the female. In six or seven weeks, the eggs hatch and after another week or so the fry leave the redd and become free-swimming.

Westslope cutthroat may reach weights of 20 lb (9 kg) but an average size is ½ to 1 lb (300 to 500 g) with an average length of 12 to 14 inches (30 to 35 cm).

2D: Brown Trout

Black or brown spots, many with light halos

Adipose fin with spots

Tail with few or no spots

Kingdom: Animalia	**Binomial name:** *Salmo trutta*
Phylum: Chordata	Brown trout are closely related to Atlantic salmon
Class: Actinopterygii	(*Salmo salar*). The genus name, *Salmo*, is the Latin
Order: Salmoniformes	name for the Atlantic salmon, while the species
Family: Salmonidae	name, *trutta*, is Latin for trout.
Genus: *Salmo*	**Common names:** German brown, Loch Leven
Species: *S. trutta*	trout, English trout, river trout, sea trout, brownie.

The brown trout was an immigrant from Germany; the first shipment arrived in 1883 as eggs sent to a hatchery in Long Island, New York. The species also made its way to New Zealand and South America. The German fish bore the butter-colored sides, red and black spots and yellow flanks that identify a brown trout today. Variations among browns are due to environment differences rather than to genetic traits.

The brown trout from Scotland was brought to America in 1883 and is still sometimes classified as a Loch Leven brown. The Loch Leven trout is a still-water strain, silvery as salmon in certain seasons.

Brown trout were first introduced to Vancouver Island, in the Cowichan and Little Qualicum systems, in the 1930s, and later into the Kootenays. In 1980, they were introduced to both the Adams River and the Lower Eve River. These populations are well established, especially in the Cowichan River, and support a strong recreational fishery.

Cover is important to these trout, and they are more likely to be found where there are submerged rocks, undercut banks and overhanging vegetation. In flowing water, brown trout use pools, runs and riffles. They are quite sedentary with a relatively small home range. Brown trout is one of the most widespread species of trout in the salmon family. The reason for the brown's great success on Vancouver Island is that this fish can live in higher water temperatures than the other salmon or trout. Brown trout sometimes do not actively feed until the late afternoon or early evening but they are opportunistic feeders and when the weather is cool they will feed during the day as well.

A good-sized brown trout being properly released.

Biologists have noted that brown trout, especially the large ones, are considered to be "resistant to angling pressure." In plain English, these fish are smart. They have earned a reputation as the most difficult of all trout to catch. Once hooked, they break out into a spectacular battle with sudden runs, eye-popping jumps and an uncanny ability to wrap fishing line around sunken objects. The largest browns feed under cover of darkness. The diet will frequently include invertebrates from the streambed, small fish, frogs and insects flying near the water's surface. The high dietary reliance upon insect larvae, pupae, nymphs and adults makes browns a favored target for fly fishers. Brown trout can be caught with artificial flies, jigs, plastic worm imitations, spinners and other lures.

The brown trout is a medium-sized fish which does not usually exceed 16 inches (40 cm) in length. In many smaller rivers a mature weight of 2 lb (1 kg) or less is common. A brown trout over 10 lb (4.5 kg) is a trophy and may exceed 30 inches (75 cm).

Tom Healy with his record-breaking brown trout.

Tom Healy's Big Brown Trout

On September 11, 2009, Tom Healy caught a 41.45-lb (18.80-kg) brown trout in the Manistee river system in Michigan, setting a new state record and, possibly, a new world record for brown trout. As of late December 2009, the fish captured by Mr. Healy had been confirmed by both the International Game Fish Association and the Freshwater Fishing Hall of Fame, as the new all-tackle world record for the species.

The spawning behavior of brown trout is similar to that of the closely related Atlantic salmon. It spawns in the fall or early winter when the water temperature drops below 50°F (10°C). A typical female digs a nest about 2.5 to 4 inches (6 to 10 cm) deep, then hovers over it until a male comes alongside. The couple then release 100 to 200 eggs and sperm simultaneously into the nest. The female then moves upstream and rapidly digs at the upper edge of the nest to displace gravel downstream to cover the eggs. She then moves farther upstream and repeats the process. The number of eggs a female produces varies from a few hundred in stream populations to several thousand in larger fish. Incubation period is temperature-dependent and varies from 148 days at 36°F (2°C) to 38 days at 52°F (11°C). Most brown trout mature in their third or fourth year, females a year later, and they rarely live more than ten years.

2E: Brook Trout

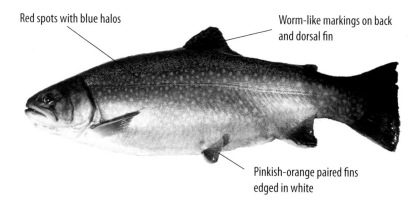

Red spots with blue halos

Worm-like markings on back and dorsal fin

Pinkish-orange paired fins edged in white

Kingdom: Animalia
Phylum: Chordata
Class: Actinopterygii
Order: Salmoniformes
Family: Salmonidae

Genus: *Salvelinus*
Species: *S. fontinalis*
Common names: Eastern brook trout, speckled trout, squaretail, coaster trout, coaster

The brook trout, sometimes called the eastern brook trout, is actually a char. It was introduced into BC in the 1920s and is now established in most parts of the province. Brook trout that are produced and stocked in the province today are all-female triploids (AF3N), to prevent any interbreeding with the closely related native char species, including bull trout, Dolly Varden and lake trout. Although this is done mainly for conservation reasons, the quality of the fish in the fishery has also improved. Many of the stocked fish can live to five or six years and in some lakes survive for up to ten years. Like all char, brook trout have spots along their flanks and lack teeth. Adults have a distinctive sprinkling of red or pink spots, surrounded by bluish halos, along the flank. They also have light green marks (vermiculations) on

The brook trout is actually a char.

their backs with a distinctive marbled pattern, and the dorsal fin is heavily marbled with dark, wavy lines. The belly and lower fins are reddish in color, the latter with white leading edges. The belly often becomes very red or orange when the fish, particularly the males, are spawning.

Brook trout have been recorded at a maximum length of 33 inches (83 cm) and a maximum weight of 14.5 lb (6.6 kg), but the typical length is between 10 to 26 inches (25 to 65 cm), with weights from 11 oz to 7 lb (0.3 to 3 kg).

2F: Dolly Varden Char (sea-run and resident)

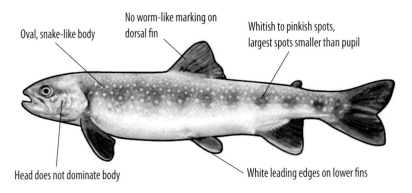

Oval, snake-like body

No worm-like marking on dorsal fin

Whitish to pinkish spots, largest spots smaller than pupil

Head does not dominate body

White leading edges on lower fins

Kingdom: Animalia	**Species:** *S. mala*
Phylum: Chordata	**Common names:** Dollies, sometimes bull trout.
Class: Actinopterygii	They are often confused with bull trout, a very
Order: Salmoniformes	similar species of char (until recently—the late
Family: Salmonidae	1980s and early '90s—they were believed to be
Genus: *Salvelinus*	the same species).

The Dolly Varden char has a trout-shaped body which, like other char, is covered with light speckles on a darker background when viewed from the side. Trout have dark speckles or spots on a light background. The Dolly's body has scattered pale pink, lilac or red spots along the flanks. There are no black spots or wavy lines on the body or fins, which are plain and unmarked except for a few light spots on the base of the caudal fin rays.

Dolly Varden have three general life-history forms. Sea-run fish migrate from freshwater to the sea and tend to remain in or near estuaries. Their return to freshwater typically involves both immature and mature individuals, and thus it is not necessarily a breeding migration. The second type of Dolly is the stream dweller that spends its entire life in streams or rivers. The last type of Dolly lives in lakes and spawns in streams in the fall, in running water.

Stream or river adults feed on the nymphs and larvae of aquatic insects, mayflies, caddis flies, stone flies and chironomids. They usually feed on drifting insects near the bottom. In lakes with cool water below 59°F (15°C), Dolly Varden forage on a wide variey of zooplankton and chironomids. As they grow they shift to larger prey, adding the drifting stages of aquatic insects and then sticklebacks and sculpins to their diet. At sea they feed on isopods and small herring and almost double their size before returning to freshwater. The average length for a resident adult is 3 to 18 inches (7 to 45 cm) to a maximum weight of 2.5 lb (1 kg). The sea-run Dolly adult averages 12 to 24 inches (30 to 60 cm) and weighs up to 5 lbs (2.3 kg).

Origins of the Name

It appears that the first recorded use of the Dolly Varden name was for a different species which is similar in appearance and is now commonly known as the bull trout. In his book *Inland Fishes of California*, Peter Moyle quotes a letter sent to him by Mrs. Valerie Masson Gomez on March 24, 1974:

My grandmother's family operated a summer resort on the Sacramento River in California. She said that some fishermen were standing on the lawn at Upper Soda Springs looking at a catch of the large trout from the McCloud River that were called "calico trout" because of their spotted, colorful markings. They were saying that the trout should have a better name. My grandmother, then a young girl of fifteen or sixteen, had been reading Charles Dickens' *Barnaby Rudge* in which there appears a character named Dolly Varden; the vogue in fashion for women at that time (middle 1870s) was "Dolly Varden," a dress of sheer-figured muslin worn over a bright-colored petticoat. She suggested to the men looking down at the trout, "Why not call them Dolly Varden?" They thought it a very appropriate name and the guests that summer returned to their homes calling the trout by this new name.

2G: Lake Trout

Worm-like markings on back and dorsal fin

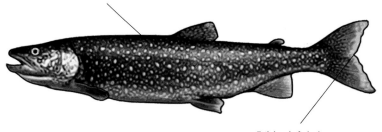

Tail deeply forked

Kingdom: Animalia	**Genus:** *Salvelinus*
Phylum: Chordata	**Species:** *S. namaycush*
Class: Actinopterygii	**Common names:** Char, gray trout, lake
Order: Salmoniformes	char, lakers
Family: Salmonidae	

This char is heavily spotted with vermiculations, irregularly light markings on the back, sides and dorsal and caudal fins that are shaped like worms. The spots on lake trout are gray or whitish but never colored. The tail is more deeply forked than in other char or trout and has light-colored spots on both halves. The head and body are covered in whitish irregular spots. The eyes are large, round and protruding. Their natural range includes the upper and middle Fraser system and the upper Skeena, Nass and Yukon drainage systems, as well as the Peace and Liard river systems. The species is absent from Vancouver Island and the Columbia system, but has been introduced into the Okanagan and Columbia drainage systems and the lower Kootenay region.

Lake trout spawn at night from early September to mid-November and, unlike most salmonids, do not require running water. They usually lay their eggs over cobbles and boulders in relatively shallow areas of lakes. The fertilized eggs, which are quite large (4–5 mm), become lodged in crevices in the rubbled bottom, where they remain for months before hatching. Depending on her body size, the female may hold from 500 to 20,000 eggs.

Young lake trout remain in shallow water along the shore for several years before moving into deeper water. At first, they feed on zooplankton. During the spring and fall, when in shallow water, they will also eat crustaceans, aquatic insects and shore-dwelling minnows. As they grow they gradually change their diet to prey on other fish such as kokanee, whitefish, burbot and sculpins. Growth rates in lake trout are variable and depend on temperature, productivity and population density. Age at maturity varies widely from around five years of age in southern areas to more than twenty years in northern BC. The typical range in length for adults is from 17 to 25.5 inches (45 to 65 cm), with a maximum length around 50 inches (125 cm). A typical range in weight for adults is 2.2 to 6.5 lb (1 to 3 kg), to a maximum of 46 lb (21 kg).

2H: Kokanee Salmon

No distinct black spots on sides

Long anal fin (12 or more rays)

Kingdom: Animalia	**Genus:** *Oncorhynchus*
Phylum: Chordata	**Species:** *O. nerka*
Class: Actinopterygii	**Common names:** Kickininee, silver trout,
Order: Salmoniformes	blueback, landlocked sockeye, silversides,
Family: Salmonidae	little redfish

Kokanee are silvery and have no dark spots on the back, side or dorsal or caudal fins. They are the non-migratory form of sockeye salmon. Some are isolated from sockeye salmon, while others remain in contact using the same water source. They have a life cycle that spans from two to seven years depending on the particular strain, with most reaching adulthood in four years.

From August to early December kokanee choose tributaries, outlet areas or the gravel area around the shoreline of a lake to spawn and complete their life cycle. Like other salmon, they die once they have spawned. Growth and size in a particular body of water depends upon the abundance of zooplankton, tiny aquatic animals from the size of a pinprick to that of a small fishhook. This is the kokanee's major food source. They feed at dawn and dusk and then migrate down to cooler water at night and during the day. Larger lakes, where concentrations are small, produce the largest fish, some to 3 and 4 lb (1.5 to 2 kg). Insect larvae or nymphs may become food sources, but not in preference to zooplankton. Thus, when a lure or bait is used to tempt kokanee into taking, it must be small and must appeal to the fish in both color and movement.

Kokanee prefer water temperatures of 50°F (10°C) or colder. In warmer lakes they will spend the summer concentrated in a very narrow band of 50°F (10°C) water or will be found close to the bottom, near underwater springs or in river channels where the water is cooler. They live in this cooler water 15 to 100 feet (5 to 30 m) below the lake surface during their entire life cycle. Adult kokanee will range in size from 8 to 20 inches (20 to 50 cm), with most in the 9 to 14 inch (23 to 35 cm) range. The typical range in weight for adults is 0.2 to 0.4 lbs (100 to 200 g) to a maximum weight of 10 lb (4.5 kg).

A nice kokanee ready for the barbecue.

Kokanee are ready to spawn from August to early December.

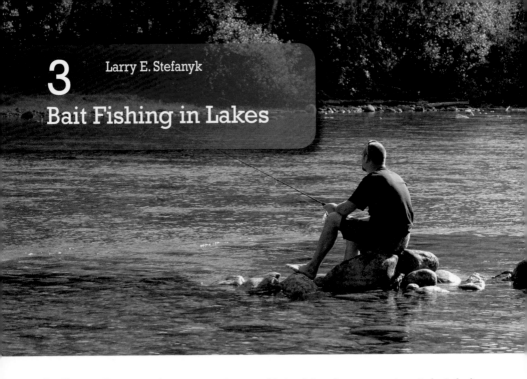

3
Larry E. Stefanyk

Bait Fishing in Lakes

Ryan Hunt patiently waiting for the big one.

Some anglers question the use of bait while others oppose it entirely. I don't believe any group of anglers has the right to force its beliefs or particular standards on others. Angling with bait is a valid part of our fishing heritage and many, including the most dedicated of fly fishers, got their start by impaling a squirming worm on a hook. If you doubt this, grab a copy of Roderick Haig-Brown's masterpiece *A Primer of Fly Fishing* and read the first chapter, "The Virtues of Fishing With Worms."

An unfortunate truth about bait fishing is that some trout are hooked deep in the gills, throat or stomach, which usually spells their doom even if they are released. Fish hooked in the gills are almost certain to die; with a trout's limited blood supply, the slightest loss is usually fatal. Trout hooked in the throat or stomach stand a better chance of survival if the leader is simply cut and the hook left in place to erode.

Upside-down Container

Take the box of worms, make sure the lid is on tight and turn it upside-down. The worms will move their way down to the bottom where the lid is, so when you open it up the worms will be on top and you won't have to dig around so much to find them.

Enter the circle hook, long associated with saltwater commercial halibut fishing. Unlike traditional J-shaped hooks, circle hooks can be ingested and then usually withdrawn without hooking any vital organs or gills. After biting the bait the fish swims away and the pull of the line tugs the swallowed hook into the mouth. The circle hook then turns and catches on the hinge of the fish's jaw.

Yet another interesting concept in the field of hooks is the anodizing process that creates bright colors like red, green and blue, all of which trout find attractive.

Then there are the upgrades in fishing lines. At one time the strongest line that could be used efficiently with lightweight or ultra-light spinning tackle was premium grade 6-pound test nylon monofilament. Now, with 10-pound test monofilament Spectra even smaller in diameter, anglers have the choice of increasing the strength of their line or going to an even smaller diameter line. Upping the line test rather than decreasing its diameter follows the general rule of using the strongest possible lines and leader tippets to reduce fish break-offs. It also means you will recover more snagged tackle.

Consistent bait fishing success often comes from using small diameter line, the smallest of sinker weights and no extraneous items like snaps and swivels. The key is presenting the bait in as natural a manner as possible. At times this means simply tying a hook directly onto the main line and eliminating the sinker. Obviously extra-long casts are out of the question, but it's surprising how far a large worm can be lobbed with a light line. And just as surprising how often it will be picked up while sinking slowly and tantalizingly toward the bottom.

Circle hooks can be withdrawn without hooking any vital organs or gills.

Bobbers can help in many situations. Round models support a lot of weight but have two flaws: their low profile in the water makes them difficult to see and their buoyancy warns biting fish that something is amiss. Better choices are slender torpedo- or cigar-shaped bobbers. Both types float high in the water, providing good visibility, and are easily pulled under by a fish.

Available in wood, cork, flexible foam plastic and rigid hollow plastic, bobbers are usually positioned on the main line by means of a tapered peg forced into a center hole or slot, or by a spring-loaded clip. A free-sliding bobber works best for fishing in deep water because the main line will keep going out until it reaches a "stopper" that positions the bait at the desired depth.

Above: Round red-and-white bobbers support a lot of weight but have their drawbacks.

Right: Choose from a selection of bobbers and dink floats for the smallest one to do the job.

The general rule for choosing bobbers is, no larger than necessary. Few things look as ridiculous as someone fishing for 10-inch trout with a fist-sized bobber on the line.

It wasn't too many years ago when "bait fishing" meant using worms, roe, cheese, corn or whatever. This has changed dramatically since the introduction of biodegradable, fish-luring products like Berkley PowerBait and Mister Twister Exude. The range of colors, shapes, sizes and scents available is absolutely mind-boggling, so your best approach is to experiment and/or ask around to determine what works best.

The beauty of soft baits and action baits is they require no refrigeration

Berkley Trout Gulp! PowerBait is a biodegradable fish lure.

and keep indefinitely as long as they are sealed in their jars or plastic bags between use. Some soft baits are buoyant so they float slightly above bottom and make a more visible target. Action baits that resemble aquatic creatures or small fish can be cast and retrieved or simply allowed to rest on the bottom.

Despite the popularity of these various commercial baits, natural baits still produce good results for many anglers. If you have ever wondered why earthworms are so universally popular, stroll along the bank of almost any creek or river after a heavy rain. In many quiet backwaters and pools you will often find worms that have washed out of the earthen banks. That is why wherever streams drain into lakes, worms become a natural food for fish.

Red wigglers, garden worms, nightcrawlers (dew worms) and manure worms are the four most common earthworms found in the Pacific Northwest. The first three are excellent baits, but manure worms (also called stink worms) are of questionable value.

The earthworm is a very popular bait.

Red Wigglers

Red wigglers (*Eisensia fetida*)—also known as red worms, manure worms, trout worms, tiger worms and compost worms—are the most common composting worm. They measure from 1.5 and 2.5 inches (3.5 and 6 cm) in length and can eat half of their body weight in a day. In the compost bin they are most active at temperatures between 59–77°F (15–25°C). They may still work their way through a bin at temperatures as low as 50°F (10°C), but temperatures below freezing will kill them off,

Red wigglers can survive colder temperatures and stay alive in the water longer than other worms.

though their eggs will keep in the compost heap through the winter to revive the population come spring. Since red wigglers can survive colder temperatures than many of their composting cousins, they make great fish bait. They can stay alive in the water hours longer than your average earthworm. They can resist temperatures as low as 35° and as high as 95° F (2°/35°C) and tend to be very active on the hook, which makes them a great choice when fishing for trout. Red wigglers don't burrow, so they stay near the top of the soil surface and are easy to find.

European Nightcrawlers

The European nightcrawler (*Eisenia hortensis*) is also known as the Belgian worm, super red, Carolina crawler, giant red worm, ENC and blue worm. It grows to be 3 to 8 inches (8 to 20 cm) long and looks like a very large, fat, red wiggler. When they are not stretched out European nightcrawlers are as thick as a pencil. They can tolerate temperatures as low as 45°F (7.2°C) but are most active between 60 and 70°F (15.5 and 21°C). They are also known to be prolific breeders, so their numbers can increase

European nightcrawlers are quickly becoming the ideal bait worm.

rapidly. ENCs are quickly becoming the ideal bait worm.

ENCs are a tough worm that can be used successfully in salt water. They have also been used for ice fishing in the most frigid waters of northwestern British Columbia and have been found to be still active on the hook after thirty minutes in the freezing water.

African Nightcrawlers

African nightcrawlers (*Eudrilus eugeniae*) are also known as Japanese tigers or super reds. They like it warmer than other earthworms, preferring temperatures of 70°F (21°C) or above, but they can be slowly accustomed to lower temperatures not below 60°F (15.5°C). They will die at temperatures under 50°F (10°C) and therefore are better suited to indoor heated environments. These worms are very lively and

African nightcrawlers are very lively but prefer warmer temperatures.

Canadian nightcrawlers can grow to a length of 14 inches (35 cm).

Alabama jumpers are so powerful they can actually jump off the ground.

make excellent fishing bait, which is why they are used heavily in the fishing industry. They have the advantage of a longer shelf life than most other worms. The fact that they grow up to 8 inches (20 cm) in length makes them a warm-weather fishing favorite, as does the fact that they can tolerate high temperatures that would kill most other worms. They have a voracious appetite and are another favorite in the compost bin. However, they'll have red wigglers for dinner. Don't mix them.

Canadian Nightcrawlers

The Canadian nightcrawler is the largest member of the nightcrawler family, often growing to a length of 14 inches (35 cm). They are popular not only because of their size but because they are easy to put on a fishhook. They are also good at attracting fish because they can remain active in the water for over five minutes. Canadian nightcrawlers must be refrigerated in warm weather because they can't withstand temperatures above 65°F (18°C).

Alabama Jumpers

Mature Alabama jumpers can grow to the size of a pencil, both in length and in circumference. They are busy, tough-skinned worms that can easily break through heavy, packed clay soil; they are so powerful they can actually jump off the ground. They do great work aerating and breaking up garden soil as long as the climate isn't too cold. Because they are so active, they aren't well suited to compost bins, but they are very desirable as fishing bait.

Worms have amazing fish appeal but there are some other important reasons for their popularity. They are very easy to find and catch or raise if you are interested in saving a few bucks or just want fresh bait readily available. Knowing where to look is half the fun of collecting earthworms and larger nightcrawlers, as they are often found in rich, soft soil and are seldom in hard or sandy soils. Piles of compost, farm manure, leaves or mulch are also good spots to search for worms. Use a garden rake to sort through these piles to find your worms. Look for worms after a rain as they come to the surface. You can also easily pick them up early in the morning—just check on driveways, sidewalks and under rocks. You can catch or purchase enough worms for several fishing trips and you can keep them alive for weeks at a time with some simple preparation. Just put them in a large container, like a five-gallon bucket. Fill the bucket at least half full with rich, moist soil, compost or similar natural debris. Feed the worms with coffee grounds and vegetable scraps. Another method is to maintain a "worm bed," a wooden box they can't escape from, sunk in the ground and covered with a tight lid. Keep the box cool, covered and slightly moist and you will have worms any time you want to fish.

An ideal way to keep a dozen or more worms is in a large coffee can. Use a can opener to remove both ends of the can. Then use the snap-on plastic lids (you will need two) to keep the worms inside. Since worms tend to go deep, simply turn the can over and open what was the bottom lid to get some bait when fishing.

Worms after Dark
When gathering worms after dark, use a flashlight with red cellophane over the lens. A white light may scare them back into their holes.

Healthy, frisky worms make the best bait. Keeping them in this state can be a problem in hot weather. A few precautions will keep them lively. One of the best methods is to place the worms in a small wooden box filled with damp moss or layers of moist burlap or newspaper. If temperatures are scorching, lay a freezer bag on top of the bedding and keep the container in a shady spot at all times.

How to Hook Up

Worms hooked once behind the "collar" last longer and present the most natural silhouette but are easily torn from the hook by bait-stealing nibblers.

Two, three or even four small red wigglers threaded onto a hook creates a writhing ball of animation that is a real attention-getter for suspending beneath a bobber or when bottom fishing. Use a small tempered steel hook because it may be totally dissolved by digestive acids within three days, making the survival of foul-hooked or released fish that much greater.

Worm hooked once behind the collar.

There are variables, of course: hook size, quality, plating and sizes of fish. Find a worm that is about twice as long as your hook shank. If the worms are too long you can always cut them to the length you want. This is something I do not suggest, as it changes how the worm is fished. When threading your worm on the hook, one end of the worm will have a smooth bump extending all the way around its body. That is the clitellum, a thick, saddle-like ring in the worm's skin. It usually has a lighter-colored pigment. Pierce the worm with the hook just below the clitellum. Continue to thread the worm onto the hook in a loose S-like shape for the length of the hook shank. Allow enough of the worm to hang off the hook so that it can move and maintain its attraction to fish. Be sure that the bulk of the worm is secured so that it does not come loose either in the water or when you are casting.

Three or four red wigglers threaded onto a hook.

Another method is to take the worm in one hand and the hook in the other hand. Now push the worm over the hook as if the worm is a sock and the hook is the foot. Once the top of the worm is at the top of the hook, you are done; the rest of the worm

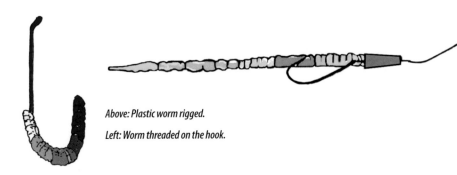

Above: Plastic worm rigged.

Left: Worm threaded on the hook.

can just be left the way it is. Both of these methods secure the worm on the hook and make it harder for the fish to steal the bait off the hook.

Artificial Worms

The artificial worm goes on the same way as the live worm, just like a sock over a foot, but this time when the tip of the worm reaches the top of the hook you need to push the hook through the plastic worm. That way the worm can hang straight down and the sharp tip of the hook is exposed.

Plastic worms are of little use in lakes if suspended below a bobber. They are very effective if they are cast and retrieved, especially when combined with a spinner or small lead head jig. Stick with worms of about three to four inches in length, preferably with a sickle-shaped tail to give added action.

Trolling

Worms trailed behind spinners or gang trolls can be threaded on in such a manner that fish cannot easily tear them free. Once attracted by flashing spinner blades, trout are seldom fussy about whether their intended meal is streaming or in a ball.

Many fish will be within a few feet of the shoreline.

Worm Casting from the Shore

Shore casting for trout is especially effective in spring, when they are living closer to the bank. There are exceptions, of course. In shallow lakes with large weed beds, the trout might find enough food to stay offshore. Trout will often remain in deep water until the surface warms into the 50°F (10°C) range. But as a rule, the shallows will be a trout magnet until the water warms. Since the shorelines of many lakes are shallow, expect trout to be near cover, fallen trees, undercut banks, large boulders and beaver houses. All are potential holds. Because the fish are feeding on stickleback, leeches, frogs and bugs, even stump beds provide cover to entice trout into shallower water.

Many fish will be within a few feet of the bank so it doesn't always pay to roar up to the edge and start casting as far out into the middle of the river or lake as you can. Try to keep the sun in front of you. When fishing with worms you want everything in the fish's environment to be as normal as possible. This means watching your own shadow and never casting it on the area you're fishing. Few things "spook" a hole as much as a human shadow. I've spooked trout out of the shallows by being in too much of a hurry. Stand as far away from the bank as you can without making it tough to get your gear back at the end of the cast. If possible, stay low and fan-cast the area—cast parallel to it. Watch your float as it approaches the bank and don't speed up the retrieve. About half the strikes you'll get will be within a rod's length of shore.

The setup for worm casting is simple. Use an ultra-light, fast-action, 4- to 6-foot (1.2 to 2 m) spinning rod and a light-duty spinning or spin-casting reel outfitted with 4- to 6-pound test line. I prefer 4—I would rather hook a good fish and lose it than not hook it at all. I use tempered-steel bronze hooks in the 10 to 14 size range because I want my hook to be inconspicuous. Avoid stainless-steel hooks as the material is impervious to water—fresh and salt—and is little affected by digestive acids.

Worms after a Rain

After heavy rains worms often cover sidewalks and roads. But picking up a slippery worm can be frustrating and time-consuming. Try using a spatula or a piece of tissue.

Putting on a little split shot helps in the casting and will keep your worm under your float. If more weight than a single split shot is required it is usually best to tie a small barrel swivel on the line, tie the lighter test to the barrel swivel and use a lighter test leader 18 to 24 inches (45 to 60 cm)long. Fasten the sinker by means of a short "drop leader" of light test line.

Theoretically, when the sinker hangs up (which it will), the dropleader will break and you only lose the sinker. But don't bet on it.

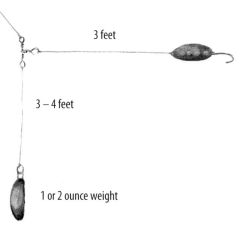

3 feet

3 – 4 feet

1 or 2 ounce weight

Monofilament tied to the front eye of the swivel.

For most applications one would tie on the barrel swivel and put the single split shot under the barrel swivel on the lighter monofiliment or fluorcarbon. If the water is fairly shallow fasten the sinker to the drop leader. For deeper water use two or more sinkers. Fasten one to the drop leader and the other(s) a foot or so above on the main line. If you use two or more on the main line, space them evenly between the swivel and bobber for better casting control. The bobber is placed above the barrel swivel at any height you wish, depending on the water depth.

Fishing Worms

The distance between the bobber/float and the hook is critical. The aim is to keep the worm just off the bottom, so experiment. Start with an arm's length distance and then add six inches at a time until you are just off the bottom.

How to Troll

Trolling requires a boat, a rod and reel, a blade string (troll) and a worm. The troll and worm are let out behind your moving boat with the amount of line varying depending on the size of the troll you select and how deep you wish to fish. The forward speed of your boat will dictate just how fast or slow the troll or worm will run and will also control its depth.

Rods, Reels and Line

Rods should be a little heavier than the one used for shore casting, 7½ to 9 feet (2.5 to 3 m) in length. A casting or spinning rod can be used. Using a heavier rod— you are dragging a "Blade String" like a Ford Fender—makes it easier on you and the trout. You can use any of three reel setups; level-wind, spin-casting and spinning. The

Trolling is a great way to relax and fish.

key is to use a little heavier line, 10- to 12-pound test with a smaller troll and a line weight of 12- to 15-pound test for a heavier troll weight.

Blades or Trolls

The troll consists of a rudder at the front end that prevents line twist, a series of free-swinging blades on a wire cable or shaft and a barrel swivel to which you tie your leader. The leader should extend at least 12 to 18 inches (30 to 45 cm) back to the lure, but may be as long as 5 or 6 feet (1.5 to 2 m). When trolled, the blades act as attractors. Fish follow the flash and sound to the source, spot the trailing worm and go after it. The shape of a blade determines how fast it will rotate and the particular sound vibrations it will produce. A round or nearly round blade such as the Colorado swings slow and wide from the shaft while narrow blades like the Willow Leaf spin fast and close to the shaft. Narrow-bladed trolls are best suited for fast trolling as they have less water resistance. A troll can be used in conjunction with just about any lure, small plug or worm.

The shape of a trolling blade determines the particular sound vibrations it will produce.

Larger and more blades should be used for deep trolling or murky water. Clear water or depths of 10 to 20 feet (3 to 6 m) require fewer, smaller blades. Nickel finishes work best on bright days or in clear water, while brass and copper finishes produce better in murky, deep or brackish (tea-colored) water. Brass, 50/50 brass–nickel or copper finishes work well when skies are overcast.

Troll slowly. Most fish will not expend any more energy than necessary to catch a meal. Try rowing instead of using your motor, which may be pushing the boat too fast. If you use a motor, make sure it will throttle down to a crawl. Also vary your speed. That does not mean going slow all the time. A lure running through the water at a constant speed, at a constant depth and giving off the same vibration pattern will not catch many fish. Fishing in a straight line will not produce as many fish either. Try

Rowing is a great way to troll slowly and give your bait great action.

running your boat in an "S" pattern. Every time the troll and worm are on the inside swing of the boat they will drop deeper and slow down; on an outside turn, they will speed up and rise. With each turn you will impart a different action to the troll and the worm.

Many "unnatural" baits also attract trout: cheese, miniature marshmallows and, so help me; small pieces of garlic sausage are some that I have seen used with varying degrees of success. There is some controversy over the use of canned corn niblets. The main concern is whether or not trout can digest them. After researching the subject I have decided that this might definitely prove a problem where anglers are chumming with corn, thereby allowing fish to gorge on it, especially in cold water when the fish's metabolism is slow.

This is not a problem here in BC because our freshwater regulations explicitly prohibit chumming with any substance. So feel free to use corn if you wish, on your hook. If you don't like natural yellow, simply color it red or orange with food dye. This makes them look similar to single salmon eggs, which just happens to be another natural bait that is popular with bait anglers, and with trout.

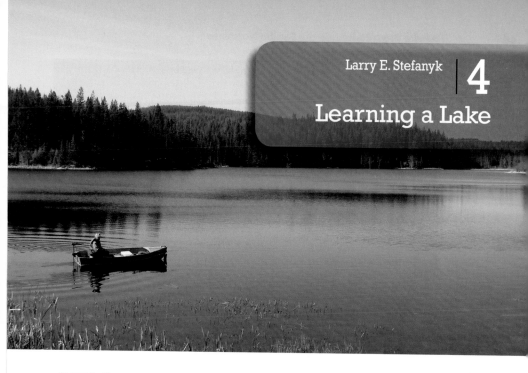

Larry E. Stefanyk | **4**

Learning a Lake

Trolling is the best way for a beginner to learn a lake and get some action—in other words, catch some trout. Most freshwater fly fishers start out using worms or roe or dragging a gang troll or casting weighted and unweighted spinners and spoons. Then, sometimes, they go through a magical evolutionary process that leads them to prefer fly-fishing to all other methods. The key word here is "sometimes." The truth is that the majority are quite content to continue with the status quo and some become amazingly proficient.

Trolling on McGlashan Lake near Kamloops, BC.

Since I started fishing I have noticed that whenever fish are plentiful, whether on salt water or fresh, virtually everyone appears to be an expert. But when fishing slows down, it's the experienced anglers, in whatever method, who continue producing results. This is especially true where trout fishing in lakes is concerned, because it is subject to a range of conditions. Water temperature (warm summer doldrums) and clarity (muddy runoff from rain and clear-cut logging or algae blooms) are the most important.

One thing you can do to become a better lake angler is to take the time to draw a map of the lake. Note the location of shallows, drop-offs, weed beds, stream channels and inlet and outlet areas. Also make a note about the wind conditions. Trout will likely be to the leeward side of a weed bed when the insects are hatching. Also note the location of the sun in relation to the shadows in the lake. Memorize and also take note of where you have observed insect activity, where you have caught fish and at what time of day.

Janice Stefanyk releasing a rainbow trout.

Rainbow trout in clear, greenish-water.

transparent water with almost no color, which is clean and clear, is excellent water for fish; water that is clear but with a slightly milky greenish-blue tint may contain limestone that can produce excellent growth rates for aquatic life and fish. Water that is a deep reddish color with a brown cast receives large amounts of tannic acid or ediron. If the water condition produces aquatic vegetation, then it should, in most cases, provide good fishing.

Having said that, trout food can be scarce sometimes and the milky gray-green common to glacial silt runoff is usually not great for producing trout food, if it is heavy.

You can use water color to read water depths. The water is normally lightest in color close to the shore and gets darker as it gets deeper. Trout will hold in the drop-offs, feeding parallel to the border.

In clear lakes, the bottom structures have their own color caused by plant growth such as green or brown algae. Sun and shadows and bottom structure can also tint or shade the water. The trout, and their food, camouflage themselves by assuming colors and patterns to help them blend in. Observing the color of the water and the lake bottom will give you clues to how trout-food imitations should be colored.

Trolling

I believe the most positive advance in trolling was the introduction of downriggers. At one time *Downriggers* only found on large boats, these have been downsized to where it is now common to *changed the* see them mounted on small cartoppers and even canoes. *way we fish.* In trolling, nothing beats a downrigger at providing precise, consistent depth controls. It also eliminates the need for a heavy-action rod and reel capable of dragging a gang troll, planer or heavy sinker. Typical downrigging outfits now consist of long, limber rods with lightweight reels, which provide much more excitement and fun while fighting and landing fish.

In smaller lakes, most anglers are quite happy trolling their lures of choice without a downrigger, relying on deep-diving plugs like Shad Raps, or something like a Tomic Wee Tad, KwikFish or spoon trailed behind a suitable-sized sinker.

When fishing a new lake, trolling is the most efficient way to cover as much area as possible and determine which places the fish might favor. Don't simply cruise around at random, hoping a fish will bite. Pay attention to drop-offs along the shoreline, inlets, outlets, islands and shoals—all the types of structure that hold and attract fish. Look for areas that offer the most attractive combinations of structure, food availability, safety and comfort, then troll close beside them if they are situated along a shoreline or right over them if they're in open water.

A general rule concerning the larger lakes is that the presence of kokanee (land-locked sockeye) almost always indicates that larger-than-average trout are available, especially cutthroats and browns. Some who target them employ tackle and setups similar to what is used for salmon—a dodger or a small or mid-sized flasher trailing a spoon, hoochie or soft plastic baitfish imitation.

Tom Moss with a rainbow caught on a Tomic Wee Tad. Wayne Moss photo

Others rely on plugs in a suitable size. They pay particular attention to the action of individual plugs by adjusting the wire nose loop, perhaps bending it slightly to one side to correct the way it tracks, or slightly downward to increase its side-to-side rolling action.

Some of the most successful anglers are those who flaunt tradition and experiment. I have often wondered who was the first person to discover that rainbow trout are suckers for a green, frog-pattern FlatFish trolled close to the bottom.

One of the best possible pieces of advice I can give you is to try to learn one lake well. When this isn't possible, take a tip from a local on how to fish the lake.

Yakima Wordens frog pattern, FlatFish.

I forgot to mention something else about trolling; when it's cold, wet and windy, you can place your rod in a holder and put your hands in your pockets, or even sip on a cup of coffee while awaiting a bite.

Try that when you're casting flies....

Casting with Bait

The other most popular tactic is casting from shore, which might involve the use of spoons or weighted spinners, or still-fishing with bait. The types of lures available are astonishing, but old reliables that are still around after many decades include Daredevil, Len Thompson and Kamlooper spoons, and Mepps, Panther Martin, Blue Fox and Rooster Tail spinners.

Len Thompson red-and-white spoon.

As for fishing with bait, the most positive advance in recent years was the introduction of circle hooks. The roundish shape with the point bent in toward the shank at a 90-degree angle creates a configuration that makes it almost impossible to hook anything on a fish except the hinge of its jaw. When a fish swallows a baited J-shaped hook, the point is driven into the soft tissue of the stomach, throat or gills as the angler sets the hook. Even if the fish escapes or is released, the wound is often fatal. A circle hook's design prevents it from penetrating internal organs or soft tissue. After being ingested, as a fish turns and starts swimming away, the baited hook simply slides over, through and past everything until reaching the jaw, the hinge of which is narrow enough for it to rotate around, allowing the point to penetrate.

Two other notable changes have been the improvements to nylon monofilament fishing line and the introduction of edible soft plastic baits. Premium quality lines are currently small in diameter, making them more difficult for fish to see, and have excellent abrasion resistance and knot strength.

Berkley PowerBait trout bait.

The range of soft plastic baits available now verges on mind-numbing, but leading the pack are Pure Fishing's Berkley Power Bait and Gulp and Breck's Mister Twister Exude, both of which are heavily scented. Power Bait, dough-like bait that is molded onto a circle hook, is suitable for still-fishing on the bottom or suspending beneath a float, as are roe imitations from both companies. Soft plastic lures come in a range of shapes, sizes and colors, and while they may be used for still-fishing they are often more productive if cast out and retrieved slowly, or allowed to sink to the bottom and then moved periodically.

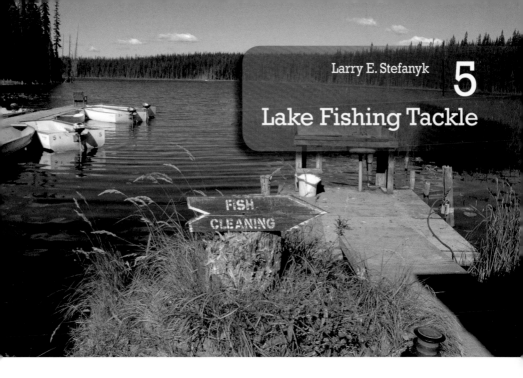

5A: Terminal Tackle

A warm summer day: perfect for fishing.

Dedicated trout anglers—those who pursue the fish year round—are possibly the most versatile members of our fishing community. They are seen prowling in, on or around salt water, brackish estuaries, lakes of every size, small streams and large, fast-flowing rivers. They may be found fishing from shore, wading, casting from a boat or trolling.

Good equipment is available in all price ranges and often offered in package deals. To fish for any trout, all you need is a light fly, spin-casting or open-face spinning outfit capable of handling small- to medium-sized lures and flies. Beginners should note that any equipment that might be used in salt water should be constructed to withstand the rigors of that environment. An unseen splash of salt water can ruin equipment, even equipment made for use in salt water, if it isn't washed in freshwater after fishing.

What follows is a rundown of all the equipment needed to enjoy the sport of angling.

Rods

"A fishing rod or a fishing pole is a tool used to catch fish."

Fishing rods were made with split Tonkin bamboo, Calcutta reed or ash wood before synthetic materials became widely available. Today they are mostly made of

Alliance fishing rod.

fiberglass, carbon fiber, graphite or, classically, bamboo. They can be found in sizes from 2 to 20 feet (60 cm to 6 m); the longer the rod, the greater the mechanical advantage in casting. An ideal rod should gradually taper from butt to tip and have a cork handle and good guides. Fishing rods are identified by their weight, meaning the weight of line or lure required to flex a fully loaded rod. A cork handle grip is light, durable, keeps warm and tends to transmit rod vibration better than synthetic material. Reel seats are often of graphite-reinforced plastic, aluminum or wood. Guides in steel or titanium or a variety of hi-tech metal alloys will round out a fishing rod.

Spin- and Bait-casting Rods

Casting rods are designed to hold a spin-casting or level-wind reel, which are normally mounted above the handle. Spin-casting rods usually have a forefinger grip trigger. They are similar to bait-casting rods and either type of reel may be used on either rod. Spin-casting rods are made from fiberglass or graphite with a cork or PVC foam handle and tend to be 5 to 8 feet (1.6 to 2.4 m) in length.

The open-face casting rod may have anywhere from five to eight larger-diameter guides arranged along the underside to help line control. The eyes decrease in size

Top to bottom: Spin- or bait-casting rod with reel. Ultra-light reel and rod combo. Level-wind reel with heavier rod.

from the handle to the tip, with the one nearest the handle usually much larger than the rest to allow less friction as the coiled line comes off the reel, and to gather larger loops of line that come off the spinning reel's spool. With the reel sitting beneath the rod, your second and third fingers straddle the leg of the reel where it is attached to the reel seat and the weight of the reel hangs beneath the rod. This allows you to hold the rod in your dominant hand, which increases control and accuracy in casting.

Ultra-light Rods

The term "ultra-light" is commonly used to refer to open-face spinning, spin-casting and fly rods that use smaller line weights. Such rods are generally shorter—from 4 to 6 feet (1.2 to 2 m)—and lighter, with a line weight from 2 to 6 pounds. Some ultra-light rods are capable of casting lures as light as ¹⁄₆₄ of an ounce, typically small spinner, wet fly tubes or bait such as worms. Fly rods from sizes up to 3-weight are lightweight rods.

Trolling Rods

Trolling involves dragging your lure or bait behind a boat. Lures weigh anywhere from ½ to 2 ounces (15 to 56 g). Balance your rod and reel because good-quality rods and reels come with the range of lure weights and fishing-line strength they are designed to handle printed right on them. Just match rod to reel.

Telescopic Rods

These rods are designed to collapse down for travel and open up to a long rod. This makes them great for transporting to remoter areas or just for traveling long distances. They are made from the same material as conventional one- and two-piece rods. Various grades of rods are available.

Telescopic rods.

Number of Pieces

Rods that are one piece from butt to tip are considered to have the most natural feel, but transporting them can be difficult. The two-piece rod, joined by a ferrule, is

Shakespeare Ugly Stick travel rod for spinning or casting.

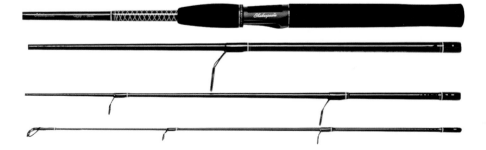

very common and sacrifices little of the natural feel, which is why most rods over 6.5 feet (2 m) are two-piece. Pack rods use the same components as one- and two-piece rods but come in four or five pieces, so they break down for easy storage and transport; they are also available in spin/fly combos.

Hardware and Fittings

Don't be in awe of a rod's price or brand name. Rather than buying a brand you should seek the quality that makes a rod seem an extension of your arm. Check the handle. If its diameter is too large or small, cramps may develop in

Travel rod and reel combo.

your fingers, hand and forearm. Look also at the cork. A good quality rod cork will be free of pitting and other imperfections. If of synthetic material, ensure it is secure on the shaft, and of comfortable shape and diameter. Look for a keeper ring, a tiny wire loop that secures the tied-on hook while a rod is not in use. Today all guides are made of aluminum oxide or silicone carbide. These are superior to metal in weight and durability, easier on line and virtually indestructible. Check the windings to make sure there are no open spots showing between the threading that secures them. Inspect the finish for abrasions like cracks or cuts, which indicate potential fracture areas when the rod is stressed. Join the sections and sight from handle to tip and make sure all guides are in perfect alignment. Ensure the reel seat accepts your reel.

Reels

"A fishing reel is a device used for the deployment and retrieval of a fishing line using a spool mounted on a fishing rod."

The first reel on record is from a Chinese painting dated 1195. Fishing reels arrived in England around 1650 and in America in 1820. Reels for trout fishing can be broken into three categories: bait-casting, spinning and center pin.

Bottom left: Old classic reel.

Bait-casting Reels

Bottom right: Bait-casting reel in pink.

There are three basic reel setups: level-wind, spin-casting and spinning. As many of today's reels are constructed with aluminum, stainless steel and/or composite materials, it's your choice for material and color.

Level-wind Reels

The term "bait-casting" is misleading, because these reels are far better adapted to casting or trolling artificial lures. Level-wind reels store the line on a bearing-supported revolving spool and mount the reel above the rod, with the handle positioned on the right side of the reel. Because the momentum of the forward cast must rotate the spool as well as propel the fishing line, this reel is normally designed for heavier lures, ¼-ounce (7 g) and up. The weight of the lure will cause the reel spool to revolve very quickly, paying out line. Once your lure lands in the water the spool, unchecked by thumb or finger, will keep turning, spitting out line that bunches up. Welcome to the word *backlash* or, another definition, *bird's nest*. As your lure nears the target, the trick is to begin to gently touch your thumb to the spool, using it like a brake. With some practice you can feather the spool with your thumb, stopping it as your lure hits the water.

These reels offer excellent control while fighting fish and, in the hands of skilled casters, will outdistance all other types of reels. With a bit of practice, you'll find them easy to cast and more accurate than spinning outfits. Some level-wind reels are fitted with anti-reverse (backlash) handles and drags designed to slow the runs of larger fish. The gear ratio in bait-casting reels was initially about ³⁄₁, later standardized at ⁴⁄₁ in most reels; today some have ⁵⁄₁ to ⁷⁄₁. The higher gear ratios allow for much faster pickup of the line, meaning you're back in the water fishing much quicker than with other reels. But this reel is not for the novice as the backlash can be a big problem. Practice and patience are needed.

Open-face Spinning Reels

It dates back to the mid-1600s, but anglers didn't use it widely until about 1870. In 1948 the Mitchell Reel Company introduced the Mitchell 300 with a design that oriented the face of the spool forward in a permanently fixed position below the fishing rod, with the line guides pointing directly to the ground. The size of the guides starts larger and become smaller closer to the tip. The reel uses a metal bar (called a

Bottom left: Level-wind reel.

Bottom right: Classic Mitchell open-face spinning reel.

Right: Daiwa open-face spinning reel.

Far right: Spin-casting closed-face reel.

bail) to hold the line on the reel. The line is not covered, which is why these reels are called open-face. As the reel handle is turned, the bail also turns, winding line neatly onto the spool.

When casting, hold the line with your index finger of your rod hand, then unlock the bail with your other hand. As you cast, release the line from your finger to let the line peel off the spool. This allows minimal friction, so anglers can cast long distances with less line tangling. At the first turn of retrieval, the bail will click in and start retrieving the line.

Most spinning reels operate best with a fairly limp, flexible fishing line. Look for reels where the handle can be mounted on either side to accommodate left- or right-handed anglers. Backlash can be a problem. So can twisted fishing line caused by the spin of an attached lure, the action of the wire bail against the line when engaged by the crank handle, or even retrieval of line. If you pump the rod up and down, then retrieve the slack line, you can avoid some of the line twist. The reel should complement the rod, balancing on it as though they were one. Match the spool diameter to the line you intend to use. Spooling 15-pound test monofilament on an ultra-light reel is futile because the tiny spool will hold only a miniscule amount of a heavy line. Filling the spool of an intermediate-sized reel with 4-pound test line is just as foolish, for it will require several hundred yards to fill it.

Spin-casting Closed-face Reels

In 1949 Zebco introduced the spin-cast reel. It was designed to solve the problem of backlash found in bait-cast designs, while reducing line twist. The new reel eliminated the large wire bail of the spin-casting reel and the line roller of the bait-caster in favor of one or two pickup pins and a metal cup to wind the line onto the spool. The reel is traditionally mounted above the rod with the line rod guides facing upwards. The line is stored under a cover and feeds from a small hole in the front, hence the name closed-face reel. These reels will give you less line tangles when you use a limp monofilament line. Casting is simple. Press and hold the thumb button, then release the button as you cast to allow the line to spool out. A rod and reel combo

Spin-casting closed-face reel and rod combo for children.

can range from 5.5 to 6.5 feet (1.8 to 2.2 m) in length, line weight from 2- to 6-pound monofilament. Lures weigh from $\frac{1}{38}$ to $\frac{3}{8}$ ounce.

This setup is generally the best combination for kids because it is user-friendly for small hands.

Center Pin Reels

The center pin is a free-spooling single-action reel. When you cast you allow the reel to spin freely, letting out line and controlling it with a light touch of thumb or finger for tension to prevent backlash. Experienced single-action reel users can sometimes cast farther and more accurately than those using spin-cast or bait-caster setups. But be warned, it is an art fraught with difficulties.

Islander center pin reel.

Used in rivers for steelhead, one has options. A dink float—a cylindrical Styrofoam float that looks like a stick of dynamite—can be fastened up from the terminal tackle. Watch the float and when it goes down, strike and strike hard. Bait varies from yarn flies to roe, depending on regulations.

One of the greatest innovations in float fishing has been the slip stopper. This allows a small rubber stopper attached to the main line to get your gear to the depth required. When you cast, the float, weights and terminal gear can be close to the rod tip, allowing maximum torque. When the line hits the water, the float stays on the surface and the line slips through until it reaches the proper depth. The stopper comes to the float and, well, stops—and your terminal tackle slips to the desired depth.

Different colored dink floats.

There are two important considerations that are often overlooked. First, be certain to load the line on your reel properly, and second, fill it to a capacity that allows for prime casting. A reel too full of line will cause endless backlashes. A reel with not enough line just won't do the trick.

And then there are always the spoons and spinners you can also use with a center pin.

Lines

"A fishing line is a cord used or made for angling."

The earliest fishing line was made from leaves or plant stalk and later thread. From the 1850s modern industrial machinery was employed to fashion lines in quantity. Linen and silk were used and a waterproofing compound was sometimes added during manufacturing. Today, lines are made almost entirely from artificial substances, including nylon, fluorocarbon, polyethylene, Dacron and Dyneema. The most common type is monofilament, made from a single strand. Fishermen like it because of its buoyant characteristics and its ability to stretch under load.

Fluorocarbon line is valued for its refractive index, which is similar to that of water, making it less visible. It is generally a bit stiffer, has less stretch and is more abrasion-resistant than monofilaments; it is also more expensive.

Braided lines, also known as superlines, are known for their small diameter, lack of stretch and great strength relative to standard nylon monofilament lines. They are great for trolling in deep water but not recommended for casting.

Fishing line is measured by its tensile breaking strength, expressed in pounds. A 6-pound line will break when 6 pounds of strain is applied to it. That does not mean that you cannot catch a 10-pound fish if you have only 6-pound line. If the reel's drag is set properly and the rod's weight is sufficient, a 6-pound fish should never put more than 6 pounds of stress on your 6-pound test line. (Unless you're an idiot, and we've all been there.)

Is line color important? It is—trout are line-shy, so most anglers use clear monofilament or line-shaded to match the color of the lake or river. Clear or light-green nylon monofilament line in 4- to 10-pound test is the workhorse line used for spinning and bait-casting lines and leaders. Generally, the lower a line's cost the less attention to detail (thus quality) during its manufacture. When loading line on reels or playing fish, remember that nylon monofilament will stretch under pressure. Always lay down several layers of Dacron or use the cork spacers that come with some reel spools to protect your reel from warping, which can occur after monofilament has been reeled onto the spool while under stress. Over time, stretched line will return to its original length, causing it to slowly tighten and warp your reel spool. To relieve

Left to right: Berkley Trilene line, Rio Fluoroflex Plus 4 x 7-pound, Sufix 832 braided-fiber line.

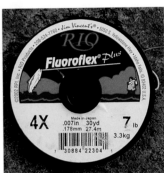

potential problems, simply remove your lure and let your line out behind a moving boat or in a stream's current, then put the line back on the reel under minimal tension.

Premium leader material is essential for success whether you are using lures or flies or casting or trolling. For most applications, a tapered leader 7.5 to 9 feet (2.5 to 3 m) long is fine if you are using heaver monofilament like 15-pound. Leaders up to 15 feet (3 m) in length may be needed in clear, calm water, especially if trout are following but not taking your gear. I prefer Rio Fluoroflex Plus tippet of 7-pound test 4x for all my trout fishing as I have landed some big fish with it without a problem.

Scientific Anglers Mastery Series tapered leaders are a staple for trout fishing.

Lures

"A fishing lure is an object attached to the end of a fishing line which is designed to resemble and move like the prey of a fish."

In early times, fishing lures were made from bone or bronze. The Chinese and Egyptians used fishing rods, hooks and lines as early as 2000 BC, though most of the first fishers used hand lines. The first hooks were made out of bone or bronze that was strong but still very thin and less visible to the fish. The modern fishing lure was first made commercially in the United States in the early 1900s by the Michigan firm of Heddon and Pflueger. Before this time most fishing lures were made by individual craftsmen. Commercial-made lures were based on their models, but produced on a larger scale.

The purpose of the lure is to use movement, vibration and color to catch the fish's attention so it bites the hook. Lures can be equipped with one single hook or a treble hook.

It is unlawful to use barbed hooks or a hook with more than one point (treble) in any river, stream, creek

Above: Classic Pflueger "Wooden Minnow" in box.

Left: Some classic fishing lures.

or slough in BC. (Note: the use of barbed hooks in lakes is permitted, unless noted in the Regional Water-Specific Tables.)

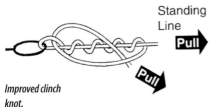

Standing Line

Pull

Pull

Improved clinch knot.

The fishing lure is either tied with a knot, such as the improved clinch knot, or connected with a tiny safety pin-like device called a "swivel" onto the fishing line, which is in turn connected to the reel and the reel to rod. When a lure is used for casting, it is continually cast out and retrieved—the retrieve making the lure swim or produce a popping action—or by being pulled behind a moving boat, called trolling.

There are many types of fishing lures. They are all manufactured in different ways to resemble the fish's prey, but are sometimes engineered to appeal to a fish's sense of territory, curiosity or aggression. Most lures are made to look like dying, injured or fast-moving fish. They can be made of wood, plastic, rubber, metal, cork or materials like feathers, animal hair, string, or tinsel. They can have many moving parts or none at all. They can be retrieved fast or slowly. There are three basic families of lures: spoons, spinners and lead jigs. From these have sprung hundreds, if not thousands, of variations.

Top to bottom: Spoons come in many different sizes and shapes. Lead head purple jig with a marabou tail. William's jigging spoon.

Jig

A basic jig is the simplest and most versatile of all the lures. It is comprised of nothing but a single hook with a lead head molded to it. Lead-head jigs can be skirted with various types of feathers, hair or synthetics, but soft plastic bodies are extremely popular. Originally designed for vertical fishing from boats, the typical jig has a hook eye at the point of balance on top of the lead head, with the hook point riding upward behind it. This not only makes the lure virtually snag-proof, but ensures that fish will be hooked in the upper jaw, usually in the lip, as the fisher moves the rod up and down to create the jigging motion. It is a great lure for jigging but not for casting.

Spoon

Spoons date back to the mid-1800s, when anglers moved their manufacture from the garage to big business. It all started with a table spoon dropped into the water by Julio Thompson Buel at the tender age of fifteen, in 1821. The spoon twisted and turned, down into the depths. Before it disappeared a great trout lunged for it, grabbed it and took off ... and the rest is history.

Spoons flash in the light while wobbling or darting due to their shape, attracting fish. One of the simplest lures, a typical spoon is nothing more than a metal blade with a hole at each end. The front hole is used for attachment to the line and the rear one accepts the hook, usually by means of a split ring. Many anglers automatically assume a spoon must be fitted with a treble hook. Nothing could be further from the truth. Single hooks not only hold better in the jaw of a fish, they cost less and seldom snag up as often.

Spoons can be divided into three categories: light, medium and heavy. Light spoons are easily activated. Heavy spoons must be worked by manipulating the rod tip, but are great for long-distance casting, fishing in swiftly flowing currents or vertical fishing (jigging). Medium-weight spoons are a compromise between these two extremes, offering reasonable casting weight and good action.

An important point to consider when selecting spoons is the shape of the metal blade. The three basic shapes are teardrop, egg (oval) and cigar (elongated). A typical cigar-shaped spoon creates a slender silhouette as it is drawn through the water, and its rapid side-to-side action is similar to a slender forage fish. Oval shapes provide the slowest side-to-side action, and their pudgy silhouettes are similar to deep-bodied baitfish. Teardrop-shaped silhouettes are not unlike those of baitfish such as shiners.

Spinners

A typical unweighted spinner consists of a blade and clevis attached to a wire shaft. One or more beads positioned behind the clevis acts as a bearing surface against which the blade can rotate. As with spoons, the shape of a spinner blade plays an important part in its action when drawn through the water. The four basic configurations are round, egg, oval and willow leaf. A round blade rotates slowly on a wide axis around the wire shaft, while a willow leaf blade lies almost flat against the shaft and spins at a higher speed. Egg and oval shapes fall between the two extremes, offering intermediate rotation speed.

Top to bottom: William's Honey Comb spoon. Mepps spinner. The 3-inch Tomic Plug #800 is very effective.

Plugs

Plugs are generally associated with bass, pike or salmon fishing, but are also effective on steelhead in rivers or trout in lakes. They offer the most intriguing shapes, actions, sizes and colors and are equipped with treble hooks or single hooks. When all is said and done, however, matters can be simplified by reducing these lures to their basic categories: surface, floating/diving and sinking. Plugs have a fish-like body shape and are run through the water, where they can make a wide variety of different movements. Body shapes range from long and slender to short and fat, and anywhere from cylindrical to laterally or horizontally compressed.

Some plugs have a dished face that imparts a side-to-side swimming motion as they are drawn through the water, while others depend on protruding lips of metal or plastic to create life-like action. A typical floating/diving model will usually have a large lip extending beyond its head. This creates a downward planing effect as the plug is drawn forward, causing it to dive deeply in a matter of seconds. The surface plug can cause a ruckus when cast on the water and retrieved. Cast out to your target, let it settle, twitch it a few times as it dives, then let it rest and reel in. A trout may follow the lure to the boat and take it at the last minute. These plugs imitate either a wounded minnow or frog or some helpless land critter. The strike to the surface plug is always violent.

Underwater plugs are designed to zigzag up or down or sideways while wiggling enticingly. Tie your plug on your line and then use a slip weight anywhere from 6 to 20 feet (2 to 6 m) from the plug. Three plugs every angler should have are the red and white, frog-colored and wounded-minnow types. If plugs become battered and scarred this does not mean that they are no longer useful; sometimes the oldest ones work the best.

Top to bottom: The Tomic Wee Tad 754 catches trout. Soft baits in various sizes and shapes.

Cutthroat caught on a Tomic Wee Tad.

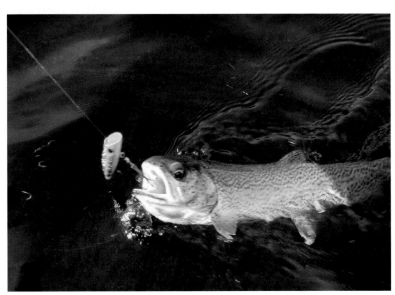

Soft Plastic Baits/PowerBait

Soft bait gives an angler several advantages over artificial lures. Soft baits feel more natural in the mouth of a wary fish, which means the fish are less likely to spit them out right away. They are made of plastic or rubber and designed to resemble worms, lizards, frogs, leeches or other creatures.

One of the top producers of soft baits, Berkley, has spent years developing and improving the most revolutionary artificial bait ever produced. Using a patented scientific process, each bait is formulated with the most advanced scent and flavor on the market. PowerBait lures have been impregnated with bite-sized pieces of scented and flavored bait that the fish tastes upon biting. The more a fish bites, the more scent is dispersed into the water.

One thing I have noticed is that bright-colored baits seem to work best in bright conditions while darker colored baits seem to perform really well in low light conditions such as dusk and dawn.

Artificial Flies

Flies are not just for fly fishermen. Artificial flies are designed to resemble all manner of insects and fish prey and can be used on a spinning outfit. The setup is simple for casting or trolling—just add a little split shot to your line. One advantage of artificial flies is that their use promotes improved survival of fish during catch-and-release fishing. This is because lures reduce the incidence of deep hooking, which has been correlated to fish mortality in many studies. Mortality is mostly caused by the handling stress and damage resulting from removing the hook from the gut or throat. The best course of action when a fish is gut-hooked is to leave the hook and cut the line as soon as possible. Hooks will then be encapsulated or evacuated from the body. Use of non-corroding steel is not recommended because a corroding hook will be easier for the fish to expel.

A fly box of leech patterns.

In Chapter 9, "Thirty Great Pacific Northwest Lures," I have included some of my picks for lake and river fishing.

Fly fishing the
Nass River in
Northern BC.

5B: Fly Tackle

Rods

"A fly rod is a thin, flexible rod designed to cast an artificial fly."

The earliest fly rods were made from greenheart, a tropical wood, and later bamboo originating in the Tonkin area of Guangdong Province in China. The mystical appeal of handmade split-cane rods has endured despite the emergence over the last fifty years of cheaper rod-making materials that offer more durability and performance. Split-cane bamboo fly rods combine sport, history and art. It may take well over a hundred hours for an experienced rod builder to select and split the raw cane and then to cure, flame, plane, file, taper, glue, wrap and finish each rod. The resultant rods offer grace, form and, with their solid mass, surprising strength. Bamboo rods vary in action from slow to fast depending on the taper of the rod. In competent hands, they reach the pinnacle of performance.

Fiberglass was popular for rods constructed in the years following World War II and was the material of choice for many years. However, by the late 1980s, carbon/graphite composite rods (including premium graphite/boron and graphite/titanium blends) had emerged as the materials used by most fly rod manufacturers. These premium rods offer a stiffness, sensitivity and feel unmatched by any other synthetic material. Each rod is sized to the fish being sought, the wind and water conditions and also to a particular weight of line: larger and heavier line sizes will cast heavier, larger flies. Fly rods come in a wide variety of line sizes, from size 2 for the smallest freshwater trout to and including size 16 rods for large saltwater game fish. Fly rods have a single, large-diameter line guide, called a stripping guide, with a number of smaller looped guides, called snake guides, spaced along the rod to help control the movement of the relatively thick fly line. To prevent interference with casting movements, most fly rods have little or no butt section extending below the fishing reel, giving them perfect balance.

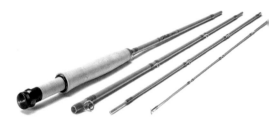

If you are planning on purchasing a new rod, put on a reel and see how the reel seat holds it to the rod. Some reels hang below the reel seat so every time you put your rod down you will scratch them. Try to purchase your rod with the reel seat raised above the butt of the rod; this will protect your reel.

Fly rods are usually longer than other forms of fishing rods. From 7.5 to 9 feet (2.5 to 3 m) is common for trout, and 9 to 10.5 feet (3 to 3.5 m) for steelhead. Lots of fly rods and reels are suitable for fishing trout; my preference is for a fast-action 5- or 6-weight, 9-foot (3-m), 4-piece rod because it is light, fun to use, can be packed for travel and is easy on my wrist. Other anglers like 7-weight rods and though I feel these are a bit heavy, if I fished only in large streams or lakes and was limited to one rod for trout fishing, it might

be a 7-weight. Because your lines are designed to match your rod, look for balance again; the manufacture will inscribe this on the rods, reels and lines.

Top to bottom: Four-piece fiberglass rod. St. Croix rods showing the fighting butt. A four-piece saltwater rod.

Saltwater Rods

The saltwater rod should have a saltwater reel seat, oversize guides and a small fighting butt. After every use, make sure you wash your rod, reel and all your gear.

When purchasing a fly outfit for a new fisher with small hands, be sure the grip fits the size of their hands; you will want an outfit that is light and easy for young people and women to hold. Casting is more forgiving than with fast action rods and when playing fish, smaller fish become "lunkers."

Fly Girl, a fly rod outfit designed for a smaller hand from Eagle Claw.

Reels

Center Pin Reels for Fly-fishing

The reel plays a minor role in fly-fishing for trout. In most cases it is a storage bin, merely a reserve for line not in use. The reel is not involved in the cast or the retrieve. The first design, patented by Charles F. Orvis in 1874, changed little from the original design; however, in recent years, more advanced fly reels have been developed for larger fish and more demanding conditions. These newer reels feature disc-type drag systems made of different type composite materials with mechanical and adjustable drag systems. Early fly reels had no drag—just a click/pawl mechanism intended to keep the reel from overrunning when line was pulled from the spool. Anglers palmed the rim, applying hand pressure to the rim of the revolving spool to slow the fish. In use, a fly angler strips line off the reel with one hand while casting and manipulating the rod with the other. Slack line is picked up by rotating the reel spool. The majority of fly reels are of single-action design with a ration of 1:1 (i.e., one complete revolution of the handle equals one revolution of the spool). They have a rather simple construction, with a simple click/pawl drag system. However, in recent years, more advanced fly reels have been developed for larger fish and more demanding conditions to permit the use of lighter leaders and tippets, or to successfully capture fish that undertake long, powerful runs.

The fly line can be retrieved using either hand. Most modern fly reels can be

Left to right: Charles F. Orvis 1874 reel. A selection of fly reels.

converted to or from left-hand or right-hand retrieve. Many fly anglers who have come to the sport after spending some years as spin-casting anglers are more comfortable with a left-hand retrieve. Right-handed "big game" fishers may find the right hand retrieve more efficient.

Fly reels are often rated for a specific weight and type of fly line in combination with a specific strength and length of backing. For example, the documentation supplied with a reel may state that it can take 150 yards (137 m) of 50-pound test backing and 30 yards (27 m) of fly line. An angler should be able to "load" the reel with the specified length of line and backing and still have sufficient room between the line and the spool's edge. Many modern reels are also designed to take interchangeable spools. Such spools can be quickly switched, thus allowing an angler to change the type of line in a matter of minutes.

Left to right: Preloaded spools make it quick and easy to change fly lines. Hardy lightweight reel with extra spool.

Some fly reels have large arbor spools (center axis of the reel) designed to reduce line memory, maintain consistent drag and assist in the retrieval of slack line. I prefer large arbor myself because it can hold up to 125 yards (114 m) of 20-pound test Dacron backing under the fly line. That backing capacity is comforting when a very large trout or salmon, possibly a fish of a lifetime, has hit my fly. Islander fly reels, made in Canada on Vancouver Island, are an excellent example of a reel that will last several lifetimes, and they come in large arbor models. Other reels are available in all price ranges and many provide exceptional value for the money. Just check out your local tackle shop.

Left to right: Large arbour reel loaded with backing and fly line. Islander fly reel LX 4.5.

Clockwise from top left: Automatic fly reels are not as popular today as they once were. Saltwater reel with fly. Fly lines.

Automatic Fly Reels

These reels use a coiled spring mechanism that pulls the line into the reel with the flick of a lever. They were popular in the 1960s but were heavy for their size and had limited line capacity. They're not a great seller today and can be hard to find. I have used one for fishing small streams for years and enjoy it.

Saltwater Reels

Some reels destined for use in salt or brackish water may be virtually destroyed by corrosion within a season. If you plan on this type of fishing, choose reels that are clearly labeled as resistant or impervious to salt water. Saltwater reels are much larger in diameter, to provide a larger line and backing capacity for the long runs salmon will make. They often use graphite, anodized aluminum frames and spools and electroplated and/or stainless steel components, with sealed and waterproof bearing and drive mechanisms.

Lines

"A fly line is a specialized fishing line that supplies the weight or mass necessary to cast an artificial fly."

The first fly lines were constructed of woven horsehair that eventually evolved into woven silk fiber. Today fly lines consist of a tough braided or monofilament core wrapped in a thick waterproof plastic sheath, often of polyvinyl chloride (PVC). In the case of floating fly lines, the PVC sheath is usually embedded with many "micro balloons" or air bubbles and may also be impregnated with silicone or other lubricants to give buoyancy and reduce wear. The typical fly line is 90 feet (27 m) long, although longer lines are manufactured. All fly lines have several distinctive characteristics. Some of these are based on industry standards and norms while others vary considerably between manufacturers.

Fly line codes consist of three parts: letters, numbers and letters. These identify the line's style, weight and specific gravity.

FLY LINE CODES

Letters:

- L-Level
- DT–Double Taper
- ST-Shooting Taper
- WF-Weight-forward Taper

Numbers:

- 1–15 denotes the weight class, in grains, of the first 30 feet (10 m) of line

Letter:

- F-Floating
- S-Sinking
- F/S- Sinking

A sample of typical line used by trout anglers might be:

- DT-5-F = double taper, five weight, floating line
- WF-6-FS = weight-forward taper, six weight, floating line with about 10 feet (3 m) of sinking tip

Sinking lines are further identified by the rate at which they sink. This indicates whether a line is slow, intermediate, fast or extremely fast.

Taper

Taper describes the change in cross-sectional diameter of a fly line from one end to another. Taper is a significant determinant in the casting performance of an individual fly line, particularly the ability to present different types of artificial flies, from the very delicate to the heavy and wind-resistant, in differing water conditions. Fly lines in general are said to be:

- Weight-forward taper—the cross-sectional diameter changes from smaller to larger to small within the front 30 feet (9 m) of the fly line. Weight-forward taper lines have only one end to which the leader is attached.

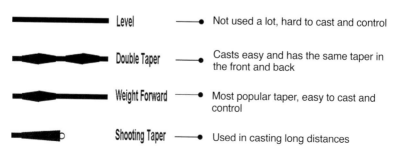

Level	→	Not used a lot, hard to cast and control
Double Taper	→	Casts easy and has the same taper in the front and back
Weight Forward	→	Most popular taper, easy to cast and control
Shooting Taper	→	Used in casting long distances

Types of taper.

For lake fishing, I recommend an intermediate sinking line. This means that the whole line will sink as time passes. I time the descent of the fly line. If it takes one minute to hit the bottom in 20 feet (6 m) of water, I can time the retrieve to fish different levels of the water table. It is my workhorse line for trout fishing in any depth of water.

I particularly like Monic, Rio or Scientific Angler floating lines, all of which were developed for use in cold water. Those who fish in lakes or large streams should also add a heavier full-sinking line or sink tip designated as a Type 3 or Type 6, for fishing close to the bottom in deeper water or for trolling. Other lines can be added as needed. For maximum casting distance and top floating or sinking performance, all lines should be cleaned following the manufacturers directions after fishing.

Backing

The fly line is typically attached to a backing—a length of braided or gelspun line wound onto the fly reel. The length and breaking strength of the backing required depends on the overall line capacity of the reel and the type of fishing. Backing may be as short as a few yards up to several hundred yards if the reel has the capacity. It can serve two purposes. One is to create a larger diameter spooling surface that allows the fly line to fill the entire fly reel. The other is to provide additional line for fighting heavy or hard-fighting fish. A fast-running or hard-fighting fish may take line from the reel and get into the backing.

Fly reel loaded with blue fly line and orange backing.

A selection of fly line leaders.

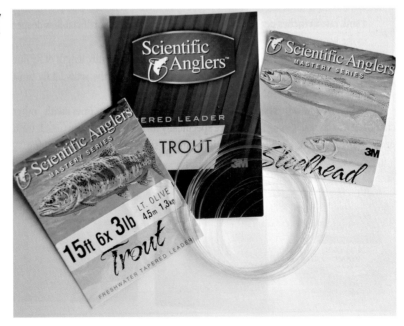

When you purchase a new reel the manufacture will let you know how much backing you need, based on the line used. If you choose gelspun backing remember to use stripping guards on your fingers to help prevent line cuts, and learn the specialty knots used for attaching the backing to the fly line.

Leader and Tippet

Level leaders are a single diameter of line that connects the fly line to the tippet or fly. They are typically much shorter than tapered leaders and are used with sinking fly lines and heavy flies. When used with sinking lines, level leaders help get the fly deeper faster. They are tapered from the wide, heavy butt to the narrow, light tippet, to help turn the fly over in casting. The purpose of the taper is to provide a continuous reduction in diameter from the fly line to the fly. With the rapid improvement in monofilament technology, leaders can now be designed with hard butts and soft tippets and with a variety of stiffness, diameter/strength and abrasion characteristics to fit virtually every fishing requirement.

There are three basic parts to a tapered leader: the butt section, the tapered section and the tippet. The butt section sometimes makes up 60 percent of the leader length and is made of stiffer, larger-diameter material. It starts the transfer of energy from the fly line into the leader. The mid section (20 percent of the leader length) is made up of short, graduated strands of monofilament stepping down quickly in diameter. It dissipates the energy transferred from the fly line to allow a gentle presentation. The final section, the tippet, is made of softer, smaller-diameter

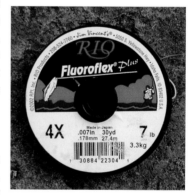

Rio Fluoroflex tippet.

material which enables the fly to set gently down and ride the current in as unrestricted a manner as possible. The leader should vary from 9 to 15 feet (3 to 5 m) in length. You should keep a selection of breaking strains from 3x to 5x on hand, depending on conditions; as a rule, the clearer the water, the finer the leader and the tippet. Leaders are also available in fluorocarbon.

Fly Tippets

The tippet connects the leader to the fly. Tippet sizes were traditionally expressed as "X" sizes in a scale based on silkworm gut leader material, nowadays superseded by nylon (see below). Monofilament is calibrated in thousandths of an inch, from 0.020" and larger (used for leader butts or in saltwater fishing) to 0.011" (old size 0X) to as small as 0.003" (8X). Fly-fishing records are classed by tippet diameter, not breaking strength, which varies between manufacturers. Anglers use tippets of different sizes and lengths depending on the size of the fly, the wariness of the fish and so on. Typically, dry fly leaders are long and fine, but leaders for deep-sunk streamer flies may be only 2 feet (60 cm) long and 0.010 inches in diameter.

Tippet sizes are referred to by "X" designations ranging from 0X (largest) to

8X (smallest). The X designation is based on the tippet diameter. An easy way to remember their correlation is subtract the X number from 11 and express in .001".

Example: Find the diameter of 4X
Solution: 11-4 = 7 or .007"

NOTE: Test strengths will vary from manufacturer to manufacturer. Diameters should be consistent throughout a length of material. Subject to each manufacturer's level of quality control, the range of variation will determine actual breaking strength. Tippet spools match the leader strength and come as monofilament, fluorocarbon and copolymer. Fluorocarbon is preferred for clear conditions and sunken flies. Copolymer tippet is fine for stained water and dry fly presentation, as it will not drag flies beneath the surface.

Balsam wood strike indicators.

Strike Indicators and Leader Weight

Strike indicators are small floating cork, yarn or foam devices attached to the leader or tippet at some point—typically 12 to 48 inches (30 to 120 cm)—above the fly to assist in the detection of strikes while fly-fishing with nymphs or other wet flies. I have fished chironomids with great success using a hot-pink and lime-green indicator. The first thing you do is double anchor your boat and measure the depth of water using something heavy attached to your fly line. Then mark the distance on your line, reel in and slide your indicator up to within 12 inches below your mark. Secure your indicator and tie on your fly. Cast out and let your fly sink to within 6–12 inches (15–30 cm) of the bottom. I use long leaders for chironomids, up to 15 to 20 feet (5 to 6 m), depending on the water depth.

Tie a small amount of lead onto the shank of your hook before dressing your fly; this weight will sink the fly to the proper depth. Weighted flies can be used in combination with strike indicators while fishing nymphs or chironomids. I like to tie a lot of my leech patterns with a little lead and the head of the hook shank; this will make the fly dip at the front of the fly head as you strip in.

Flies
"An artificial fly or fly lure is a type of fishing lure."

Like fly lines, there are basically two types of flies, dry flies and wet flies, with more combinations than there are stars. Dry flies are designed to float on the surface and are meant to imitate an adult insect that has landed on the water. Wet flies are designed to sink. Artificial flies are constructed by fly tying, in which furs, feathers, thread or any of very many other materials are tied onto a fishhook. They may be constructed to represent all manner of potential freshwater and saltwater fish prey, including aquatic and terrestrial insects, crustaceans, worms, baitfish, etc. Effective artificial fly patterns are said to be killing flies because of their ability in sub-surface presentation, imitating aquatic insects, insect larvae, leeches or even small fish called streamers.

Fly tying is a common practice in fly-fishing; many anglers even think of it as an important part of the fly-fishing experience. Fly fishers who tie their own flies either follow patterns in books, natural insect examples or their own imaginations. The technique involves attaching small pieces of feathers, animal fur and other materials on a hook in order to make them attractive to fish. This is done by wrapping thread tightly around the hook and tying on the desired materials. A fly is sized according to the width of the hook gap; large or longer flies are tied on larger, thicker and longer hooks.

In Chapter 8, "Thirty Great Pacific Northwest Fly Patterns," I have included some of the top flies for lake and river fishing.

Top: Brown bead-head marabou leech.

Above: A box of hand-tied trout flies.

Left: Fly tying bench with material.

Fishing on a crisp spring day.

5C: Fishing Tools and Gadgets

I have tried to list all the gear and gadgets you need or want in order to have a great experience on or near the water, starting with your fishing license.

Freshwater License

In British Columbia, freshwater licenses are valid for the current year from April 1 to March 31, commencing on the date purchased. You may purchase a one-day, eight-day or annual license. If you are under sixteen years of age and a resident of BC, you can sport fish without any license or stamp and do not need to be accompanied by a license holder. Another great thing if you are under sixteen is that you are entitled to your own quota of fish. For more information, pick up a copy of *Freshwater Fishing Regulations Synopsis*.

To purchase your angling license online or for further information, go to www.fishing.gov.bc.ca. Anglers may also obtain electronic licenses from their local Service BC Centre or any license vendor who offers this service. For a listing of Service BC centers and license vendors, go to http://a100.gov.bc.ca/pub/lvs.

To fish for salmon in freshwater, a provincial Non-Tidal Angling License is required. If you wish to retain any salmon caught in freshwater, your license must be validated with a Non-Tidal Salmon Conservation Stamp. Consult a copy of the freshwater or saltwater fishing regulations synopsis for the appropriate fishing licenses and regulations for the water you intend to fish.

Saltwater License

A tidal water sport fishing license is required to fish for any species of finfish. They are valid for the current year in British Columbia from April 1 to March 31, commencing on the date purchased. To purchase your angling license online or for further information, go to www.pac.dfo-mpo.gc.ca/recfish/Licensing. Tidal water sport fishing licenses are available province-wide from sporting good stores, resorts, service stations, marinas, charters and department stores.
A list of vendors is available on the DFO website. http://www.pac.dfo-mpo.gc.ca.

Tide Guide

"Tides are the alternating rise and fall of sea level with respect to land, as influenced by the gravitational attraction of the moon and sun."

If you are fishing for sea-run cutthroat trout, tides are very important, because if you are planning a trip to fish on a high tide you may not have any beach to stand on.

Samples of tide and bite guides.

Rod

"A fishing rod or a fishing pole is a tool used to catch fish."

Fighting Butt

Add versatility to your favorite fish rod with this removable extension butt that fits on the end of your rod handle. It can range from 1 to 6 inches (2.5 to 15 cm).

A four-piece fishing rod.

Fighting butt on one rod.

Reel

A reel holds your monofilament line or fly line and is attached to your fishing rod.

Tackle Box with Lures

A tackle box holds everything you need for a six-month fishing trip in one small container. Some tackle boxes are as big as your cooler.

A spin-casting reel.

Fly Boxes and Flies

Fly boxes are designed to store and carry artificial flies in an organized manner. The typical fly angler carries one or more fly boxes while fly-fishing. Fly boxes are available in a wide variety of sizes, styles and configurations. (Some fly fishermen get a little carried away and carry enough fly boxes to hold up to 500 flies for a one-day fishing trip.)

A tackle box full of trout gear.

Bait

Do you have your worms? How about your PowerBait?

Strike Indicators, Bobbers and Floats

Great for still fishing, just cast out and enjoy the day.

Weights

Slip weights attached to your line help take your lure or fly down to where the fish are.

Fly box with flies.

Clockwise from top left: Berkley PowerBait. Red and white floats for trout fishing. A selection of weights. Store-bought worms.

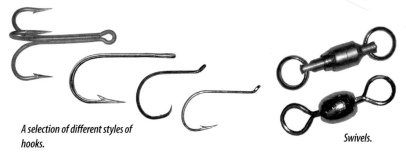

A selection of different styles of hooks.

Swivels.

Hooks

Most lures are purchased with hooks and you can change treble hooks to single hooks without changing the action of the lure.

Swivels

This is a must for all monofilament lines when fishing with all lures. This little piece of metal with two eyes that spin will prevent line twist on your main line. I use a leader on my main line, joined by a swivel.

Snaps

I don't use snaps when I freshwater fish as they add more weight to the lure and can affect its movement.

Scale

It's always nice to know the weight of your catch.

Measuring Tape or Ruler

This is a great tool for bragging rights, I have a ruler on my boat gunnel just for that purpose. Another tip is to measure your fishing rod near the butt end and use it as a measuring stick. I use my hand extended from my thumb to my baby finger (8 inches, or 20 cm) to measure my trout before I release them.

Needle-nose Pliers

Used for a variety of tasks, especially the safe removal of hooks, tightening knots, crimping sleeves and cutting leaders and line.

Hemostats

Used to remove hooks from the mouths of fish and other clamping tasks.

Top to bottom: Two snaps with swivels. A scale. Needle-nose pliers with pouch. Hemostat with wrist strap.

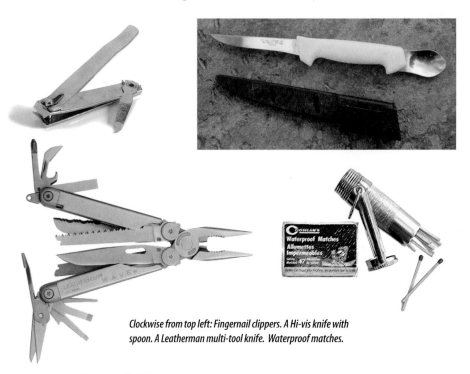

Clockwise from top left: Fingernail clippers. A Hi-vis knife with spoon. A Leatherman multi-tool knife. Waterproof matches.

Fingernail Clipper

A small clipping tool can be used to cut tippet material and other fishing lines cleanly.

Knife

A must when fishing. I carry a Leatherman on my belt at all times and have a large knife in my boat for cleaning fish. This knife is designed for cleaning fish and has a spoon on the end of the handle for the entrails.

Disposable Lighter or Waterproof Matches

You never know when you will need them, so always have them handy.

Fishing Log or Diary

Great for comparing trips—successes and otherwise—and for keeping track of which lures or flies worked.

Waterproof journal.

Left: Sharpening stone with pumpkinhead leech. Right: Nail knot-tying tool.

Left to right: Loon Outdoors floatant for dry flies. Tippet dispenser. A Fish Hawk thermometer.

Hook Sharpeners

Sharpening steels are used to sharpen hooks.

Knot-tying Tool

Used to assist in the tying of fishing knots.

Floatant

This liquid, paste or dry agent can be applied to artificial flies in dry fly-fishing to help prevent waterlogged flies.

Wetting Agent

A liquid designed to cause the sinking of flies and leaders.

Tippet Holder

A mechanism to hold one or more small spools of tippet material, as fly anglers typically carry a variety of tippet sizes at one time.

Thermometer

These are used to determine the temperature of the water we are fishing.

Landing Net

Typically constructed of cord or rubber mesh, a handheld net assists in the landing of fish and facilitates catch-and-release angling.

Wooden landing net with a nice rainbow trout.

Right: Lanyard loaded for fishing.

Far right: A selection of retractable gear keepers.

Lanyards

Lanyards are used to hold a variety of tools and gadgets around the angler's neck.

Retractable Gear Keepers

These are used to organize individual tools and gadgets while keeping them accessible on the water.

Magnifiers

Polarized sunglasses.

Help you to thread fine tippets and tie on small flies and lures.

Polarized Sunglasses

These protect the angler's eyes from the sun's rays and provide better underwater visibility while fishing. Try to get a pair that black out all sun from the sides. Use a lariat on your glasses, so that when you bend over or accidentally knock them off your head, they don't end up on the bottom of the lake or ocean.

Personal Flotation Device

Anglers should wear PFDs when fishing in a boat or other floating device such as a float tube, and wear a certified life preserver. I wear my PFD when I am wading—it's light and I don't know it's on, until I need it.

Sunscreen

Most sunscreens with an SPF of 15 or higher do an excellent job of protecting against UVB. SPF—or Sun Protection Factor—is a measure of a sunscreen's ability to prevent UVB from damaging the skin. Here's how it works. If it takes 20 minutes for your unprotected skin to start turning red, using an SPF 15 sunscreen theoretically prevents reddening 15 times longer—so it'll take about five hours, not 20 minutes, for you to turn crimson.

Mustang Survival flotation device.

Another way to look at it is in terms of percentages: SPF 15 blocks approximately 93 percent of all incoming UVB rays, SPF 30 blocks 97 percent, and SPF 50 blocks 98 percent. These may seem like negligible differences, but if you are light sensitive or have a history of skin cancer, those extra percentages will make a difference. And as you can see, no sunscreen can block all UV rays.

During a long day on the water, you should use around one half to one quarter of an 8-ounce (250-ml) bottle. Sunscreens should be applied 30 minutes before sun exposure to allow the ingredients to fully bind to the skin. To make them more effective you'll have to consistently reapply at least every two hours, and use a higher SPF. This is a must today for your own protection.

Top: SPF 30 suncreen designed for fly fishermen.

Bottom: Sunscreen for your lips prevents wind chap as well as sunburn.

A day on the river with the right equipment.

Tom Vaida from Victoria landed a 5.4-pound (2.5-kg) rainbow using a black leech pattern at Elk Lake near Victoria, BC.
Ward Bond photo

5D: Clothing and Apparel

"Layered clothing is a manner of dressing using multiple garments that are worn on top of each other."

Layered clothing is particularly relevant in cold climates, where it must at the same time transfer moisture, provide warmth and protect from wind and rain. This system is a must for West Coast anglers fishing for steelhead in the fall/winter or beach fishing for sea-run cutthroat on a cool winter day.

Two thin layers can be warmer yet lighter than one thick layer, because the air trapped between layers serves as thermal insulation. Usually at least three layers are required: the base layer provides comfort by keeping the skin dry, the mid layer provides warmth and the outer layer protects from wind and water. The purpose of the inner layer is to draw the sweat away from the skin to the next layers, which makes the wearer feel warmer and more comfortable. Synthetic materials such as polyester and microfiber-based fabrics are good choices.

Middle layers provide maximum warmth, and multiple thin mid layers can work better than one thicker layer and can

Gill's base layer.

facilitate adjustment of warmth. The mid layer should be more loose-fitting than the inner layer, as this leaves insulating air between the layers. Wool is the traditional mid layer material because it has good insulation even when wet, absorbs moisture but does not feel wet even when it holds significant moisture. It also transfers moisture. Fleece or other synthetics have many of the features of wool but are lighter. They provide good insulation even when wet, absorb very little moisture and dry quickly.

The outer layer is called the shell layer, but only if it blocks wind or water. Ideally it will let moisture through to the outside (breathable), while not letting wind and water pass through from the outside to the inside. Soft shell materials block water only partially and are not "waterproof," just water resistant. They are usually more breathable and comfortable, as well as being thinner and cheaper, than completely waterproof materials. Hard shell materials are waterproof and somewhat breathable. Their essential element is a thin,

Fleece jacket.

porous membrane that blocks liquid water but lets through water vapor (evaporated sweat). The more expensive materials are typically more breathable, the best-known brand being Gore-Tex.

The practical benefit to layering is that the wearer can shed layers according to changes in temperature and keep warm and cool depending on the day or activity.

Shirts and Pants

On warmer days, our shirts and pants have very different requirements than layering, because they must block the radiation from the sun and allow for sufficient air circulation. When fishing for trout on hot days wear light, long-sleeved, vented

Jack Derish was fishing with his eight-year-old grandson, Kole MacKinnon, at a lake near Port Alice on Vancouver Island when Kole caught the biggest fish of the trip—a rainbow 20.5 inches (52 cm) long, 5.5 inches (14 cm) deep and 6 pounds (3 kg) in weight.

Left to right: Gloves can make or break a trip on a cold day. Stripping finger guides can save the day especially when fishing in salt water. This pack has it all: a chest pack and a backpack.

shirts because these hi-tech items will keep moisture and heat away from your body, making fishing more comfortable and enjoyable.

Hats

Big-brim hats are a must because they keep the sun off your face and ears. They can also protect your face from a fly that has gone wild during casting.

Gloves

Anglers use a variety of gloves to protect their hands from the sun and cold.

Stripping Finger Guards

Prevents grooves and cuts on your stripping finger. They are used more in saltwater applications as the salt sticks to the fly line and will wear into your stripping finger.

This fishing vest works as a flotation device and holds your gear.

Fishing Packs

There is a wide variety of small to large packs specifically designed for anglers who carry accessories, supplies, lunch and other gear while on the water. These include fanny packs, backpacks and chest packs.

Fishing Vest

There is a wide variety of vests specifically designed for fly anglers, which they can use to carry accessories, supplies and other gear while on the water.

Waders

Waders will keep anglers dry while they are wading or otherwise in contact with water. Waders may be chest high, hip high or merely tall boots. They may have a stocking foot requiring the use of a wading boot or shoe, or have integrated boot feet. Most waders are made of breathable Gore-Tex or neoprene. Neoprene waders are essential to prevent hypothermia when fishing a saltwater beach out of a float tube, pontoon boat or other inflatable craft where much of your body is often in cold water. They are not as popular as they once were since they do not breathe and are not the easiest to get into or out of.

Wading Belt

For safety, wear a wading belt to stop water from filling your waders in case you slip on a rock; your waders will fill quickly with ice-cold water. Some waders have a built in wading belt.

Wading Boots

Wading boots protect the angler's feet. They typically have some form of gripping mechanism on the sole to provide a margin of safety on slippery surfaces; this may be made of felt and/or felt with removable metal studs. When tying your boots, try using an elastic cord with a stopper to secure them—when a knot gets wet and your hands are cold, it's not fun to undo.

Gravel Guards

Some waders have built-in rock guards, which keep small gravel from getting into your boots, making walking uncomfortable, if not impossible. These usually consist of a piece of neoprene—a tube or a flat piece with a zipper—which fits around your ankles and over the top of your boots.

Top to bottom: Waders drying after a day on the water. Our family wading boots. Simms neoprene tube gravel guards.

6 | Phil Rowley

A Still-water Kit Bag

A beautiful day to wet a line.

Variables are part of a still-water fly fisher's life. Some you control, some you do not. Fly fishers have no control over environmental variables such as water temperature, barometric pressure or wind. On the other hand, they can control equipment. From personal experience, focusing on what you can control better prepares an angler for what you cannot control. Fly fishers who are confident in their equipment from a quality, performance and availability point of view are better prepared for Mother Nature's curve balls, and better able to focus on the challenge at hand. Rods and reels are a natural. However, on any given day or outing it is the little things or details that so often make the difference. In equipment terms, this means a well-stocked and organized kit bag. The still-water nerve center, if you will.

The first stop on any kit bag tour is the bag itself. A suitable kit bag must be portable and compact with enough compartments, pockets and sections to house a wide array of gear. Compartmentalized bags allow fly fishers to sort and store equipment in a logical, easy-to-find fashion.

Phil's kit bags.

Discipline is required to make sure items are put back in their place. This is not always easy during the course of a day, and contents often become dishevelled.

Look for a bag with good strong zipper systems. A reliable set of zippers ensures items stay on board during the trip from the car or boat or during a walk through the woods to the shoreline. Be wary of bags that have pockets that zip around 90-degree corners. These can be challenging to close once loaded, and in some instances cause the zippers to split. A shoulder strap is another handy feature because this allows rods, landing nets, coolers and kit bag to be portaged in one trip, an event all fishermen are familiar with. Water resistance is paramount, especially if the kit bag is also home to camera equipment. Most quality gear bags are waterproof and some come with waterproof covers to protect your gear on a damp day. If fly-fishing during torrential rain is your thing, choose a completely waterproof bag.

At first glance there appears to be lots of room in an empty kit bag. One might ask, "How am I going to fill this thing?" Don't worry, it won't take long. There are six main categories to consider when outfitting a gear bag: reel spools/lines, leaders and tippet, accessories, fly boxes, safety and comfort and miscellaneous items.

The number of extra spools and lines fly fishers stash in their bag depends on the time of the year, the physical makeup of the lake, the number of fly rods and a dash of personal preference. I prefer two rods strung and ready, typically a floating line, with or without an indicator, and a clear intermediate. Experience has taught me two rods are best, especially when fishing with more than one person. In addition to the rigged rods include an extra floating line, which can be particularly handy during a chironomid emergency. Alone on the boat, anglers can work two floating lines, one with an indicator and one without.

Working down the depth chart, a traditional intermediate would be next. Depending upon the manufacture, these sink slower than most clear intermediates, which tend to sink at type 2 rate. Intermediates are the best choice for creeping scuds, leeches or damsel nymphs over shoals or along shorelines. A clear-tip line is also an excellent addition. Such lines are ideal for long-leader nymphing and for working flies through the shallows, and offer a different retrieve angle that can make all the difference. A selection of full sinking lines, typically type 3 and 6, rounds out your line selection. The type 6 line is ideal for working deep reaches, stripping leeches and dragon patterns over the shoals or crawling buoyant flies over sunken weeds and debris.

Top: Kit bag compartments.

Bottom: Samples of leaders and tippets.

Leaders and tippet are the critical connection between fly and angler and are sometimes overlooked. Depending upon your leader setup preference, carry butt material for long leader setups or braided loops. I use both types of leader connection depending on the line and presentation. For example, for a floating-line, long-leader system I always begin with 2 to 3 feet (60 to 90 cm) of .025" to .030" butt section and add a tapered leader and tippet for length.

Carry a good selection of tapered leaders from 9 to 15 feet (3 to 5 m). Breaking

Some of the accessories in a kit bag.

strains should vary from 3x down through 5x, depending upon conditions. As a general rule the clearer the water, the finer the leader and tippet. Tippet spools should match leader strength in both fluorocarbon and copolymer. Fluorocarbon is the preferred choice for clear conditions and sunk flies, while copolymer tippet is best for stained waters and dry fly presentations because it does not drag flies beneath the surface (which is often the case with fluorocarbon).

Hemostats or forceps are used to remove hooks from fish.

Accessories are the catch basin for many items in a well-stocked kit bag. Thermometers are critical tools because water temperature dictates fish activity and feeding as well as insect emergences. Knowing that the preferred temperature range

of rainbow trout is 55–65°F (12–18°C) allows fly fishers to avoid non-productive water. Using a traditional thermometer on a string, anglers can vertically probe the water and locate fish. When it comes to nippers have a good pair or, even better, two. This is an accessory I lose often, either in the rubble of the boat or accidentally over the side. Placing nippers on a retractor and attaching them to the shirt or jacket is advised.

Hemostats or forceps are used to crimp barbs, remove hooks from fish and friends, transfer fly lines and even set indicator depth. A bell sinker also works for fine-tuning indicator depth. If possible look for a pair with cutters and other handy add-ons. To transfer a fly line using forceps, reel the leader back to the reel. Clamp the forceps on between the stripping guide and the reel to prevent the leader from snaking back through the guides, then cut the leader and replace the spool. Reattach the leader to the new line and you are ready to go—you'll have no more adventures standing in a boat feeding line through rod guides. If you don't have a hemostat, try using a clothes peg.

Knot tiers for forming nail knots are handy if you like to attach leaders or butt sections to your fly line. As for indicators, carry a good selection of sizes, types and colors. Corkies and yarn are personal favorites. Yarn indicators cast easily and work well in shallow clear waters, where the splat and look of a corky may spook wary trout. When using floating lines in windy conditions weight is often needed to aid presentation.

Include a selection of split shot or non-toxic putty. Barrel swivels are another option. A small bag of 12 to 16 swivels should suffice. Other accessories include floatant, leader sinkant and line cleaner. Use both paste and powder floatant. Apply paste floatant prior to casting. Dry fly powders are a desiccant that quickly dry out sunk or trout-slobbered flies. Sinkant degreases leaders and tippet, a necessary step when fishing dry flies on calm clear days.

Throat pumps are a valuable accessory but should only be used on fish larger than 14 inches (35 cm) and if the angler is comfortable doing so. A vile or white tray allows for clear inspection of the contents, which can help in fly selection and determining feeding depth. Bottom-dwelling contents would suggest presenting patterns just above the weeds. Conversely, emergers and adults would suggest that the fish are cruising near the surface.

After years of experimenting I prefer smaller fly boxes that are easy to store in the kit bag. Use a label maker to identify the contents so you don't waste time looking for a favorite pattern. Clear compartmentalized boxes are ideal for dry flies as they tend not to squash hackle. Choose a sorting system that makes sense. I tend to group my flies by food type: chironomids, caddis and mayflies, leeches, dragons and damsels, scuds, boatmen and backswimmers and dry flies. These groupings were in a state of flux but in recent years have remained steady and reliable.

Labeled fly boxes.

Safety and comfort items typically have nothing directly to do with fishing but everything to do with having an enjoyable day on the water. Polarized sunglasses are probably the one exception. In addition to providing eye protection from errant flies, these are critical to penetrating the sun's glare and allowing you to see into the water, so you can spot underwater obstructions, weed beds, drop-offs, migrating invertebrates and cruising fish. Keep the glasses in a protective case when not in use and make a regular habit of cleaning the lenses.

Sunscreen and lip balm are recommended kit bag additions, especially for the fair-skinned. Band-aids manage small nicks and cuts as well as providing fore finger relief from line burns caused by fleeing trout. A small bottle of Aspirin, Advil or Tylenol handles any dehydration headaches that pop up. A roll of toilet paper in a ziplock bag is a welcome sight for obvious reasons. Finally, keep a small towel in the bag for wiping wet hands. On cool days letting hands dry through evaporation leads to frigid digits in short order.

Packed kit bag.

With every storage system there are a few items that slide neatly into the miscellaneous category. Never leave the shore without a camera. A DSLR or small point-and-shoot system can provide lasting memories that add to the experience. Include a pen and notepad in a plastic bag to record detailed notes of the day's experiences and observations. This habit reduces the learning curve because important items are not forgotten. Keep track of everything, including weather patterns, diet analysis, hatches, successful patterns, structure types, leader setups, presentation techniques and any general observations. This information is key to a fly fisher's growth and development. Last but not least, don't forget the fishing license.

A well thought-out and stocked kit bag plays a pivotal but often unrecognized role while fly-fishing still waters. Knowing it is complete provides an anchor on which to rely. There are enough uncontrollable aspects to a day's fishing. Having this one thing in your favor keeps some of these variables at bay, enabling the angler to focus on what's really important—catching fish.

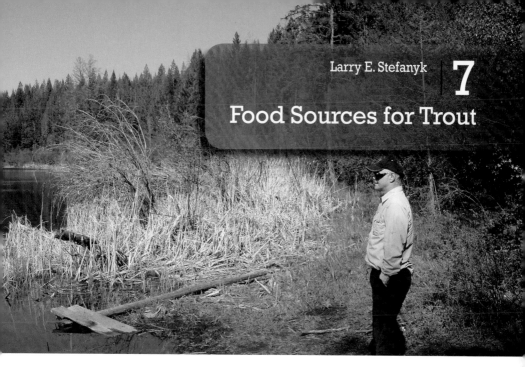

Food Sources for Trout

W hen I arrive at a lake I like to look along the shoreline and answer some questions regarding insect activity. Aquatic insects will show themselves if water temperatures have risen enough to start activity. I check out the wash area of the shoreline, flip over a rock or two or examine the area around reed beds, looking for the pupal skins or "shucks" of insects that have hatched recently. They give me a clue as to what fly pattern to use. I don't wet a line anywhere until I first look and see if there is any activity. If I don't see surface activity, either fish or insect, I pack up and go home.

Assessing the insect activity upon arriving at a lake helps determine successful fly patterns.

Just kidding.

I head out and tie on an attractor or searching pattern, the most common being Doc Spratley's, Halfbacks, Carey Special, Montana, Wooly Buggers or a Leech pattern. I also mimic the natural creatures I am imitating in both speed and action when I retrieve.

The following are the most important food sources for our waters. I have given you fly patterns to match the insects and some suggestions on how to fish the fly to represent the food source.

7A: Dragonflies and Damselflies

Dragonflies and damselflies are prominent inhabitants of lakes, ponds and some streams. Darner dragonflies are the largest dragonflies, the common green darner being one of the most widespread and numerous. The blue-eyed darner and the variable darner make up half of the darners. They are widespread in western Canada. Dragonfly nymphs are quite large and often occur in great numbers. Nymphs live as

Darner dragonfly.

long as three years, swimming around and eating other insects. They range in size from 25–50 mm (1 to 2 inches) and in color from brown to olive brown.

Dragonfly adults emerge out of the water. Unlike damselflies they are such strong flies that they are seldom taken by trout while emerging.

There are three types of dragonfly nymphs of which western fly anglers should be aware. The appearance and behavior of each are radically different.

Dragonfly Nymph.

Aeshnidae

The "climbers" (the family Aeshnidae) have long, tapered bodies. They search for their prey, moving about by jet propulsion: they take in water through their mouth and expel it through their anus. This causes them to move in spurts, so a good tactic is to cast an appropriate nymph and use the count-down-and-retrieve presentation, moving the fly with 6- to 12-inch (15- to 30-cm) strips with a pause between each strip. This is the type of dragonfly nymph that is most commonly imitated by fly fishermen.

In shallow lakes use a dry line with a long leader and fish above weed beds and shoreline debris. Use a full-sink line to probe deeper waters and the fish will strike these flies with force. Hook sizes can be 2 through 12 on 3X- or 4X-long hooks in colors ranging from green to dark olive. Brown Wooly Worms, Carey Special (try using a Peacock herl body), Doc. Spratley and Matuka Leeches are all effective patterns to imitate this dragonfly nymph.

Doc Spratley fly.

Libellulidae

The second type of dragonfly is the "sprawler" (the family Libellulidae). Sprawlers are boxy in appearance, being wider and shorter than their Aeshnidae cousins. As you might expect from their couch-potato shape, they're not very active still-water dwellers. They nest quietly among aquatic plants, then spring up and nail unsuspecting prey when it comes along. Sprawlers are naturally camouflaged, so choose an imitation that is the same color as the lake bottom where you are fishing. Let the fly sink to the bottom and sit there. Then give it a quick tug, like a nymph leaping from ambush to inhale an unfortunate midge larva. If that doesn't catch the interest of a passing trout, let the fly settle back down and try again, or retrieve the fly very slowly with a hand-twist retrieve. Patterns used should be tied on shorter hooks; the Wooly Worm tied on a standard hook in sizes 8 to 12 1X long is a good pattern to try. Another great pattern is a Rabbit Leech, weighted, tied on a 3X-long hook in sizes 4 to 10.

Red Butt Wooly Worm.

Gomphidae

The third type of dragonfly nymph is the "burrower" (the family Gomphidae). Like sprawlers, nymphs are broad and flat, with very long, thick bodies, large thoraxes and two pairs of long clear wings held perpendicular to the body in flight and at rest. Brown and black are common colors, mottled and banded with darker shades. The nymphs live in sediment and ambush their prey using similar tactics to sprawlers. They climb through aquatic vegetation stalking their prey. Both dragonflies and damselfly nymphs will climb reeds, rocks and branches to emerge. Inspection of these areas will reveal the shucks if "hatching" has occurred. You can use a pattern like the Ultimate fly or a dragonfly nymph.

Left to right: The Ultimate fly. A dragonfly nymph pattern. A damselfly.

Damselflies

Damselflies are closely related to dragonflies and have a similar life cycle. However, damselflies are smaller and have more slender bodies than dragonflies and are more numerous. Trout eat both nymphs and adults. The nymphs are usually found near weedy margins of still water or very slow-moving portions of rivers or streams. They can swim slowly but usually cling to weed stems and ambush their prey. They have slender bodies from 5/8 to 2 inches (15–50 mm) long, with thick wing cases and thoraxes, long legs, two pairs of long clear wings held parallel to the body at rest, a large head with small but prominent eyes and flipper-like tails. The most common colors are browns, greens and yellow-greens. These nymphs swim to within a yard of the surface and then head toward vegetation to crawl up and emerge as adult damselflies.

Damselfly and dragonfly nymphs usually have the same coloration as the bottom or vegetation they frequent. Dubbed marabou or seal hair makes excellent bodies and these flies are all in my fly box: Marabou Damsel, Stump Damsel, Chenille Olive Wooly Worm, Seal Fur or a Green Carey Special in hook sizes of 10 to 12. Most dressings for this nymph are green or olive and a few are brown. My favorite is the Carey Special with an insect-green chenille body and a pheasant rump hackle tied sparse.

Dragonflies emerge from vegetation.

7B: Mayflies

Larval mayflies, often called nymphs, live underwater from streams to large lakes and mostly feed on plants or organic debris. Their body color may be green or brown but may vary according to the food they are eating. They are elongated and flattened or cylindrical, and have long legs and plate-like gills on the sides of the abdomen.

They usually have three long thin tail projections, but a few species only have two, and a short set of antennae. The flattened forms attach themselves to rocks or other substrates in streams and the cylindrical forms are better swimmers.

Larval mayflies may live a year or two, or even up to four years, molting several times before they leave the water. Size and coloration are endless, though many nymphs are of a brownish hue. Nymphs are available most of the season, usually in shallow waters, near weed beds or near the bottom. Your best

Mayfly nymph.

success often comes when the nymph pattern is fished in the evening on the shallow shoals just by a drop-off. Add a little life in still water with pulsing movements of the rod tip, or with short strips of line. Use a dry line with 8- to 12-foot (2.6–3.6 m) leaders. Nymphs should be tied on 2X- or 3X-long shank hooks, ranging from sizes 10 to 18. Popular nymphs are the Prince, March Brown, Zug Bug, Pheasant Tail, Gold Ribbed Hare's Ear and Hendrickson.

Left to right: Pheasant Tail Nymph. March Brown Nymph. Small purple bead-head micro leech.

A dark micro leech is a great mayfly nymph pattern.

In rivers and streams, cast into the current and allow the nymph to tumble along the bottom. When it reaches the end of its drift retrieve it slowly to imitate it crawling along the bottom. You will often get most of your strikes on the swing.

Subimago (Dunn) is the first winged stage of the mayfly. It has a dull appearance. The nymph emerges by crawling out of the water on plant stems, sticks or rocks. Dunns are seldom available to fish but trout will try to pick up strays if they can.

Unlike most other insects, mayflies molt again after reaching the winged stage, to a fully adult stage called the imago or spinner. The imago has large triangular front wings with many cross veins, which it holds upright and together over the thorax. Subimagoes have cloudy colored wings while imagoes (spinners) have clear wings. Some species may have the winged pattern. Hind wings are much smaller than fore wings and are absent in a few (mostly small) species. The thorax and the abdomen of mayflies are bare and shiny. Legs vary

If there's a heavy hatch on, pick a fish outside the main feeding lane where there are fewer bugs per fish. Best not to be one fly competing with fifty real bugs. If there's a light hatch on, pick a back eddy and find the main seam and the one rising fish. You'll usually get the bigger fish with the second situation.

in size, with the front legs the longest and held forward when at rest. Body color is quite delicate and varies with species, including yellow, green, white and black.

Spinners live just long enough to mate and for the female to lay eggs. After emerging from their old skin, they leave the water and take flight for the first time. As this is happening they are vulnerable to trout that pick them off at the surface. The best conditions for fishing mayfly spinner patterns are calm, warm evenings. Size of hooks commonly range from 10 to 18 tied on a standard dry hook; you can likely get by in most situations with these patterns.

The Adams is the most basic and fundamental dry mayfly pattern. It represents any medium-sized, medium-colored (grayish-brown) mayfly and often works very well during hatches of various mayfly species. Suggestions: Light Cahill (for light-colored mayflies), the Blue-Winged Olive (for olive-colored mayflies), CDC, Tom Thumb, Blue Dun, March Brown Soft-Hackle and Gray Wulff.

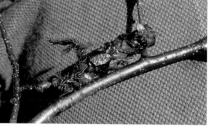

An Adams dry mayfly pattern.

7C: Caddis Flies

Caddis Larva

The caddis larva is a grub-like creature that builds cases or "retreats" of nearly infinite design. They build their retreats from weeds, pebbles, wood debris, pieces of leaves or other materials that they find in lakes, rivers or streams. They can live encased in this tubular structure for up to two years, molting and changing their cases as they grow.

The larva moves about and feeds by protruding its head and using its long legs to crawl slowly along. When disturbed it retracts into its casing. Hungry trout will eat caddis larvae, case and all.

A caddis larva case on a branch.

Patterns should represent the insect as well as its house. Use a floating fly line with a long leader and retrieve line with a slow hand-twist retrieve. Use a weighted fly to put the fly on the bottom, then retrieve very slowly along the bottom with occasional twitches to imitate a crawling, foraging larva. Suggestions: Golden Ribbed Hare's Ear, Zug Bug, March Brown, Carey Special in sizes 8 to 16 in brown, tan, green, black, yellow and gray, tied on 1X- or 2X-long hooks.

Above : Caddis larvae build cases from pebbles, wood and other debris, moulting their cases as they grow. Below left to right: Cased caddis larva fly. Copper Carey Special.

Adult Caddis Flies

Often called sedges, adult caddis flies have two antennae and are easily identified by the mottled-colored wing, which is folded over the top of the body in a V shape.

Total length is ⅜ to ⅞ inch (9 to 22 mm) with a modest body portion, thick wing case/thorax area, prominent head, long legs and no tail. Color generally spans the yellows, browns, greens and blacks, with a tan-colored nymph being the most abundant. Many species live completely exposed on sand and gravel, while others attach themselves to rock and weed during the day and will seek shelter and become more active at dusk.

The caddis fly is an insect that trout feed on heavily. During a caddis hatch there is no better pattern to use than the Elk Hair Caddis in gray. Black, cinnamon, green, yellow and brown are also common colors with hook sizes ranging from 6 to 18. Elk Hair Caddis, Deer Hair Caddis, Stimulator, Traveler Sedge, March Brown and a Tom Thumb pattern will all work.

Top: Adult caddis sitting on a reed.

Bottom: Elk Hair Caddis.

7D: Stone Flies

Stone flies vary in size from very small to gigantic, depending on species and habitat. Nymphs have two claws at the end of each leg, two sets of wing pads, two short, heavy tails and two antennae that look like armor plating. Nymphs of the larger species live in fast, riffly water with lots of oxygen. Because stone flies are voracious predators, their active crawling is mainly in search of prey. This and their fast-water habitat means that many nymphs are dislodged and drift in the current, only to be eaten by trout. An effective method is to use short casts upstream and then let the fly tumble back down with the current. Use no drag and no imparted action, and a floating line with a wet tip and a short leader of 4 to 6 feet (1.2 to 2 m). During emergence activity fish feed on the restless nymphs. Try using a Gold Ribbed Hare's Ear 12 through 16 in dark brown or black or a Montana Stone, Golden Stone, Elk Hair Caddis in the same size.

Stonefly.

Right: Double Black Pearl Black Stonefly.

Far right: King Double Bead Thin Skin Golden Stonefly.

Adults will be hidden on the undersides of leaves or other stream foliage where mating occurs. In the evening they become active and the females release the eggs when the abdomen touches the water. Many females are trapped in the surface film, resulting in active feeding by trout. Pattern: Golden Stone sizes from 4–10 3X long.

7E: Terrestrials

Grasshoppers

In areas with lots of grass near a river or a lake, hoppers—with their large heads, prominent eyes, boxy build, large legs and wings—are abundant from mid summer until the first frosts. If a few hoppers fall onto a river they have a difficult time getting airborne and will drift until they make a meal for a trout. Trout may be interested in food other than hoppers, even if these big bugs are present. In fact trout eat far more beetles and ants than hoppers.

Grasshopper.

But if hoppers are available and if trout want them then you can make for some outstanding dry fly-fishing. Most times it's not enough to simply let your imitation drift down the river, you will need to place it within inches of the river bank and preferably have it land with an audible "plop." Any hopper pattern will work, like Madam X tied in sizes 6 to 10. Colors range from green, yellow and cream to tan and brown.

Madam X.

Ants

Many ants live in trees near rivers or lakes, and when the wind blows it often blows a few of them onto the water. On many lakes and streams a dry fly that imitates an ant or termite is an excellent choice in the summer.

Another good time to use an ant pattern is during an ant hatch. Trout will gorge themselves on ants until they cannot fit another one in their stomach. Remember, once the trout gets a full tummy on ants, it stops eating, so get on the hatch early. Tie on any pattern 10 to 16 in black or red-brown.

Top: Black ant.

Above: Flying ant.

Above: Siminiuk's black ant.

Right: Flying ant.

7F: Waterboatmen and Backswimmers

Both inhabit still water and reach maturity in late summer and fall. With their brown-olive bodies and dark brown wing cases, backswimmers closely resemble their near relatives, the water boatmen, in both appearance and behavior. There are important differences, however: backswimmers are bigger, swim on their backs and use a pair of large rear legs for propulsion, and when they are on the surface their abdomen penetrates the film. These differences are important if you are tying flies. First consider the size; then match the color of the top of the insect rather than the bottom. Thirdly your pattern should poke through the surface to make a floating imitation.

Backswimmer.

Like waterboatmen, backswimmers have large legs that they use like oars. Like waterboatmen they also lack gills and carry a bubble of oxygen with them when they dive beneath the surface in search of food. Look for them in shallow, weedy areas of lakes where the water is less than 5 feet (1.5 m) deep. Short casts are better than long casts when presenting this fly.

Try to touch your fly with your hands as little as possible to avoid leaving human scents. In fact, some "old-timers" used to say that you should wash your nymphs and wet flies with soil to remove the human and head cement odors.

Mimic the insect's up-and-down behavior with a lift-and-settle retrieve that draws the fly back to the surface in short darts. Then let the fly sink without any action. A floating line and a long, fine leader will keep the fly in the zone; then use short, two-inch strips to bring it back to the surface. Shades of tan, green or brown are most common; hook size is 16 through 20 on a standard 1X hook. Corixid, notonectid and backswimmer are all good patterns.

7G: Midges: Chironomidae, Mosquitoes

Larvae

Midge larvae live at the bottom of lakes, including deep lakes. They feed on organic debris or microscopic plants and animals and are microscopic and worm-like with a many-segmented body. As they develop, the larvae can grow anywhere from a quarter to over one inch (8 to 25 mm) in length before pupating, which can take up to three years depending on the species. Some are colored bright red by hemoglobin, earning the name

Chironomidae larva.

"bloodworms." Bloodworms are usually red but can also be brown or dark green. Larvae midges can hatch in early spring and again in the fall. They live on the lake bottom, except when strong winds reach this area and sweep them up, making them vulnerable and a major food source for trout. To fish them, use the same techniques as with the pupa stage. Patterns: bloodworm, bent bloodworm.

Above: Bead-head bent bloodworm.

Right: Trout with bloodworm pattern.

Pupae

The pupa stage is the most important from a fly-fishing perspective as the trout feed voraciously on these small, emerging insects, largely because of the sheer numbers that may be present throughout the water column during an emergence. This generally occurs from early April through late July, though much depends on lake latitude and elevation. Smaller and shorter emergences will continue through to at least the end of September.

Chironomid pupa.

Pupae range in size from ⅛ to more than one inch (4 to 25 mm) and have a thin body, thicker wing case/thorax, white gills in the head area and no tail. The most common colors are red, black, green and tan, depending on environment. The pupa emerges from the larval (bloodworm) tube and rises directly to the surface. Here the head splits open and a tiny mosquito-like fly emerges, which will live for at most a few weeks.

When chironomid fishing I anchor from the bow and stern and use a strike indicator to help detect strikes. I use a floating line with a large lime-green/hot pink strike indicator with a leader and tippet anywhere from 10 to 20 feet (3 to 6 m) long, depending on the depth of the water I'm fishing. In order to get the chironomid pattern to the desired depth, I measure the depth of water I am fishing using a weight on my fly line and then mark my line to indicate the bottom. I adjust my strike indicator on the leader and use a bead-head fly pattern or split shot to help me sink the fly until it is just off the bottom.

A strike indicator is not always necessary. If you do not wish to use one, tie a weighted chironomid pattern to your floating line, cast it, then allow it to sink to the desired depth. Begin a slow "figure-eight" retrieve—pause—then continue. Another method is to use an intermediate sinking line and a long leader with tippet. Cast out and time your descent and retrieve with the same slow figure-eight retrieve—pause—then continue.

Try keeping your fly rod tip at or just under the water while retrieving a fly in still water. You'll feel a lot more takes than you would otherwise. The same goes when trolling flies in a boat or tube. Keep that tip as low as possible, with your line taut so you can feel any bumps while it is sinking. The only exception to this is when performing a technique near the end of a retrieve with the last 10 feet (3 m) of fly line. Slowly raise the rod tip until it's sky high, while continuing to retrieve. This will imitate an emerging insect or a fleeing prey. Fish that have been following your fly will often slam it hard enough that it's not a big problem that your tip's nowhere near the water.

Fish it slowly, taking many minutes to retrieve a cast. There is a saying about chironomid fishing: "if you think you're retrieving it too slow, retrieve it ten times slower." In late summer I won't use an indicator because the chironomids are usually bigger and the trout tend to hit them fairly hard. The largest pupal patterns, known locally as "bombers," are dressed on 12-3XL to 8-3XL hooks. The Tunkwa and Leighton lakes out of Kamloops are known for their bombers.

Bomber chironomid.

Chironomid pupa color is important. The most common colors are black, maroon, green and brown, or various shades of each. Patterns are tied on hook sizes 18 to 24 or smaller as chironomids are found in lakes but are more common in rivers and especially productive tailwaters. However, the larval and pupal stages of many chironomid species found in the still waters are commonly represented on 16 to 10 hooks such as the Mustad Signature C49S or Tiemco 2457. Pupal bodies with ribbings of copper, red copper, green copper, silver and gold wire or holographic tinsels in the same colors are effective. Body colors are black, maroon, brown and shades of green. Pupal gills or breathing filaments can be imitated well with white metal or pearlescent plastic beads, white antron or ostrich herl. If I had one pattern to use it would be a black floss body with a red copper wire rib and white bead-head tied on a Mustad Signature C49S or Tiemco 2457 in sizes 14 to 10.

*Brown
Pheasant Tail
chironomid.*

Adult Chironomidae

Adult chironomidae are mosquito-like in appearance. They have fairly long bodies, up to half an inch (12 mm) overall, and are usually gray, green or black, with one pair of clear elongated wings lying parallel to the body at rest and no tail. Many chironomids form large swarms, often at dusk, though I have seen them swarm over lakes in the afternoon. Patterns: Lady McConnell.

*Right: Adult
chironomidae.*

*Far right: Lady
McConnell.*

Mosquitoes

The mosquito is closely related to the chironomid but is not a common food source for trout. Mosquito pupae are only slightly heavier than water and can easily rise to the surface by wriggling their bodies rapidly from side to side, because they must obtain their oxygen directly from the atmosphere. They do this through a siphon tube that they extend through the surface of the water. If wave action occurs it will likely break this surface contact and drown the mosquito. Because of this, these insects are restricted to marshes, ponds, swamps, puddles and pools that don't have wave action and are not normally found on our interior fishing lakes.

The period of transformation from pupa to adult is very short. The pupa skin splits at the thorax, the adult works its way out and the mosquito is poised for flight. The same fishing techniques employed with chironomids are applicable to mosquito imitations. The adult mosquito is not a food source because trout usually avoid egg-laying adults. Pattern: Mosquito in sizes 14–18.

Mosquito.

7H: Scuds: Freshwater Shrimp

Scuds, sometimes called "freshwater shrimp," are freshwater crustaceans. There are two kinds in interior lakes, Hyella and Gammarus. At a casual glance the only visible difference is in their size; the Hyella never grow as large as the Gammarus. Trout feed on both but a large Hyella imitation would be tied on a size 18 to 20 hook.

Our lower-elevation lakes tend to be high in dissolved salts and calcium and are generally very productive for shrimp. Lakes with lily pads tend to be more acidic and usually have lower populations of shrimp. In some lakes scuds are active all year round and are an important part of the food chain, making up 20 percent of a fish's diet. Since the shrimp have no natural defense mechanisms except camouflage, they usually hide in the Chara weeds and are more active during periods of low sunlight or after dark.

> If your fly box gets dunked, set it out in the open to dry as soon as you can. Those hooks will rust fast and nothing's worse (or more expensive) than a box full of rusty flies.

Scuds will swim in just about any position: upside-down, right-side-up, backwards, forwards, sideways. They'll dart and can move quickly when startled.

Gammarus shrimp are semi-transparent; their entire digestive tract shows through their shell. Although they scavenge on animal material, their primary food is often plant matter and blue-green algae. The plants and algae cause most shrimp to appear as various shades of green, sometimes into bluish hues. However, the immediate surroundings can sometimes offset that color.

Of note is the orange coloration of the eggs carried within a pregnant female. When the shrimp die these turn pinkish to orange. The shrimp will swim for 5 to 10 inches (12 to 25 cm) and then stop to rest and breathe. When stopped they sink toward the bottom, usually in a curled position. After a few seconds they will uncurl and swim another short distance. This swimming and sinking is very erratic and is a good way to retrieve a fly representing a shrimp. Use a floating, neutral-color fly line with a

Top: Freshwater shrimp.

Bottom: Pregnant shrimp with young. Jack Shaw photo

strike indicator in shallow water or a slow-sinking line with a short leader in deeper areas. Scuds aren't great swimmers and when they move they flip their tail. A good presentation is to combine 2- to 5-inch (5- to 12-cm) jerky strips with a steady hand twist, a short rest and repeat. The hand twist keeps tension on the line, important because strikes will be difficult to feel. Since scuds usually inhabit the weeds and vegetation on the bottom they are seldom found free-floating in the water, so don't tie scud patterns with weights. When the water is off-colored you can use a brightly colored, highly visible fly, or darker flies on light-colored bottoms for contrast.

Patterns: Werner Shrimp, Mylar Shrimp, Pearl Shrimp in sizes 8 to 16.

Right: Rowley CDC shrimp.

Far right: Pink marl shrimp.

7I: Snails

Trout don't feed heavily on snails, but will if they're around. Streams and spring-fed lakes with high calcium carbonate levels can be loaded with snails because calcium carbonate is the essential mineral snails need to build their shells. In this sense, scuds and snails prefer the same types of water, so when you find lots of one, keep an eye out for the other.

Snail.

Snails like shallow water with a minimum of wave action. Trout can feed on them by "grubbing"—cruising the bottom snout down and simply plucking the snails off the floor, or gulping them down when the snails are dislodged from their bases by waves crashing on the shore of a large lake. Larger fish tend to feed on snails up to 6 inches (15 cm) long, as they have stronger digestive tracts than smaller fish and can break down the hard shells more efficiently. A Tom Thumb in size 12 to 16 on a floating line using a dead drift approach is a good technique.

Tom Thumb.

7J: Leeches

Leeches are distant cousins to aquatic earthworms and the more familiar common garden worms and nightcrawlers. They live in lakes and the slower portions of some rivers. The leech's body is similar to that of the common earthworm, with a segmented form and strong muscular structure that provides support. The leech is flat from top to bottom and can change its appearance from long and snake-like to squat and contracted in an instant. This is one of the leech's primary defensive reactions. Leeches swim with their bodies extended. The rear of the body is wider and flatter than the front. This paddle-like appearance makes the leech a competent swimmer. Leeches swim in an undulating fashion and are quite rhythmic in their motion. While they grow up to 6 inches (15 cm) in length, few are longer than 4 inches (10 cm), and trout feed primarily on those that are about 2 inches (5 cm) long.

Olive/ brown leech underwater.

A leech is a good meal for a fish, and a well-presented leech imitation will get a trout's attention in almost any month of the year. Leeches tend to swim near the substrate and usually stay near the shallow regions of their aquatic habitats to avoid predation. Unfortunately, they are primarily nocturnal. Dawn, dusk and cloudy days are other good times for a leech pattern, but I have caught trout on leeches during the day as well.

Small black leech.

Leeches swim at moderate speeds in short and erratic bursts. They can move quite fast when they are pursued so I fish them at high speed on the theory that a trout will think another trout is after the leech, which will trigger a greed-based aggressive reaction. When trolling a leech I will stop the forward momentum of my boat, let my leech pattern sink and then strip in. Wooly Buggers work well when it comes to size and pattern. I use small patterns; the largest leech pattern I tie is a size 6, 3Xl, which offers a slim, natural-looking profile. A 2- to 3-inch (5- to 8-cm) leech is only the diameter of a pencil when fully extended. Materials such as marabou and rabbit fur imitate the undulating nature of the leech.

Left to right: Bead-head fur micro leech. Olive leech. Bunny leech.

7K: Forage Fish: Sticklebacks

All trout eat small forage fish. They will not always attack a small fish out of hunger; they often attack out of aggression or curiosity. Trout longer than about 12 inches (30 cm) prey almost exclusively on fish, where these are available, and adult trout will devour smaller fish up to a third of their length. A small fish will attempt to escape its predator with frantic motions that often trigger the instinctive, aggressive response of a larger trout. Spoons trolled or jigged will set off this response. By moving the rod tip you can dart and swim the imitation-spoon or change its direction with the simple movement of the rod. A fast retrieve will imitate a small fish trying to take evasive action with a quick, erratic burst of speed.

Stickleback.

Sticklebacks are forage fish for trout that are well worth imitating. They range in size from 2 inches (5 cm) and up. Sticklebacks are pale olive with a darker back and dark vertical bands on the sides, red tints near the gills, and large eyes. Breeding males develop bright-red bellies.

Use a count-down-and-retrieve presentation. Sticklebacks are not fast swimmers and tend to

Hook eyes clogged with head cement should not be opened with another hook because this dulls the point. Use a safety pin that you can keep pinned to your fly vest.

be still much of time, or to swim in little jerks. Try fishing with this pattern in the afternoon, when they seem to be the most active. Olive Wooly Bugger, Zonkers in yellow-green or similar streamers will work. Be sure to capture the deep-bellied appearance of the natural fish when tying an imitation.

7L: Baits

Eggs

Artificial eggs come in a variety of colors. Red, yellow and the fluorescent colors are all top producers. Hooks from 8 to 14 with short shanks can easily be concealed

entirely within a single egg. For fly fishermen a single salmon egg pattern usually runs 5 to 7.5 mm, a trout egg 3 to 5.5 mm. Matching the size can make a difference: an egg pattern that is too big will not fool a trout. Fish with a split shot above the leader's tippet so the lead will tap the bottom to make the egg act like the real thing, rolling in the current.

Cheese

Another favorite bait is soft cheese, because cheese oils rapidly disperse with the currents, luring

Trout eggs. trout. The cheese can also be shaped around a salmon-egg hook.

Marshmallows

While marshmallows don't resemble any form of trout food, hatchery or natural, they can be cut or torn into smaller pieces and easily formed to cover a salmon-egg hook. They have a high air content and tend to float, so a small piece of split shot must be added to the line about 12 to 18 inches (30 to 45 cm) above the hook.

Pink and lime egg pattern.

Corn

Fresh corn, yellow or white, doesn't seem to work well at all, but for some reason canned, whole-kernel yellow corn makes great trout bait. Cover the hook with two or possibly three kernels. Corn has slightly negative buoyancy, so use split shot to maintain the proper depth.

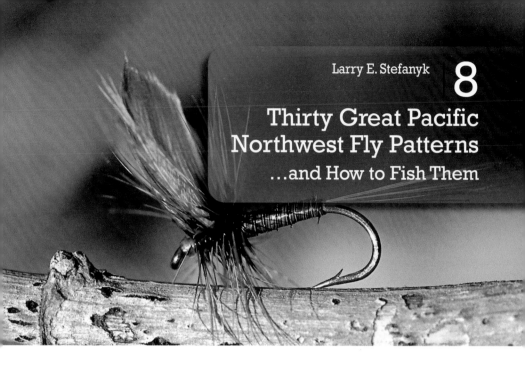

Thirty Great Pacific Northwest Fly Patterns
...and How to Fish Them

Some fly anglers walk up to a river, a lake or the ocean, wade out as deep as they can and start casting. Unfortunately, they probably just walked through the best fishing. Trout do most of their feeding in less than 10 feet (3 m) of water and eat many aquatic insects and small feed fish within 20 feet (6 m) of the bank or shore in shallow water.

Most people assume trout that live in lakes spend all their time at the bottom in deep water. This is just not true. Trout need two things: safety and food. Your best opportunity to find trout is by a drop-off near the shore in water that is anywhere from two feet (60 cm) to 25 feet (8 m) deep. The fish come out of the cover of deeper water to pick up food and then head back into cover. In early morning and late evening, when light is low, they will cruise this shallow lane, holding to it longer while looking for food.

8A: Midges and Mayflies

1. Adams
Hook: Mustad R43-94831, (1X fine), Nos. 12–20.
Thread: Black.
Tail: Brown and grizzly fibers, mixed.
Body: Dubbed gray muskrat or rabbit.
Wings: Grizzly hackle tips.
Hackle: Brown and grizzly mixed.

The Adams is one of the most generic dry flies and resembles many different kinds of trout food. One should always carry a bunch of Adams in sizes 14–18. A female Adams flies is tied the same way, but with a small bit of yellow dubbing at the rear of the body to imitate a mayfly ready to lay its eggs. A dry fly presentation in a lake has to be more delicate than in most rivers. The lake is usually a lot calmer. Use a floating line with a 12- to 15-foot (3.6- to 5-m) leader and dress your fly with floatant.

Cast the fly and let it sit. If nothing happens after a minute or two, gently pick up the fly and cast to a different location. When you see a cruising trout, cast ahead of it and let the fly settle before the fish arrives at that point. During a hatch, locate the feeding trout. Wait until you see a rise then cast to it, using a soft fly presentation. Slapping the water with your fly or fly line on a cast will put the fish down.

> When stringing up your rod, strip more line than you need off the reel, then double your fly line over a foot or so back from the tip and run that through the guides. If the line slips out of your fingers, it won't slip all the way back through your guides. You're also a lot less likely to miss a guide than you are with the leader.

With the soft presentation it is important to have a straight leader and tippet and to keep the slack out of your line so you can feel the take as the fly sits on the surface.

Also try drift fishing with the wind with this pattern. Cast into the wind at a 45-degree angle. The wind will "drift" your fly in a natural motion and you will also cover a lot of water.

In rivers and streams cast about 2 feet (60 cm) upstream of the "ring" that indicates a trout is present. The fly goes by in the current and the fish has to make a quick decision. The quicker the trout's decision, the more success you will have.

> When tying on a new fly, stand in fast water so that when you drop the fly before getting it secured to the line, you know it has been carried away. This saves you about an hour sifting through the tall grass or the river stones because you know "it couldn't have gone far."

I use a somewhat different technique when I fish rivers and streams. All fish will take some of their food as it passes them in the current. I like to move the fly a little faster than the speed of the current. The trout will usually miss the fly on the first take simply because the fly is going faster than their normal fare. The first appearance of your fly has interested the trout and when it misses it, it will usually turn for another go. I use a floating line and a leader the length of my fly rod. I roll cast upstream with only about 20 feet (6 m) of fly line. The shorter length allows me total control over my fly. I cast, then lift the rod, taking up slack as the fly moves downstream toward me. When the rod is at my shoulder height I roll cast again. I cover about 7 feet (2.1 m) of water at a time and then move to the left or right and repeat the cast. After I have covered 7 to 8 feet I move up the stream 8 feet and repeat the process. I "shotgun" the river with casts, covering every bit of water where a trout could be lurking.

I very rarely miss hooking a feeding trout using this method. A good friend who fished small streams in Alberta for fifty years taught it to me. He caught a lot of trout with it, and so do I.

2. Light Cahill
Hook: Mustad R43-94831, (1X fine), Nos. 12–18.
Thread: Tan or yellow.
Tail: Light ginger hackle fibers.
Body: Dubbed cream seal fur.
Wings: Wood-duck flank fibers.
Hackle: Light ginger or cream cock hackle.

Light Cahill is a traditional Catskill-style dry fly, and still an effective fly for catching trout. It matches the hatches of mayflies that are encountered in spring.

Use the same dry fly presentation you would for the Adams.

3. Mosquito
Hook: Mustad R43-94831, (1X fine), Nos. 12–18.
Thread: Black.
Tail: Grizzly hackle fibers.
Body: Moose mane—dark & light wrapped together or grizzly saddle stem.
Wings: Grizzly hackle tips.
Hackle: Grizzly.

Use the same dry fly presentation you would for the Adams.

4. Royal Wulff
Created by Lee Wulff
Hook: Mustad R43-94831, (1X fine), Nos. 10–18.
Thread: Black.
Tail: Brown bucktail.
Body: Peacock herl, then red floss, then more peacock.
Wings: White Bucktail, upright and divided.
Hackle: Brown Bucktail, upright and divided.

The Royal Wulff dressing is a variation of the famous Royal Coachman. While it doesn't really imitate anything, it can catch trout when they aren't feeling picky. The most common variations of the Wulff-style flies are the Gray Wulff (gray body, blue-dun hackle) and White Wulff (white body and tail, badger hackle).

Use a floating line and dress the fly with floatant. When casting in fast, riffly water, the trout don't have too long to look at the fly. Wulff patterns work well because they are designed for rough water. However they are too highly dressed to work well on slow, clear water or when trout are feeding selectively. When casting upstream and letting the fly drift by the waiting trout, it is important to have the slack out of your line so you can feel the take, because the fish usually take the fly aggressively. This is not your best choice of a fly for lake applications because it is big and bushy.

5. March Brown Soft-Hackle

Hook: Mustad R43-94831, (1X fine), Nos. 12–16.
Thread: Brown.
Tail: Three pheasant tail fibers.
Body: Cream hare's body.
Rib: Fine copper wire.
Hackle: Brown partridge.

March brown nymphs live in riffles and near rocky areas in rivers and streams; as they near maturity, they migrate to slower water. During the migration, they can lose their grip and drift in the current. For this reason trout will congregate in places where fast riffles start to slow down, in the seams between the fast and slow water. Try fishing your fly where the current changes speed. Sizes 12 and 14 seem to be the most popular. You can change the shape of your fly by trimming down the body to make it thinner if needed. Try to match the naturals that tend to adapt to the color of the streambed. Most nymphs are dark, some nearly black. Try coloring the legs with a black felt marker if your fly is the wrong color.

Start by fishing the slower water first using a dead drift with flies that are lightly weighted. Cast them slightly upstream and mend a little slack into your presentation. Then work your fly out into the faster current. I use a 9.5–foot (3-m) 5- or 6-weight rod with a weight-forward line. A natural-colored fly line works better than a bright one. I use a leader the length of my rod and a fluorocarbon tippet.

6. Pheasant Tail Nymph

Hook: Mustad S60-3399A, (1X STD), Nos. 12–16.
Thread: Brown.
Tail: 2–3 pheasant center tail fibers.
Body: 2–3 pheasant center tail fibers.
Rib: Fine copper wire.

Over 600 species of mayflies dwell in North America, and most of their nymphs are small and brown. This creates a wide range of living creatures of which trout are fond. In rivers the fly can be presented near the surface, but it is usually most productive when fished near the bottom on a dead drift with an indicator or tight line presentation. To achieve the right depth you may need to use a weighted fly.

In a lake use a floating line or intermediate sinking fly line and do a very slow retrieve to imitate the nymph's swim to the surface. This is a very effective fly in the middle of the day. Pay particular attention to shallow areas near weed beds.

This fly can also be fished with a spinning rod and float. Add a small split shot about 18 inches (45 cm) above the fly and place the float approximately 5 feet (1.5 m) above the fly. Cast out and either let the wind drift it or retrieve the line very slowly.

7. Halfback

Hook: Mustad S80-3906, (3X STD), Nos. 2–10.

Thread: Black.

Weight: 15–20 turns lead wire diameter of hook shank (or non-weighted).

Tail: Ringneck pheasant tail fibers.

Body: Peacock herl.

Wing Case: Ringneck pheasant tail fibers.

Hackle: Hen or saddle, brown.

Thorax: Peacock herl.

Use a floating line or intermediate sinking fly line and do a very slow retrieve to imitate the emerging nymph swimming to the surface of the lake. Sometimes "takes" can be difficult to detect. Try using a small indicator on a dry line, treating it like a dry fly, mending line when it looks like it might drag and striking when it disappears. Also fish the shallows with this same technique.

8. Elk Hair Caddis

Hook: Mustad R43-94831, (1X fine), Nos. 10–16.

Thread: Tan.

Body: Tan fur or wool.

Wings: Natural brown bucktail.

Hackle: Ginger.

The Elk Hair Caddis is the go-to fly in imitating adult caddis in BC. It has caught countless trout. This fly floats well in rough water but will also work reasonably well in slower water because adult caddis often fall or are blown into rivers or lakes. A useful variation is the hot butt caddis, which has a poly-yarn butt-end in bright colors not found in nature that makes it somewhat easier to spot in low light conditions. Use a floating fly line, casting near the bank just downstream or downwind from overhanging vegetation.

9. Stimulator

Hook: Mustad R74-9671, (3XL), Nos. 4–18.

Thread: Fire orange.

Tail: Natural elk hair.

Body: Dubbed yellow Antron wool.

Alternate body colors: Black, golden, green, orange and red.

Wings: Natural elk hair.

Body Hackle: Furnace saddle hackle.

Thorax Hackle: Grizzly hackle.

Thorax: Amber Antron wool.

Stone flies emerge on land, so adults are not available to trout when they hatch. They spend several weeks crawling around in bankside vegetation and are often blown off or fall out of overhanging vegetation and are then eaten by trout.

Near dusk female salmon flies often gather in hoards and then drop to the river to lay their eggs. Standard dry fly presentations are used. The fly should be heavily doped with floatant so it will ride high in the surface film. Stimulators float well in rough water, but on calmer drifts you'll do better if you trim the hackle on the underside so the fly will float a little lower.

Adult caddis can also be fished with a spinning rod and the float technique.

10. Tom Thumb/Humpy
Hook: Mustad R75-79580, (2XL), Nos. 4–14.
Thread: Black.
Tail: Deer hair.
Body-wing: Deer hair.

The Tom Thumb is another fly that can represent a number of different aquatic insects that are trout food.

Use the same dry fly presentation you would for the Adams.

8B: Dragonflies, Damselflies and Caddis Flies

11. Hare's Ear Gold Ribbed Nymph
Hook: Mustad R75-79580, (2XL), Nos. 12–18.
Thread: Tan or brown.
Tail: Guard hairs from hare's ear.
Body: Hair fur from hare's ear.
Rib: Narrow gold tinsel.
Wing case: Brown turkey quill.
Legs: Picked body fur.

A traditional pattern, the Hare's Ear can be tied to suggest many different species of nymphs and can be weighted (with a bead-head) or unweighted. Dark brown is the most productive body color but dark olive and tan will work. Keep the patterns sparse. Fish with a sinking line and keep the fly on the bottom. Trout are most likely to mistake this fly for a mayfly nymph.

12. Zug Bug
Hook: Mustad S60-3399A, (1X STD), Nos. 6–16.
Thread: Black.
Tail: Three peacock herl fibers; clip so tail is equal to two-thirds the length of the body.
Ribbing: Oval silver tinsel.
Body: Peacock herl.
Throat: Brown hackle.
Wing case: Gray partridge.

Zug Bugs suggest many different insects, including cased caddis and free-living caddis larvae. Fish with a full-sinking line cast and then count the seconds until the fly reaches the proper depth. If you start hooking bottom or picking up weeds your fly has dropped too deep and you should use less time while sinking the fly. Then begin your retrieve using a hand twist. Twist the fly

> I always wait until I'm in the water to tie on my fly. You can't tell from the truck what the fish might be feeding on and what the water conditions are like.

line one way, then the other. Another method is to use a dry-line presentation and a strike indicator. Using a dead drift, keep your fly near the bottom. The retrieve to use is the hand twist.

In streams or rivers cast upstream using an intermediate fly line and use a short length of fly line around 15 to 20 feet (5 to 6 m). As soon as the fly hits the water mend the line so all the line and leader is upstream from the fly. As the fly passes by keep the line tight by lifting and lowering the rod. If the fly stops, lift the rod to set the hook. If nothing happens move two or three steps upstream and cast again. That way you will cover all the water.

13. Red Butt Wooly Worm

Hook: Mustad R74-9671, (3XL), Nos. 8–16.

Thread: Match body color.

Rib: Narrow copper, silver or gold tinsel or wire.

Body: Green, olive, maroon, purple, yellow/olive, black, white or brown chenille.

Hackle: Grizzly or ginger, palmered.

Tail: Your choice of colors.

Wooly Worms represent a lot of different trout food: dragonfly nymphs, damselfly nymphs, leeches or baitfish. If you fish lakes you should have lots of these in your box, with a mix of colors, sizes and weights. A bead-head can be added or add weight under the fly's dressing. In lakes try putting a strip of Flashabou down each side. Another variation is the Krystal Bugger, which uses a body of black Krystal Chenille. Using a floating or intermediate line and an unweighted or lightly weighted fly, retrieve very slowly—about an inch or two of line each second. This can be very effective

> If you're buying the "hot" local fly, be sure to buy more than one. The first one will always end up in a tree or on the bottom of the stream.

but is like watching paint dry, not terribly exciting. The takes can be so soft they feel like a slight hesitation. Tighten up slightly by pulling the line with your free hand and don't strike using your rod; the set might spook a following trout.

You can vary the retrieve until you find what works best at the moment. Try a 4-inch (10-cm) pull followed by a short pause. With larger flies you can make a longer pull. Next try short and rapid 2-inch (5-cm) pulls with barely a pause between each pull. Also do a super-fast retrieve using both hands while clenching the rod to your body. Using a full sinking line or an intermediate line, cast at a 45-degree angle to your direction of travel. Let the wind push you across the lake while dragging the fly behind you. If you are using an electric motor, give yourself a push for a few feet and then retrieve using one of the techniques mentioned above.

14. Black/Green Montana Stonefly
Hook: Mustad R74-9671, (3XL), Nos. 6–14.
Weight: 15–20 turns lead wire diameter of hook shank
  (or bead-head).
Thread: Black.
Tail: Black hackle or marabou.
Body: Black, brown or green chenille.
Thorax: Orange, yellow, red or green chenille.
Case: Same as body color.
Hackle: Black or brown hackle.

This nymph pattern imitates the salmon fly that crawls around on the bottom—so you know where to fish it. Weight it heavily under the body and then flatten the weight with pliers to give it a squat, flat body like the natural nymph. For extra weight you can put on a bead-head. Some patterns also use rubber legs, but I have caught more trout on this fly than all the other flies in my fly box, and it has no legs. My color of choice is a black body and case with an electric green thorax.

Use the same presentation as for the Wooly Worm.

15. Carey Special
Hook: Mustad R75-79580, (2XL), Nos. 4–12.
Thread: Black.
Tail: Ringneck pheasant rump fibers.
Body: Maroon, brown, or black chenille.
Hackle: Ringneck pheasant rump feathers.

This is a traditional northwest lake pattern. The Carey Special is the number one fly in BC lakes. It could represent a dragonfly nymph or a still-water caddis.

16. Doc Spratley
Created by Dick Pranckard
Hook: Mustad R75-79580, (2XL), Nos. 6–12.
Thread: Black.
Tails: Guinea hackle fibers.
Body: Black, red, purple or olive-brown, green wool or chenille.
Rib: Medium flat silver or gold tinsel.
Wings: Ringneck pheasant tail fibers.
Legs: Natural guinea hackle fibers.
Head: Peacock herl.

The Doc Spratley is one of the most popular flies in British Columbia. The pattern probably originated to imitate caddis hatches or dragonfly nymphs, but the Spratley can be used to represent most insects as well as leeches. When tying it, vary your hook sizes in order to cover a broader spectrum of insects. Smaller sizes, when trimmed down, are good chironomid imitations. Also vary your body color and style with thin and sparse combined with fat and stocky. Larger hook sizes make useful representations of nymphs and leeches.

17. Damselfly Nymph

Hook: Mustad R73-9671, (3XL), Nos. 8.
Thread: Black.
Body: Dubbed seal fur, brown olive, green drake and Naples yellow.
Tail: Same as body.
Body: Same as tail.
Rib: Fine oval gold.
Thorax: Peacock herl.
Wing Case: Dark turkey or brown plastic raffia.
Legs: 8–10 fibers ringneck pheasant tail.
Head: Peacock herl.

As its name suggests, this fly imitates a damselfly nymph. It's extremely useful in lakes and slack-water portions of rivers. Damselfly nymphs are active throughout the spring. In July, they migrate to above-water objects such as standing timber, rocks and the shore. Adults emerge out of the water. After July most mature damselfly nymphs have hatched, so trout no longer expect to see them. The most common body colors are olive and yellow-olive. A bead-head is sometimes helpful, but in some waters and situations it will make the fly sink too fast. Damsel nymphs are not fast swimmers so a leisurely retrieve is appropriate. Use a very slow but steady retrieve. Slowly strip in a foot of line, then pause a second or two and strip again. The fly should be somewhere between the weed tops and the top few inches of water.

8C: Streamers

18. Muddler Minnow

Hook: Mustad R74-9671, (3XL), Nos. 4–14.
Thread: White, gray or red Kevlar or heavy rod wrapping thread.
Tail: Brown mottled turkey quill.
Body: Medium flat gold tinsel.
Rib: Medium-width oval gold tinsel.
Under Wing: Brown calf tail.
Upper Wing: Two matched brown mottled turkey quills.
Hackle or Head: Deer hair.

The Muddler is one of the most useful streamer patterns an angler can carry. It suggests a wide variety of baitfish that trout eat, especially sculpins. It is suitable for both rivers and lakes. Muddlers can produce fish when presented shallow or deep, on a sink-tip line or a floater.

19. Zonker
Hook: Mustad R74-9671, (3XL), Nos. 2–8.

Thread: Black or white.

Wing & Tail: A strip of natural rabbit, gray or olive rabbit still on skin.

Body: Medium-diameter braided pearl or copper Mylar piping.

Throat: Grizzle cock hackle to match wing.

Eyes: Painted (optional).

Zonkers are a great baitfish imitator. The silvery or copper Mylar is tantalizing and the way the rabbit fur moves makes them attractive to predatory trout. They work well in both rivers and lakes. In lakes most of the time you should be fishing somewhere between 2 to 6 feet (60 cm to 2 m) deep and near some form of cover or structure. In rivers with undercut banks, let the fly drift under the bank as deep as you can, then strip it fast.

20. The Matuka Sculpin
Hook: Mustad R74-9671, (3XL), Nos. 2–4.

Thread: Black.

Weight: Optional.

Tail: 4–6 grizzly feathers dyed olive green hackle tips.

Body: Cream angora yarn.

Ribbing: Thin gold wire.

Wings: 4–6 grizzly feathers dyed olive green hackle tips.

Collar: Dark deer hair dyed dark olive.

Head: Dubbed olive hare's ear.

Eyes: Optional.

Matuka-style flies imitate small baitfish. There are many variations, including different body colors, spun and clipped deer hair heads, gills, etc. The fly can be weighted or not. In rivers this is a good fly to use with a sink-tip line; let it sink into undercut banks, then start stripping, or let it swing deep like a wet fly.

Always watch where the birds are hanging out in the lake, as they may be feeding on a hatch.

In rivers this is a good fly to use with a sink-tip line and a heavily weighted fly. Make your cast upstream of the lie and let the fly swing across it. Mend, if necessary, just enough line so the fly sinks into an undercut bank and drifts into the hole.

8D: Chironomids: Larval and Pupal

Red Ribbed Peacock Bloodworm.

21. Bloodworm / Blood Midge

Hook: Mustad R73-9671, (3XL), or R74-9672, (4XL),
    Nos. 12–22.

Thread: Black or red.

Tail: Black bear tail or red marabou.

Body: Fine dark maroon, olive, black or tan chenille or
    single-ply wool.

Rib: Fine copper wire or single strand of Peacock herl.

Hackle: Dark brown feathers from cock pheasant.

This fly imitates the larval stage of the blood midge, which is red or olive in color and found in most of our lakes. The most effective way to fish these lakes is from a boat because most have very soft muddy or marl bottoms that make wading difficult. Anchor your boat at both bow and stern to minimize movement and drift. To fish the bloodworm stage successfully you must get your fly to the bottom or very close to it. A floating line and long leader without a strike indicator allow effective coverage of the entire water column because the majority of larval and pupal emergences occur in water less than 26 feet (8 m) deep. Use a floating line and a tapered leader that is at least 25 percent longer than the depth of water being fished.

Bomber Chironomid.

Chan's Bloodworm.

Cast out an unweighted pattern and allow it to sink to within about a foot of the bottom. Then use a very slow hand-twist retrieve or strip retrieve to move the pattern horizontally through the water. This technique is extremely effective. The larvae and pupae move very slowly up through the water column. Strikes are often very soft because the trout are basically inhaling pupae. You can use a wind-drifting method by casting, as usual, at about a 45-degree angle to your boat.

Floating lines and strike indicators are a deadly combination for fishing larval and especially pupal patterns. Measure the water depth and then attach the strike indicator to the leader so the fly is about a foot (30 cm) off the lake bottom; then gradually tug the fly higher if you have no luck at those deeper levels. I tie a small swivel between my leader and tippet. This little bit of weight will keep my fly down and in the zone. Cast the fly out and allow it to sink. Then wait. Movement can be enhanced by wind-drifting with the indicator setup. When you feel resistance, or see the strike indicator head the other way, raise the rod tip and set the hook.

Carry a hook stone to sharpen hooks that become dulled from bumping rocks or catching too many fish.

Another technique is to use a clear intermediate fly line and long leader when fishing water in the 16- to 26-foot (5- to 8-m) range. Use the countdown method with your watch to determine where your fly is relative to the lake bottom. Once on the bottom start the continuous slow hand-twist or strip retrieve, bringing the fly right up to the surface. This technique brings the pupal pattern through the entire water table.

Deep-water chironomid fishing takes place from 26 feet (8 m) to more than 50 feet (15 m). These emergences take place during the summer. Type 3 to type 7 full-sinking or density-compensated sinking lines are used with a shorter leader up to 10 feet (3 m). Allow the fly to sink and begin the slow but continuous hand-twist retrieve, bringing the fly right up to the surface. Takes are usually hard, making this an exciting way to fish.

22. Black and Silver Chironomid
Hook: Mustad R43-94831, (1X fine), or C-535, Nos. 14–16.
Thread: Black.
Tail: Gray hackle.
Under Body: Peacock herl.
Over Body: One strand four-ply white tapestry wool.
Ribbing: Fine silver tinsel.
Thorax: Peacock herl.
Shellback: Ringneck pheasant tail fibers.
Gills: White Antron.

Use the same presentations for the Bloodworm.

Rising chironomid pupae come in a variety of sizes and colors. The most common colors are black, green and brown. Light spinning outfits and plastic bubble floats can also be effective. Just vary the length of leader to different depth zones and let the wind drift the fly around.

23. Two-Tone Green Chironomid
Hook: Mustad R43-94831, (1X fine), or C-535, Nos. 12–16.
Thread: Green.
Body: Lime green Flashabou and dark green Flashabou.
Rib: Fine silver tinsel.
Thorax: Peacock herl.
Shellback: Ringneck pheasant tail fibers.
Tying Tips: Use three or four strands of Flashabou to build up the body of the fly. Apply Sally Hanson's "Hard as Nails" nail polish or Superglue to the finished fly.
Gills: White Antron.

24. Glass Bead Chironomid

Hook: Mustad R43-948r31, (1X fine), C-535 or C49S, Nos. 14–16.

Thread: Black.

Body: Black Flashabou or Super Floss.

Alternate body colors: Olive, brown, maroon, red, lime green, tan and orange.

Rib: Thin silver, gold, copper or red wire.

Thorax: Peacock herl.

Head: 10 crystal bead.

Gills: White Antron yarn.

8E: Leeches

Egg-Sucking Leech Green.

Egg-Sucking Leech Red Hot Bugger.

25. Egg-Sucking Black Marabou Leech

Hook: Mustad R73-9671, (3XL), or R74-9672, (4XL), Nos. 2–10.

Thread: Black.

Flash: Two strands pearl Flashabou.

Weight: 15–20 turns lead wire diameter of hook shank.

Tail: Marabou black.

Body: Marabou black or black chenille.

Hackle: Black, palmered on body.

Rib: ½" oval gold.

Head: Fluorescent orange, lime green chenille or red bead.

This is a good fall pattern. Nearly all lakes have leeches and they are naturally nocturnal, so when a fish spots one during the day it represents a fortunate meal. Use a full-sink line and a heavily weighted fly. Let the fly sink. It should travel within 2 feet (60 cm) of the bottom. The head and or front half (only) of the fly should be weighted. A bead-head is optional. When retrieved both methods will move the fly in an up-and-down undulation that mimics the way real leeches swim.

Use the count-down-and-retrieve or slow retrieve presentations. Vary the retrieve until you find what works best at the moment: slow and steady, fast, strip-and-pause or quick, short 2-inch (5-cm) strips. As the marabou waves in the water it contributes nicely to the overall effect. Leeches swim at moderate speeds with short and erratic bursts of speed and pauses. For this reason some anglers always retrieve the leech quickly in the belief that a trout will see it speeding along and try to beat another trout to it. Also use a floating fly line and a slow hand-twist retrieve with a few quick strips. Using an intermediate sinking fly line and simply trolling a leech behind any boat will produce fish.

Black Bunny Leech.

Egg-Sucking Rabbit Leech.

26. Black Bunny Leech

Hook: Mustad R74-9672, (4XL), Nos. 2–6.

Thread: Black.

Weight: 15–20 turns lead wire diameter of hook shank (or
non-weighted).

Tail: Rabbit fur dyed black.

Body: Black rabbit strip.

As a general-purpose streamer, this is a superb fly. It is useful in lakes and in slower portions of rivers. The rabbit fur moves in a lifelike fashion. Good color choices are white, burgundy, purple, black, red, brown, dark-olive and yellow-olive. This is an excellent fly for winter steelhead. It's easy to tie and you will lose several each trip if you use it right. For most winter conditions, use a bead-head or nickel eyes for added weight.

27. Chartreuse Wooly Bugger

Hook: Mustad R74-9671, (3XL), Nos. 2–10.

Thread: White.

Tail: Bottom half white, top half chartreuse marabou.

Body: Chartreuse marabou.

Weight: 15–20 turns lead wire diameter of hook shank.

Rib: Fine copper wire.

Hackle: Chartreuse saddle.

A good fly that will work in other colors like red, burgundy, purple, black, brown and dark olive. Use a sink-tip or full-sinking line and a count-down-and-retrieve and a slow retrieve presentation. Make the fly move with quick darts giving it a short, fast strip, then let it sit and strip again. The main thing is to be at the right depth and to make the fly move like it is alive.

28. Blood Leech

Hook: Mustad R73-9671, (3XL), or R74-9672, (4XL),
Nos. 6–12.

Thread: Black.

Tail: Dark maroon mohair wool.

Body: Dark maroon mohair wool.

Unlike many patterns that are called a "leech," the Mohair Leech and the very similar Mini Leech really do resemble leeches. Most of the leeches that trout eat are only an inch or two long and are quite thin. Good color choices include red, burgundy, purple, black, brown and dark olive.

29. Micro Leech
Hook: Mustad R75S-9674, Nos. 12–14.
Thread: Black.
Tail: Any color: black or burgundy marabou.
Body: Any color: black or burgundy marabou.
Rib: Copper wire.
Head: Gold ⅛ inch bead.

Floating lines and strike indicators are a deadly combination for fishing Micro Leeches. Know the water depth and then attach the strike indicator to the leader so the fly is just off the lake bottom. Cast the fly out and allow it to sink. Now wait. Movement can be enhanced by wind-drifting with the indicator setup. Remove the slack in your line and wait. When you are ready to retrieve your line use short and rapid pulls; when you feel resistance or see the strike indicator head the other way, raise the rod tip and set the hook. Another technique is to use a clear intermediate fly line and a long leader. Use the countdown method using your watch to determine where your fly is in relationship to the lake bottom. Once on the bottom, start the continuous short-and-rapid-pull retrieve, bringing the fly right to the surface. This technique brings the Micro Leech through the entire water table.

8F: Backswimmers and Waterboatmen

30. Corixis Waterboatman
Hook: Mustad R43-94831, (1X fine), Nos. 12–14.
Thread: Brown.
Body: Brown or yellow dubbed seal.
Back: Ringneck pheasant tail.
Rib: Yellow silk thread.
Swimmerettes: Single fiber of a dark brown turkey wing.
Hackle: Single piece of silver tinsel ³⁄₃₂".

This pattern imitates adult waterboatmen, which feed on submerged plants in still, shallow waters. Although they spend most of their time underwater, these insects come to the surface to breathe. The frequency of their breathing can be anywhere from a few minutes to an hour. After getting a gulp of air they descend, often trailing a string of bubbles behind them. Waterboatmen propel themselves by kicking their legs and are of most interest to trout in the fall.

Use a floating fly line and a strike indicator. Cast into water 3 to 4 feet (1 to 1.2 m) deep and let the fly settle near the bottom. Then use a twitching lift-and-settle retrieve.

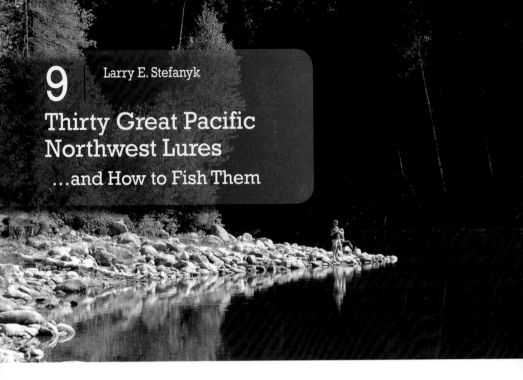

9

Larry E. Stefanyk

Thirty Great Pacific Northwest Lures

...and How to Fish Them

Bait Casting

River casting from the shore.

The term "bait" casting is a misnomer because it may also involve casting artificial lures such as plugs, spoons, spinners and jigs as well as bait. There is a multitude of gear available today for trout fishermen to choose from and a lot of the lures catch more fishermen than fish.

One of the most popular tactics is casting from shore, which might involve the use of spoons or weighted spinners, or still-fishing with bait. The types of lures available are astonishing, but old reliables that are still around after many decades include Daredevil, Len Thompson and Kamlooper spoons, and Mepps, Panther Martin, Blue Fox and Rooster Tail spinners.

Spinners

Casting into a lake from the shore.

Fishing spinners, one of the most popular types of equipment for catching trout, take a little practice. Start by making some short casts and then begin a slow, steady retrieve, keeping an eye on your rod tip. A vibrating tip means the spinner is working. As the lure gets closer, watch it underwater to match the movement with the tip vibration. A rotating spinner blade creates sound waves that attract the attention of fish that may be unable to see them. As they swim closer to investigate, the flashing lure becomes a visible target.

Right: Panther Martin Black with Green Dot Spinner.

The shape of the spinner blade determines its speed and angle of rotation. While there are dozens of variations on the market, all stem from four basic shapes: round (Colorado), egg (Indiana), oval (French) and long (Willow Leaf). Round blades rotate slowly and swing widely around their axis, which creates a fairly bulky silhouette. They also create the most drag of all spinners when drawn through the water. Lures with long blades that rotate quickly and close to the shaft create a slender, bait-like silhouette and can be retrieved at fairly high speeds. Because of its low drag, the Willow Leaf is popular on multi-blade trolls. Egg- and oval-shaped blades are intermediate between the two extremes and are found on most popular lures.

Left to right: Samples of spinner blade shapes: "Willow, "Indiana" and "Colorado."

Spinners make a flash in the water that is intended to mimic the flash made by smaller fish. Trolled or cast from the shore, they will catch trout. In-line spinners are the lure of choice when fishing for trout on spinning tackle. The rotation of the spinner blade can cause the line to twist and lead to bird's nests, so use a swivel to counteract that potential problem. Two brands of trout spinners that are very popular for catching rainbow trout are Mepps and Panther Martin.

Worden Rooster Tail ⅛-ounce (4-g) Midnight Black spinner.

Rooster Tail spinners

Rooster Tail spinners are quite effective when used as bait for trout in river fishing scenarios. The key to success when using these lures is to make sure that they are very small. The perfect Rooster Tail for trout fishing ranges from ¹⁄₁₆ to ⅛ ounce (2 to 4 g). I've always had more success with dark colors such as greens, browns and blacks, but as with all fishing, experimentation is the key to finding the best color pattern for any given day.

Because of their action, spinners should always have a snap swivel attached to the eye if there's no barrel swivel. When casting you should try to vary the depth of each retrieve until you find the fish. A 1-ounce (28-g) spoon or spinner on a tight line will sink about a foot (30 cm) per second. A ¼-ounce (7-g) lure will sink 5 feet (1.5 m) in 3 seconds, 10 feet (3 m) will take 6 seconds and so on. You can also count the number of seconds it takes to reach the bottom, then subtract two seconds of sinking time on the next cast until you have covered the full water table. Sometimes the trout are a little hard to catch. Your line might be too visible, so try switching to a smaller diameter line. Remember—on overcast days, early mornings and late evenings, brass or copper finishes work well, while nickel finishes are my choice on bright days or in clear water. Try not to retrieve your lure at a constant speed and in a straight line. Twitch the rod tip every few seconds, slow down the retrieve, stop the lure and start again, use different actions and speeds to entice a strike.

Snaps with barrel swivels.

Spoons

Spoons are effective because they closely resemble and imitate the actions of crippled baitfish, which make up a large part of a trout's diet. There are an endless number of spoon designs and they all catch trout. I prefer a smaller size. A thin,

lightweight spoon will provide the most erratic, darting baitfish motion in the water, but can be difficult to cast. A heavier spoon is easier to cast and its extra weight will carry it deeper. Casting

Tomic Spoon 3 ½ inch #246.

accuracy is important to success; try to cast a couple of feet from a finning fish and have the spoon tumble into its zone. Cast directly across a stream or river and let the spoon tumble into the current. Your line should be taut as the trout will hit the spoon hard, and you will either have him or not. As you are retrieving the spoon it is advisable to continue the tumbling operation by raising and lowering the rod tip and allowing the lure to drop while reeling in, especially across a deep, still pool.

In lake fishing a spoon should wobble from side to side; this action seems to produce the best results. Check the retrieve, because the spoon should not be allowed to spin.

Rigging your Spoon for Trolling

A barrel swivel placed 6 feet (2 m) up from the spoon.

I suggest not putting a swivel next to your spoon because it can change the action. Instead tie on a small barrel swivel six feet (2 m) up from the spoon and use tippet material from the barrel swivel to the spoon. The spoon is let out anywhere from 50 to 100 feet (15 to 30 m) behind the moving boat and will stay near the surface. This technique is very effective during low light periods.

Using the same setup for your spoon with the small barrel swivel, attach a keel sinker up your line. When you hit a trout and reel in, the keel weight will slide to the barrel swivel. A suggestion is to have the barrel swivel positioned no longer than the length of your fishing rod. As you lift the rod with the fish, the swivel will be near the top eye of the rod and the trout will be close to you.

The last method is to use a downrigger, fishing the spoon by itself or in conjunction with a small flasher. The downrigger allows you to work all depths with no weight on the line when the fish is hooked. If you are using this method with only the spoon, position your spoon at least 15 to 20 feet (5 to 6 m) from the clip. Some anglers use as much as 40 to 60 feet (12 to 18 m). If you decide to use a flasher, the shortest length of leader between the spoon and the flasher should be 18 to 30 inches (45 to 75 cm). A shorter leader produces a more frantic and faster spoon action while a longer leader up to 5 feet (1.5 m) results in a slower action.

A keel sinker will slip down your line with a little pressure.

Some spoon colors are designed for particular water conditions or depths. Silver-plated spoons reflect a higher percentage of light and work in a variety of different light conditions and depths. Fish-scale spoons look natural and have the iridescent sheen of baitfish; they work well in all depths. Glo finishes (especially the florescent green strip) are very effective in deep water. With all of these spoons, one of the best things you can do to improve your catch rate is to keep the hooks sticky-sharp.

Bait

As noted in Chapter 4, "Learning a Lake," the range of soft plastic baits available now verges on mind-numbing, but leading the pack are Pure Fishing's Berkley PowerBait and Gulp and Breck's Mister Twister Exude, both of which are heavily scented. PowerBait, dough-like bait that is molded onto a circle hook, is

Above: Downriggers will get your lure down to any depth.

Left: Berkley PowerBait.

suitable for still-fishing on the bottom or suspending beneath a float, as are roe imitations from both companies. Soft plastic lures come in a range of shapes, sizes and colors, and while they may be used for still-fishing they are often more productive if cast out and retrieved slowly, or allowed to sink to the bottom and then moved periodically.

Other bait for trout can range from live bait to "unnatural" baits like cheese, corn, miniature marshmallows or homemade dough baits, all of which have been known to work. I have not covered worms, another important bait, here, as they are extensively chronicled in Chapter 3, "Bait Fishing in Lakes."

Red Wiggler worms.

Jigs

Using jigs to catch trout can be most successful. Use very small setups with jig heads of $\frac{1}{32}$ to $\frac{1}{16}$ ounce (1 to 2 g), or even smaller for the mini-jigs. The bodies on the jigs can be made of either hair and feathers or soft plastic. Try matching the body color of a foraging fish. Use a bit of caution when fishing with jigs, as obstructions such as rocks, logs and overhanging branches can cause frequent snags and lost gear.

Hooks

When a fish swallows a baited J-shaped hook, the setting of the hook sometimes drives it into the soft tissue of the stomach, throat or gills. If the fish escapes or is released, this hook may be totally dissolved by digestive acids within three days.

Jigging a cast lure.

*Top to bottom:
J-shaped hook.
Circle hook.*

Avoid stainless steel hooks. The material is impervious to fresh or salt water and is little affected by digestive acids. The area around such hooks becomes ulcerated, usually resulting in the death of fish that would otherwise have lived.

One of the most positive advances in recent years has been the introduction of circle hooks. Their overall roundish shape, with the point bent in toward the shank at a 90-degree angle, makes it almost impossible to hook anything on a fish except the hinge of its jaw. A circle hook's design also prevents it from penetrating internal organs or soft tissue. When the fish bites and starts swimming away, the baited hook simply slides over, through and past everything until reaching the jaw, the hinge of which is narrow enough for the hook to rotate around, allowing the point to penetrate.

I highly recommend using barbless hooks in lakes. Some anglers complain that single barbless hooks lose fish. One can counter this by saying that more fish are hooked with barbless hooks than barbed. In other words, more fish seem to be lost during the fight because you hooked them in the first place instead of simply rolling them on the strike.

*This rainbow
was caught on
a barbless hook
by the author
and safely
released.*

It is unlawful to use barbed hooks or a hook with more than one point in any river, stream, creek or slough in BC as per the provincial regulations. Note: the use of barbed hooks is permitted in lakes, unless noted in the Regional-Water-Specific Tables.

Thirty Great Pacific Northwest Lures... and How to Fish Them

Vancouver Island lakes hold big fish! Brandi Miller's rainbow trout weighed in at 5.4 pounds (2.5 kg). She caught it on a spoon while trolling drop-offs. Gibran White photo

Here is my list of some of the top lures for lake and river fishing in the Pacific Northwest.

1. Gibbs/Nortac Ruby Eyed Wiggler HB Hammer Brass 2–2¼ inches (5–6 cm)

Fish can't resist this lure with its darting and wiggling motion. It is fitted with two ruby-colored beads to imitate a bug or beetle. It comes in four sizes with a dozen color combinations.

2. Rapala Countdown CD-5 Rainbow Trout 2 inches (5 cm) in length; ³⁄₁₆ ounce (6 g)

The controlled depth technique was introduced to the world with this lure. Whether the fish are suspended at certain depths near the weed tops or on bottom structure, this lure can get you to them consistently. The CD01 size is specifically designed for smaller fish and is ideal for casting or trolling to depths anywhere from 1 to 13 feet (30 cm to 4 m).

3. Yakima Bait Company—Worden's Lures— Rooster Tail Midnight Black ⅛ ounce (4 g)

Since the 1950s Worden's original Rooster Tail has been one of the most productive spinners around, and it still is. Used to catch just about any game fish, the Rooster Tail's pulsating hackle tail and attractive spinning action will make fish strike even when nothing else will work. It's available in 10 sizes and over 100 different colors.

4. Luhr Jensen—0314 Krocodile Rainbow Trout ⅙ ounce (5 g)

The Krocodile operates on a simple premise: big fish eat smaller fish. This spoon is very productive. It can be cast and retrieved, jigged over structure or trolled. Choose the size that best mirrors available forage. Sizes range from ⅙ to ½ ounce (5 to 15 g) with a great selection of finishes available.

5. Yakima Bait Company—Worden's Lures—FlatFish F-4 Skunk 1½ inch (3.8 cm)

For over fifty years the FlatFish has been around and catching fish with its one-of-a-kind swimming action. Available in 14 sizes and over 100 different colors, the FlatFish is now more versatile than ever.

6. Brecks International Inc.—Trophy I and Trophy II Electric Red

Genuine silver-plated Trophy I (½ oz; 15 g) and Trophy II (¾ oz; 22 g) are excellent casting and trolling lures. They are most effective when trolled or retrieved at a slow speed where their unique design provides maximum action, flash and enticing vibrations. This wide-bodied spoon emits strong vibrations and its large surface and heavier weight allows for longer casts and holds its depth upon retrieve or while trolling.

7. Rhys Davis/Baitrix-Trout

This combines the holders of Rhys Davis and the artificial bait of Baitrix. All the bait products are hand-finished for assurance of quality, consistency and attention to the smallest detail. They're as lifelike as lures get. Available in Fire Tiger, Hologram Green, Hologram Orange and Spot Tail.

8. Gibbs/Nortac—Humpy #1-1½ Red/Yellow/White/Brass ⅜ ounce (12 g)

This heavy spinning lure has a similar shape at either end and is curved to produce a good wobbling action. Made of extra-heavy metal, it dates back to the early 1970s and is available in one size only.

9. Brecks International Inc.— Mepps BF2D Black Fury Dressed with Chartreuse Fury hackle ⅙ ounce (5 g)

Introduced in 1962, this lure offers a medium-depth running, solid brass-machined blade on a black muted background. Available from ⅛ to ½ ounce (4 to 15 g) with a good selection of color options.

10. Deadly Dick Classic Fishing Lures # 2 Red ½ ounce (15 g)

This lure has unbeatable action when casting or trolling and comes in 8 sizes ranging from 1/16 to 3 ounces (2 to 85 g). There is a great combination of colors available.

11. Gibbs/Nortac—Gypsy ½ inch (1.3 cm) 50/50 Nickel/ Brass

Great for casting or trolling, the Gypsy comes in four sizes. The two smaller sizes, the 1 (1⅜ inch / 3.8 cm) and 1½ (1⅝ inch / 3.8 cm), come in 10 colors while the 2¾ (2¾ inch / 7 cm) and 3½ (3½ inch / 9 cm) come in 18 different color combinations.

12. Leo's Flies and Tackle— Rondell Flasher Wedding Band

The spinner blade, beads and rhinestone rondelle combine nicely to attract trout; attach a worm and it is a trout catcher. Available in many color combinations.

13. Yakima Bait Company— Worden's Lures—FlatFish F-4 Frog 1½ inch (3.8 cm)

Charlie Helin invented this lure over fifty years ago and the FlatFish is still around and catching fish with its one-of-a-kind swimming action. It's available in 14 sizes and over 100 different colors.

14. Gibbs/Nortac—Gypsy Spoon Army Truck Glow 1½ inch (3.8 cm)

Great for casting or trolling, the Gypsy Spoon comes in four sizes. The two smaller sizes, the 1 (1⅜ inch / 3.5 cm) and 1½ (1⅝ inch / 3.8 cm), come in 10 colors while the 2¾ (2¾ inch / 7 cm) and 3½ (3½ inch / 9 cm) come in 18 different color combinations.

15. Brecks International Inc.—Mepps Aglia Shallow Runner Brown trout B3 ¼ ounce (7 g)

For fifty years fishermen have been using the Mepps Aglia (pronounced *Ag'lee a*). It's available in six sizes: 0 and 1 are perfect for smaller streams, 2 and 3 Aglia are ideal for lake and river fishing and 4 and 5 are irresistible to large rainbow trout and steelhead. The Aglia blades are available in polished brass (gold), genuine silver plate and various "hot" colors.

16. Brecks International Inc.—Mister Twister Night Crawler Natural or Bubblegum 4 or 6 inch (10 or 15 cm)

Nightcrawlers are favorite bait for just about any species, and Mister Twister is a great substitute for the real thing.

17. Gibbs/Nortac—Ironhead Green #100 2⅜ inch (6 cm) length, one ounce (28 g)

Constructed of heavy gauge brass for casting accuracy and control, the Ironhead is ideal for rivers, streams and lakes. Even in fast, deep water, this lure gets down to where the fish are. Designed with an enticing frantic motion at any speed of retrieve, this heavy spoon is great for steelhead in fast-moving waters. Comes in three sizes—066 (⅔ oz / 19 g), 100 (1 oz / 28 g) and 150 (1½ oz / 42 g)—and four color combinations.

18. Luhr Jensen—Krocodile Brass/Fire Strip ⅙ ounce (5 g)

Krocodiles can be cast and retrieved, jigged over structure or trolled. Choose the size that best mirrors available forage and then pick the perfect finish from an extensive palette.

19. Gibbs/Nortac Fishing— Original Wedding Band #8 Sparkler Fire Tiger with Ruby Red Beads

These multipurpose little spinners are a must for trout. The sparkle reflects from the bowl of highly polished Indiana blades as they revolve around a genuine European rhinestone rondelle. They are sized according to hook and available in many color combinations.

20. Brecks International Inc.— Mepps Little Wolf Silver
1½ inch (3.8 cm) ¼ ounce (7g)

The Little Wolf design maintains a wobble and prevents roll-over with a perfect balance. It's great for casting or trolling. Its reverse-curve design features 10 distinct highly reflective surfaces that disperse light equally in all directions. Solid brass silver-plated or hot colors and glow patterns will give you a long duration.

21. Brecks International Inc.— Mooselook Wobbler #20 Silver Front/Copper Back 140 medium
3⅛ inch (8 cm) ¼ ounce (7 g)

John A. Green developed the Mooselook Wobbler in 1938 on Lake Mooselookmeguntic in Maine, from where it takes its name. It's a Canadian favorite in all lakes and has been a classic trout and salmon spoon for over sixty years. Try trolling it at a wide range of speeds. Imitate your baitfish profile using the Pee Wee—¹⁄₁₅ oz (2 g), Midget—½ oz (15 g), Junior—⅙ oz (5 g), Medium—¼ oz (7 g) or Large—⅜ oz (12 g) models. Mooselook comes in about 20 different colors so experiment with color to find the right combination for your water. Pumping your rod occasionally can trigger strikes from followers, as your Mooselook appears to be darting away or fluttering back like a wounded baitfish.

22. Hot Spot Lures—Apex Kokanee Special 75 Chartreuse
1½ inches (3.8 cm)

Nine color combinations available in 1- or 1 ½-inch (2.5- or 3.8-cm) lengths.

23. Gibbs/Nortac Fishing—Gypsy Frog
#1—1⅜ inch (2.5–3.5 cm) length

Great for casting or trolling, this lure comes in four sizes. The two smaller sizes, the 1 (1⅜ inch / 3.5 cm) and 1½ (1⅝ inch / 3.8 cm), come in 10 colors while the 2¾ (2¾ inch / 7 cm) and 3½ (3½ inch / 9 cm) come in 18 different color combinations.

24. Tomic Lures—Casting Spoon

This casting spoon is made from nickel-plated brass and comes rigged with welded rings, a swivel and a stainless-steel single hook.

25. Luhr-Jensen—Kwikfish #0979 Fire Tiger

The wide, slow-trolling action of the Kwikfish lure will target smaller trout in the smaller sizes; the middle weight lures larger trout, steelhead and lunker lake trout. For maximum success, tune the screw eye on the face of the plug to achieve an even side-to-side action. Using small adjustments, turn the screw eye in the opposite direction to that which the lure is favoring until it tracks straight.

26. Thompson-Pallister Bait Co.—Len Thompson Original Series 00 Red & White Spoon ½ ounce (15 g)

Len Thompson started selling his lures in 1929; the company that still bears his name has sold about fifty million lures since. Famous for its Yellow & Red (Five of Diamonds) and Red & White models, the line has expanded to include "The Platinum Series," nickel-plated spoons finished in very high contrast, often with fluorescent paint jobs in today's most desired patterns.

27. Tomic Lures—Tomic Plug 3-inch #800

The Classic is the original design of the Tomic Plug; the 3-inch (7-cm) model weighs ⅜ oz (12 g). All plug bodies are manufactured from extremely strong and lightweight plastic. Airbrush artists finish each lure by hand with durable lacquers. The Classic series has an erratic side-to-side swimming action that fish love. Mainly a trolling lure, the Classic comes rigged with a single stainless hook and is great for down-rigging or top-water trolling. Fast troll or retrieve provides the best action.

28. Hot Spot Lures—Apex Trout Killer

An Apex with specialized rigging is designed to catch trout every time. Comes in 21 color finishes and in 1- or 1 ½-inch (2.5- or 3.8-cm) sizes.

Far left: Wayne Moss with a trout caught on a Tomic plug.

29. Tomic Lures—Tomic Spoon 3.5 inches 246

The Tomic Spoon (formerly called the Road Runner) is a lightweight trolling spoon (the 3.5-inch / 8.5-cm spoon weighs ½ oz / 15 g) made from nickel-plated brass. It comes rigged with welded rings, a swivel and a stainless-steel single hook.

30. Yakima Bait Company—Worden's Lures—Spin–N–Glo

The original winged drift bobber has been a favorite of anglers for decades. Available with soft plastic wings or stiffer, light-reflective Mylar wings, the Spin-N-Glo spins in the slightest of currents, adding floatation and motion to any fishing rig. Its buoyancy makes it a floating bait that will entice trout to feed. It comes in a variety of sizes and colors.

Peter Willing fishing for rainbow trout at Langford Lake near Victoria, BC. His Apex Trout Killer brought in this incredible fish weighing 8 lb 1 oz (3.6 kg). Kevin Tisdale photo

10 | Ralph Shaw

Lake Fishing for Trout in the Pacific Northwest

Dugan Lake near 150 Mile House in the Cariboo region of BC.

The Pacific Northwest has thousands of lakes that are home to cutthroat, rainbow, brook and lake trout as well as Dolly Varden and kokanee. Cutthroat, rainbow and brook trout are the major species in most lakes. Kokanee (land-locked sockeye salmon) are also common in many of the larger lakes. Dolly Varden char are native to many of the lakes, but their populations are in decline throughout coastal waters. Some of the lakes on the southern half of Vancouver Island contain good populations of smallmouth bass. A few lakes have fishable populations of brown trout.

This chapter's major emphasis will be on lakes with good populations of rainbow and cutthroat trout. The Freshwater Fisheries Society of BC is doing an excellent job of stocking hundreds of lakes throughout the province with yearling catchable triploid rainbow trout, brook trout and large numbers of cutthroat trout. They also stock selected lakes with kokanee salmon. Their policy of stocking only lakes that have open access to the public is sound management. The society also sponsors

The author landing a trout at Hefley Lake outside of Kamloops, BC.

learn-to-fish programs and promotes the Family Fishing Weekend, held every year on the Father's Day weekend in June. Both are great ways for newcomers to learn about the sport of fishing.

As an essential part of your fishing equipment you should have a copy of the current *Freshwater Fishing Regulations Synopsis*. Take the time to read the regulations as they apply to the lakes or streams you choose for your fishing.

I spend a lot of time fishing lakes, primarily because I find still-water angling to be a soul-enhancing way of bonding with nature. The complex ecosystems of lakes make angling days adventures of ever-changing moods and surprises. Our large lakes at low elevations can be actively fished twelve months of the year, if you have the physical and mental attitude needed to challenge open waters all year long. Most of the smaller, low-elevation lakes are ice-free for at least ten months of the year. The lakes at higher elevations in many mountainous valleys are frequently iced over for several months, making fishing there a summer experience that's usually done from open shorelines or float tubes.

> When you hook a fish that is strong enough to overpower your drag, don't crank the drag down to a heaver setting as this is a good way to lose your fish. Set it so that it won't backlash or free-spool and palm it to put more pressure on the fish.

Beaver dams often create all the characteristics of still waters, but fall under stream regulations. This means they have a single barbless hook rule and a 30-cm (12-inch) size limit, with a daily bag limit of two fish in British Columbia.

10A: Tactics for Successfully Angling Lakes

Large Lakes

Usually found at low or medium elevations, large lakes many miles long and wide are important fishing destinations for many anglers. Examples include Shuswap Lake, Okanagan Lake, Arrow Lakes, Quesnel Lake, Lac La Hache, Shawnigan Lake, Cameron Lake, Horne Lake, Comox Lake, Buttle Lake and Victoria Lake.

There is much excellent fishing in all of our large lake systems. The rules of engagement that apply to successfully fishing these large bodies of water are somewhat different than those for smaller bodies of water. Because most large lakes lie in valleys and many are sandwiched between mountain ranges, they are subject to challenging thermal winds. For this reason, it is probably prudent to be in a seaworthy boat when you venture onto the main body of the

This large lake lies in a valley sandwiched between a mountain range.

lake. A big plus is that they tend to stay cooler throughout the warm summer days, thereby avoiding the warm temperatures associated with parasites and off-flavor flesh when you keep fish to eat. Lakes that have been raised by hydroelectric dams are subject to major changes in shorelines and lake depths. Water depth changes can vary with rainfall and seasonal drawdowns. Hazards in lakes behind dams can be stumps from pre-flooding and land clearing and surprise changes in shoreline water depths.

The most successful method of fishing large lakes is trolling. When you fish a large lake do not think in terms of the whole body of water. Instead break the lake into fishable parts, such as waters near feeder streams and rivers, submerged reefs and discrete bays that may have many of the characteristics of much smaller bodies of water.

Trolling is a successful method for fishing large lakes.

It is on the larger bodies of water that outboard motors and electric trolling motors come into their own, simply because of the distances from one fishing area to another. Depth sounders and fishfinders also pay big dividends, especially if you are not familiar with the contours of a lake. Shoal areas and islands offer rich feeding grounds for predator fish such as large cutthroat trout. Various Willow Leaf, Wedding Band and Ford Fender lake trolls up to 6 feet (1.8 m) in length rigged with worms, bucktails and lures can attract large lake trout from the deep water.

Traditional bucktail streamers can be amazingly successful.

Many of the small wooden or plastic plugs and FlatFish produce good catches. In large lakes with kokanee populations the traditional bucktail streamer patterns are amazingly successful.

Most lakes have healthy populations of baitfish, which are important food for large trout. The Rhys Davis Teaser head with a Baitrix trout imitation will work wonders with these big trout when trolled using a Luhr-Jensen/Les Davis-Sun Flash Flex-i-Troll.

Les Davis Sun Flash Flex-i-Troll with a rainbow trout caught on the Rhys Davis/ Baitrix trout pattern.

Fly casting with sinking lines off ledges near feeder streams will work wonders with Rolled Muddlers, Clouser minnow and leech patterns.

Small and Medium Lakes

It is inviting confusion to try to classify lakes as medium or small. For our purposes we will classify lakes of less than 1,200 acres (500 ha) as medium and those between 250 and 25 acres (100 to 10 ha) as small. These smaller bodies of water are nutrient factories for freshwater fish, and are small enough that you can become intimate in your associations with them. Many such lakes are multi-use; they can be used for swimming, canoeing, rowing, sailing, kayaking and, for the purposes of this book, trout fishing in all its glorious manifestations.

In doing some of the research for this chapter I went

An angler fishing from his canoe shows off his catch.

fly-fishing on a high-use lake on a Sunday to test the idea that you can fish while many other people are using the lake for their own enjoyment. On the Sunday in question I anchored my punt in the middle of a popular fishing bay. At one time I was surrounded by four kayakers and six canoeists. We were visiting over the still water and none of our activities interfered with others' enjoyment of the lake. The lake had a no motor restriction that put everybody on an even playing field. You have a different problem when sharing a large lake with various speedboats and their water skis.

If you wish to become a good still-water angler you would be wise to select a small lake in the 200 acre (80 ha) range, with a good fish population. Hopefully it will be close to your home so you can fish it often.

Have a fishing love affair with these bodies of water and fish them at all seasons of the year, in good weather and foul. You will find a lake is a small ecosystem with its own set of rules for the plant, insect, bird, amphibian, fish and mammal

I generally only have about three or four fly patterns in my still-water fly box on any given outing. Those patterns might change around a bit during different times of the year, but I keep my choices to just those that are appropriate for the task.

communities that inhabit it. Going fishing early in the morning, during the day and in the evening will show you feeding patterns and variations in certain species. For example, large bass and trout will frequently move into shallow shoals in the evening as they hunt for baitfish, salamanders, frogs, crayfish and large flying insects such as sedges. Yet if you fish the same body of water between 10 A.M. and 4 P.M., your fish will be in much deeper water feeding on chironomid pupae, sedge pupae, dragonfly nymphs and leeches.

During the warm part of the day in the early part of the year you will discover that different hatches occur at varying times of the day. These will dictate the fly patterns you use. Depending on the season, you will soon discover that fish take different lures

and flies at different times. If you fish with worms it will soon become apparent that some areas of your lake are much more productive than others.

Electronic depth sounders and fishfinders can help you discover the structure of your lake and where fish hang out. Use them if you must, but avoid becoming addicted to the scene on the sounder at the expense of watching feeding birds or surface splashes for clues. One of the best tools you can have for learning where to fish your chosen body of water is a contour map of the lake bottom. These can be found in fishing map books, which are available for most of the lakes in the province.

A fishfinder showing fish at 5–6 feet (1.5–1.8 m).

10B: Suggestions to Improve your Catching Skills

Shore Fishing

It's one of the most popular forms of angling lakes throughout the province. You can purchase several types of rod holders to assist you in enjoying this relaxing style of fishing. Spinning and casting outfits are usually used while shore fishing. If you're

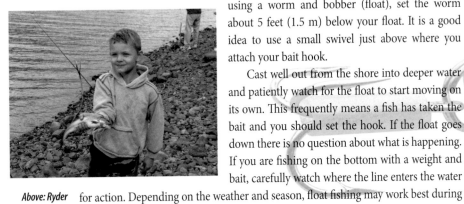

using a worm and bobber (float), set the worm about 5 feet (1.5 m) below your float. It is a good idea to use a small swivel just above where you attach your bait hook.

Cast well out from the shore into deeper water and patiently watch for the float to start moving on its own. This frequently means a fish has taken the bait and you should set the hook. If the float goes down there is no question about what is happening. If you are fishing on the bottom with a weight and bait, carefully watch where the line enters the water for action. Depending on the weather and season, float fishing may work best during the middle of the day and bottom fishing during the evening. But there are no firm rules. Make it a regular habit to check your bait and keep it fresh. It is against the law to use anything other than worms, roe or scented plastic baits.

Above: Ryder Samuels holds a prize cutthroat trout caught fishing from shore.

Right: Homemade rod holder.

Trolling with Gang Trolls

Trolls vary in size from simple little spinners with beads to strings of shiny blades up to 6 feet (2 m) in length. They are designed to fish all levels of a lake. In large lakes they are frequently fished from downriggers. They are primarily designed to fish with worms, but flies and lures can also

Lake Troll, sometimes
called a gang troll.

be used. Depending on the body of water and local regulations, most trolling is done from motor-driven boats. It is an idyllic way to fish large bodies of water as you watch the passing landscape.

One advantage to fishing with worms—they are like bread and butter—is that they work throughout the season. When trolling with worms it is a good idea to check your bait frequently after a couple of good bites (obviously this is not necessary if you are using a fly or a lure). If you are a novice angler, learn to treat your worms with care. Keep them cool in the fridge or have a large worm-friendly container with a food source to keep them healthy between trips.

Lures, plugs, FlatFish and spoons are primarily trolling tackle. Casting spoons and jigs can be shore cast or used from boats in drop-off locations such as inlet or outlet streams. Children can become proficient is using these hands-on kinds of fishing tackle, especially from riverbanks and the shore. One big advantage they have over trolling, which can be boring for young people, is all the activity involved with casting.

Top: Gibbs/Nortac Cowichan Lake Troll.

Bottom: Tomic Plug #176.

Fishing with flies is a growth activity throughout the province and elsewhere in Canada. There is a complex array of choices for pursuing this addictive type of still-water angling. It can become an all-absorbing activity that has all kinds of spin-offs, such as tying your own flies.

If you are a complete novice at this absorbing pastime, a simple way to catch some fish is just trolling a fly from a boat on a sinking or weighted spinning line. Don't be overwhelmed by the jargon of fly fishers. Anyone who can hold a rod can absorb the basics of fly-fishing—from very young anglers to aging seniors. If you choose to get deeply involved with this fascinating type of fishing, join a local fly-fishing club. You will meet many anglers willing to help you learn the finer points of this addictive hobby.

From this author's perspective it is truly a simple and basic way to fish. Fishing flies are generally clever imitations of actual insects, small fish or other bait. You will hear fly fishers talk about catching trout on tiny flies. The reason they use tiny flies is to imitate the food the fish are eating. It is that

Jay Mohl with a fly-caught rainbow trout.

Rainbow trout from Howard Lake, which is located above Canim Lake in the Cariboo, BC.

simple. One of the challenges of this fishery is to choose the correct imitation for the time and place you are fishing. I will try to help you select the best flies to fish and give some suggestions for successful use of fly patterns.

Leeches

Virtually all freshwater lakes, ponds, sloughs and beaver dams have good populations of these ancient creatures. They are important fish food that is available

12 months of the year. I have at least 20 different leech patterns in my fly boxes and I believe all of them will catch fish.

(Berkley PowerBait makes an imitation flavored leech that would most certainly confuse a leech looking for company.)

Fly patterns come in many sizes and lengths. The most common colors are black, brown, olive green and a maroon blood color, in hook sizes of 8 to 10 on 3X long shanks. When you are trolling a leech, troll slowly. When a fish nibbles at the fly, let it really bite it before you set the hook.

Above: Olive green leech on a rock.

Right: Berkley Gulp Alive 3-inch (8-cm) Black Leeches.

Leeches are frequently tied with small beads at the head, giving rise to the term bead-headed. Micro-leeches are a relatively new addition to our leech patterns as they are tied with bead-heads on smaller hooks like numbers 12 and 14, 3X long shank hooks, and can be deadly for both rainbows and brook trout. When casting them, use a fairly fast sinking line; retrieve your fly in short pulsing pulls with occasional pauses. Sometimes the strike is violent enough

Jack Shaw on Six Mile Lake outside of Kamloops, BC. Note the anchors on the bow and stern of his boat.

to break your tippet; and at other times it is a series of nibbles prior to taking the fly.

No fly box should be without at least half a dozen leeches. From my experience I would put them on a par with angleworms as a season-long fly.

Chironomids

Over forty years ago the late Jack Shaw started fishing with flies tied to match these small insects. He started a fishing revolution that continues right up to this day. Chironomids are important trout food. They are a very large family of small flying insects that look much like mosquitoes. Their various races number in the thousands. Each individual lake system seems to generate species all its own.

Always string your rod before you put on your waders and take it apart before you take off your waders. Keeping an order to your preparation processes keeps you from forgetting things—like rods on the roof of your truck.

While we think of the interior lakes as the birthplace of this type of fly-fishing, the patterns also work equally well on the lakes of Vancouver Island. One thing I find is that there appear to be smaller races of these little insects in Island waters compared to interior waters. Anglers who want to fish this important fly pattern should use more flies in the 14 to 18 range in Island lakes, whereas in the interior they would use more flies in the 12 to 16 range. As a general rule on the Island, the earlier in the season you start with this pattern, the smaller your flies will be, though there are always exceptions.

Chironomid season runs from early March right up to late June and then again in October and November. If fishing early in the season you should use the larval stage of the insect, which is called a bloodworm and is very simple to tie. The technology of fly-line development reaches high challenges for the dedicated angler. A committed chironomid fly fisher may use a dry line, a sinking tip line, a slow sinking line and a fast sinking line all in the same day. He or she may also fish depths ranging

Jack Shaw's Blood Worm.

from 15 to 50 feet (5 to 15 m). Depending on the type of boat, the angler will probably use two anchors to keep the boat steady, one anchor off the stern and one off the bow.

It may sound a little intimidating but it really isn't that bad. The dry line fishing will in all probability involve a strike indicator (a fly-fishing term for a tiny float) and a long leader. There is also another way of fishing a dry line that was championed by Tom Murray. You simply use a long leader, cast the line out and let it drift around.

The sink-tip line is used for wet-line fishing in fairly shallow waters or when the fish are feeding in mid-depth waters up to 15 feet (5 m). Finally there are sinking or wet lines, which are designed to sink at varying rates and hold the fly at a desired depth in the water below your boat. One of the most important tools you need in this type of fishing is a wristwatch to time the descent of your fly.

In spite of the mystique associated with chironomid fishing it can be mastered with a little patience and dedication. It is a forgiving sport in that you don't have to be an accomplished fly-caster to cast far from the boat. I would also suggest you learn to cast while sitting down in your boat. In the deep water of this fishery, the fish are not boat shy.

A 3-pound (1.5-kg) rainbow trout out of Leighton Lake near Kamloops, BC.

To assist your fly in sinking it is a good idea to tie a small 14 swivel about 18 inches (45 cm) from the fly as you tie on your tippet. Fluorocarbon tippets of 4 pounds work well unless you are targeting large fish; in that case you may need 6 pound to avoid break-offs when you set the hook.

Keep your fly in the water. Always.

To locate where these insects are hatching simply watch where the swallows are feeding on the lake. Also watch carefully for emerging insects as you move about the lake. When you find them, anchor and begin to fish. Change patterns after a few casts if you have no takers. Try to match the color and size of the insects in the water about you. When you catch a fish it is a good idea to check its stomach contents to more clearly pinpoint the color and size of insects you are trying to imitate.

The newer patterns of these small insects use weighted beads to help sink the fly to the feeding zone. Some beads such as magnesium are quite costly so be careful how you use them. Many chironomid fly bodies are tied in black, brown, green, yellow or clear plastic, to name a few. Most patterns have a red copper, gold or silver wrapping of fine wire, thread or tinsel.

Black and Orange Chironomid.

One of the saving graces of chironomid fishing is that it is usually best during banker's hours—10 A.M. to 4 P.M.

Dragonfly Nymphs

Fish don't eat the dragonflies we see flitting about the water or around the neighborhood. Instead they feed on the nymph stages in the life cycle of these large predator insects. Dragonflies live in the nymph stage in our lakes for up to four years before emerging as adults. It is during their long aquatic life cycle that they are important fish food. The nymphs are tied in rusty brown colors, olive green and light green with seal hair dubbing and pheasant wing cases.

Deer hair is also an important material in some types of nymph patterns. These are large flies in 6 to 10 on 3X long hooks. The pattern is fished off a wet line right off the bottom. Dragonflies are important predators in their own right and are found on lake bottoms where smaller insects live. They present a nice meal to a foraging trout and occasionally you will find a dragonfly nymph mixed with chironomid pupae. This suggests that the big insect may have got in the way of a feeding trout and became food itself. A moderately fast retrieve with pauses will attract action from big trout. This pattern is also good for trolling along a weed bed or shoal. It can be fished throughout the season from spring right up to late fall. During the fall, fish it off shoals into deeper water, as the nymphs migrate from shallow to deep water in the winter.

Top left: Dragonfly nymph.

Bottom left: One of the best is this rust-colored dragonfly nymph pattern.

Caddis Flies (Sedges) and Pupae

Caddis pupae are high on the list of important trout foods. They are grazers along rocky shoals, weed beds and algae-covered rocks. When they emerge from the larval stage in May and June they create some great fishing opportunities for the dry fly versions of the insect. Sedges vary in size from about ½ to 1½ inches (12 to 37 mm) long depending on the species. Trout eat the larval stage as well as emerging adults.

Wooly worms and some specifically tied pupae patterns work well and are popular flies for targeting trout feeding on caddis pupae. If you look into clear waters and see small bundles of weeds or stick-like bits of wood moving around on the bottom you are looking at grazing caddis pupae. At this stage we fish them with wet flies on sinking lines in the same general area you would find dragonfly nymphs.

The retrieve for sedge pupae is slow and steady with few pauses. When fish strike the fly they normally do it with no hesitation. This pattern is well adapted to slow trolling over shallow weed beds and rocky shorelines. The dry fly version is made to copy the actions of emerging sedges and creates some of the finest dry fly-fishing anywhere you find these interesting insects.

Top to bottom: Caddis larva in pebble retreat. Chenille Olive Wooly Worm. Brown sedge pupa pattern.

Many fishing trips are planned to coincide with sedge hatches, which provide some of the best dry fly-fishing

Ralph Shaw and his grandson Danny with a nice catch.

opportunities a season will offer. Casting a dry fly pattern such as a Tom Thumb to feeding trout during a traveler sedge hatch is one of the most exciting experiences I have had in over seventy years of fly-fishing.

At the end of the day, loosen the drag on your reel. This applies to spring-and-pawl and disk-drag reels, and will save your reel.

The lakes of British Columbia have a worldwide reputation for being the natural home of rainbow trout. They also enjoy an enviable reputation for being home to native cutthroat trout. In recent years we have added a third species of trout-like fish to our lakes that is building an enviable reputation as both a superb fighting fish and excellent eating—the brook trout, a member of the char family.

These trout were first planted in select lakes to provide a catch for ice fishermen so they wouldn't target rainbow trout during the winter. It worked, and brook trout soon became very popular throughout the spring and fall fisheries as well. They take all the flies we use for other trout and give a good account of themselves in the process.

The strike of a 3-pound (1.5-kg) brook trout can frequently be a leader-breaking experience. They have an added quality in that they are excellent on the table. In most of the lakes I have fished them they tend to school, hanging out in favored locations most of the time. Once you find a school of biting fish you are in for some memorable fishing.

I t's a late spring day, cloudy and about 55°F (13°C). You are on your favorite trout spot. You scan the body of water and see rings forming all around. You notice fins and noses quietly breaking water with the odd slurping sound. You feel the excitement start to build as you begin fumbling your fishing gear around like you had ten thumbs. This is a day of which we all dream.

Using a floating fly line.
Rory Glennie photo

Fishing for rainbow trout, whether you are fly-fishing, trolling or casting your favorite spinner for these magnificent fish, is always a great experience. I find myself craving fishing a dry fly for feeding trout.

Before we head out in search of that trophy rainbow we have to learn what type of fishing we're going to do and the best gear for the job. Whether we are going to be using gear or fly, having a bit of knowledge of what is available will save us money and frustration. I am going to cover gear first. You don't have to break the bank to get out and catch trout. Many companies offer spinning rod combos at an affordable price. These combos are actually good quality and easy to use. If you're looking at a spinning rod you will find that a medium-light, medium or medium-heavy one with a length of 6 to 8 feet (2 to 2.5 m) will suffice.

You want your reel to hold about 110 to 200 yards (100 to 180 m) of 6- to 8-pound test monofilament. For young kids or beginners you may want to look at a closed-face reel. These reels are some of the easiest to use. They have a push button with a cover on the front. The cover helps with tangles and keeps

Closed-face reels are great for beginners.

the line hidden from curious fingers. When you become more experienced you may want to go to a spinning reel or even a level-wind. The level-wind is the most difficult to use but it tends to cast a little farther and has smoother drags.

Now that you have chosen what rod and reel you want to use, pick some lures. As you walk down the trout section of your local sporting goods store you may find yourself getting overwhelmed.

Make sure that your tippet spools have not been around for years. Whether you use mono or fluorocarbon, tippet ages—especially when it's exposed to the sun—and gets brittle.

There are lures that catch fish and lures that catch fishermen. You can make it as easy as some number 4 or 6 bait-holder hooks, a medium-sized bobber and a size b or bb split shot. Good trolling gear would be a Willow Leaf or Ford Fender lake troll followed by a FlatFish or Wedding Band and worm. I like the Rooster Tails, Panther Martins or Mepps. If you are going to use spoons you want to try the Red Devil, Five of Diamonds or William's Wobbler. When I choose colors for any gear I look for silver, copper, brass or 50/50. I like to choose natural colors as well so I look for blacks, browns or olive. It doesn't hurt to have a bright color like red, blue, pink or chartreuse in your tackle box as well.

All spoons, spinners and trolls come in many different sizes and weights. An easy way to remember what size you may want is big lures for big fish and small lures for small fish. This is just a guideline. You don't want to use a five-inch spoon if your target fish are only 12

The Gypsy 50/50 in silver and brass is a winning spoon.

to 14 inches (30 to 35 cm) long. For weight you want a lure that best matches your rod. Most rods have the best lure weight written on them just above the handle. If the lure is too light it will not cast and if it is too heavy you will end up with the same problem—and you will find your line breaks easily, causing you to lose a lot of gear.

Fly-fishing is altogether different. With gear, we use a rod to throw a weight out to the fish and that weight carries the line. In fly-fishing we use the rod to cast the line out to the fish and the *line* then carries the fly. For trout you want a rod 8 to 10 feet (2.5

Fly Girl rod and Islander reel with a 2-pound (1-kg) rainbow trout.

to 3.2 m) long with a 4 to 6 weight to start. A good guideline to go by for choosing a rod weight is the higher the weight the bigger the fly and the bigger the fish, and the smaller the weight the smaller the fly and the smaller the fish.

When you choose your rod you want to match it to your reel and line. You may want to look for a reel that you can get spare spools for at a reasonable price. With fly-fishing you will want different lines to help you get the fly to where the fish are feeding. If they are feeding on the surface you want a floating line; if they are feeding below you will want to use a sinking or a sink-tip line. In lakes I prefer a full sinking line and in moving water I like sink-tip lines.

Once you have selected your rod, reel and line you will want to pick up some tapered leaders, or make your own. A tapered leader is a semi-invisible extension of your fly line that allows you to tie your fly and place it in the strike zone without spooking the fish. You will find a lot of fly fishers also use a tippet. The tippet is an extension of your monofilament leader. It's the last piece of line tied to your fly. You add it so *A selection of* you can change flies or extend your leader without using up your expensive, maybe *leaders.* homemade, tapered leader.

The last must-have is your favorite flies. Your local tackle shop will have the top flies for your area. You will find that size, color and hatches change in different areas, elevations and bodies of water.

Other things you may want to have before you head out to your favorite trout spot are forceps for removing hooks; a pair of pliers to de-barb your hooks; extra line, leaders or tippet; and a good knot book.

If you are wading you may want to invest in a pair of waders and boots. Don't forget to use a wading belt if you are wading in a river—it could save your life. It's also good to have a pair of nippers and a nail knot tool. Again this is just touching the surface, I could write a whole book on gear and how to choose the right gear for the job. I want to try to keep it simple for those who are new to the sport so they are not overwhelmed.

First Key Point: Read the Water

No matter if you are fishing lakes or rivers, large or small, you have to know what the fish are doing at all times of the year. You should know where they are going to hold. Look for structure, whether in rivers, lakes or still waters.

The author wearing a pair of breathable waders.
Lisa Andrade photo

Eve River on Vancouver Island.

If I am fishing a river I look for anything that breaks the current. Trout will expend a lot of energy trying to hold in the current so they will look for anything that will give them an ambush point, cover from above or a break from the current. Large boulders, logs and back eddies are all good places to begin your search.

Remember to bring a spare rod and reel. A broken rod or a reel is a real bummer, but with a spare outfit you can still get in a day of fishing.

As you gain more experience reading water you will find so many areas that hold trout that you will catch a lot more fish in a smaller area. Once you've learned to see these key holding areas you will find that the patterns are the same around every bend of any river, big or small. The head of a pool or the tail-out and undercut banks are a few areas to study and concentrate your efforts.

Rivers are constantly changing, from water depth to course. Fishing moving water can be dangerous as conditions are constantly changing due to rain, drought and bank stability. With snow melt or rain the water can get high and dirty really quick, making fishing difficult. But as the river drops and clears, fishing can turn great just as fast. The high, fast water moves insects into the river from the banks or from under rocks. A key thing to remember is to look for your main holding areas like boulders, logs and stumps or other structure that break the current. Also look for foam. Foam is also called "a food highway." The head or tail of riffles or pools and pocket water are also great areas to concentrate on. Whether you are using gear or flies, a properly placed cast in these areas will

Lynette Jones caught her very first fish, a beauty of a cutthroat, in Upper Campbell Lake. It was cooked over an open fire and made a great lunch. Kevin Tisdale photo

usually produce rainbows. Larger fish will also hold in the best areas where the most food can be found.

If you find yourself on a lake or your favorite still water, it is just as important to find the key holding areas for trout. These spots will provide cover from sun, birds and other predators. They are also areas where food is most plentiful. My favorite spots are where moving water is flowing in or out of the lake; shoals, which are the first spots to warm up and where insects begin to hatch; and drop-offs that provide cover for trout to ambush food such as leeches or minnows.

A sunken structure.

Lakes and still waters have a lot of sunken structures like trees, roots or rocks that can hold trout. Finding such structure can be difficult but when you do they can produce. A good fishfinder can help a lot. It will also give you a good indication where fish are holding on any particular day. Other areas to concentrate your efforts are the shoreline and deep-water zones. As you learn to read water the next step is to find out what exactly the fish are feeding on.

When food is plentiful, fishing for rainbows can be easy. Rainbow trout prefer water around 64°F (18°C) but will feed in waters as warm as 73°F (23°C). This temperature range allows us to enjoy really good fishing most of the year. Rainbows will move from the bottom of a body of water to the top in search of food. They search for aquatic life such as leeches, mayfly larva, damselflies, dragonflies and stone flies when these insects are moving around to complete their life cycles.

To find out what fish are feeding on throughout the year you can go out to your favorite fishing hole and spend the day trying all the lures or flies in your arsenal. Or you can educate yourself by reading some of the many books and articles that have been written on this subject. You will still have to do a bit of research but it is quite simple. Talk to local fishermen and find out if they have been successful and what they have been using. You should also read up on the aquatic life of the area you are fishing. Knowing water temperature and hatch cycles will help narrow down what lures or flies will be successful, and a thermometer and a stomach pump will help pinpoint the lure or fly of choice.

> Don't use your fly keeper ring on your fly rod— run your leader around the butt section of your reel seat and up to one of your guides. This way the leader will always be out of the tip-top and you'll be ready to cast.

Lakes

In the early part of the year shallow, muddy shoals are the first to warm up and get the desperately needed sunshine, especially if the lake has been frozen over. These areas are the first to experience new life, whether it is vegetation or aquatic life such as leeches and the larvae of aquatic insects. Rainbows will move from the deeper areas of lakes to feed on this new life. These shoals tend to be anywhere from 3 to 20 feet

Shallow muddy shoals are the first to warm up in the spring.

(1 to 6 m) deep. As the days grow longer and the water warms, smaller lakes at lower elevations are first to start teeming with life. The nice thing about fishing these waters is that whether you are using bait, casting spinners or spoons, trolling or casting your favorite fly, anyone can get out and catch rainbow trout from the shore.

The author with his son and his first fly-caught trout. Lisa Andrade photo

If you are new to fishing and are overwhelmed with information and you are just looking to spend the day on your favorite river or lake with your family or friends, I can help. Take a rod and reel and add a bobber, a weight and a good sharp hook. Now you need something to attract fish. My first choice would be a worm. If you cannot find worms or don't like putting live bait on your hook there are things like power bait, roe paste or even plastic baits. The recipe for success is to place the bobber about 18 to 24 inches (45 to 60 cm) from your hook with a small weight about 12 inches (30 cm; the distances are not that critical) from your hook. Cast your rig into the water, wait until the bobber moves and then set the hook. An important thing to remember is that you don't have to cast into the middle of the lake, because the trout will cruise close to the drop-off between the deep water and the shallows.

Casting Spinners or Lures

Deadly Dick size #2.

If you choose to cast spinners or lures a few good choices would be Rooster Tails, Panther Martins, Blue Fox spinners, Krocodile spoons, Five of Diamonds, Red Devil and the Deadly Dick. All come in various sizes and colors; good choices would be natural colors such as black, browns, olive and greens, but silver, gold and bright colors can be more productive at times. Remember to keep an open mind and keep trying gear until you find the right combination.

If you're going to try to fly-fish then I would recommend you try to find any bugs or shucks (the empty shells left behind after a insect hatches) to see what is going on in the lake and then try to "match the hatch." If you are new to fly-fishing and are not sure what to look for, try some searching patterns. A searching pattern resembles a couple of different insects, or simply attracts fish. A few examples would be a good old leech pattern, Wooly Bugger, Muddler Minnow or Doc Spratley. Stay with natural colors such as black, brown or olive but don't be afraid to try a little red, chartreuse or orange. The bright colors can trigger strikes.

Lisa Andrade caught this trout on a lightweight rod and spinning reel using a lure.

You can troll flies as well using the same patterns, but tie a rabbit-fur strip on your leeches or Wooly Buggers on a sinking line. Whether you are in a boat, pontoon boat or a float tube you can troll your fly by letting line out behind you and slowly moving along the shoal, shoreline or drop-off.

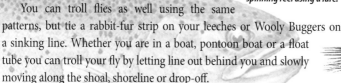

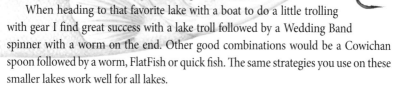

Doc Spratley.

When heading to that favorite lake with a boat to do a little trolling with gear I find great success with a lake troll followed by a Wedding Band spinner with a worm on the end. Other good combinations would be a Cowichan spoon followed by a worm, FlatFish or quick fish. The same strategies you use on these smaller lakes work well for all lakes.

No matter your preferred method of fishing you must cover the water to increase your odds of catching fish. Spin fishing is a great way to cover water quickly and effectively.

Trolling in a pontoon boat with a fly.

Bill von Brendel uses a figure-eight retrieve. Note his rod tip is near the surface.

Casting at a 45-degree angle across the current and using the current to provide action and sweep the lures in front of feeding trout is the most productive method. If you are fishing in BC remember our moving waters have a single, barbless hook law and the use of bait is banned unless stated in the regulations. Lakes have different, specific regulations, so make sure you look up the body of water you are fishing to see if there are any closures or bans on certain fishing methods. If you are fly-fishing a good way to cover the water is to start your cast really short using the swing method. Cast out at a 45-degree angle and let the current move your fly downstream. Lay your cast out farther and farther until you have reached a distance you can effectively cast to with little effort and few line tangles. This method works well for attractor or flesh patterns.

Another effective rig for lake trout trolling is the spoon-fly combination. Simply remove the treble hook from your spoon and replace it with 12 inches (30 cm) of monofilament holding a flashy wet fly or streamer. The spoon attracts the fish from great distances, while the fly actually draws the strike.

In the first part of this chapter I have covered beginner to intermediate fishing methods. These will definitely help you catch fish. If fishing with gear seems less confusing and a lot simpler, that's because it is. When you are fly-fishing you want to match the hatch. This means you want to imitate the food source on which the trout are feeding. In doing this you have to learn some entomology and different casting techniques so you can mimic the movement of various aquatic insects in each stage of their lives. If you are just starting out fly-fishing I highly recommend taking a course from a reputable instructor. Look for someone who is a certified casting instructor through the Federation of Fly Fishers (FFF).

Now that you are learning to read the water you have an idea of what lure or fly to use. When you cover the water effectively, you naturally become better at fishing.

Here are a few examples of different casts and retrieves to help you enjoy fly-fishing and be successful. I know for a fact that if you can get out and catch a few trout you will be hooked.

Once you have located fish and worked out what they are feeding on you have to choose your favorite fly pattern. In spring you will find yourself fishing chironomids.

Chironomids move out of the mud on the bottom of the lake and slowly drift upward to the surface to break free of their shells and hatch into adult midges. The cast is simple. Lay out a simple straight cast. Do not try to cast farther than you can control. You want the fly to sink down near the bottom. Get the fly down by using weighted patterns or sink-tip lines. Then start to retrieve the line through the feeding zone. A natural retrieve for chironomids is a very slow, upward one. I like a figure-eight retrieve because you keep control of the line and it doesn't end up on the ground or the bottom of the boat.

A figure-eight retrieve is very hard to explain, but once you see it done it is very simple. You start with the hand not holding the rod. Pinch the line in your thumb and forefinger and rock your hand back, placing the line in your palm. Release the line with your thumb and forefinger and rock your hand forward, pinching the line again. Repeat this over and over until you retrieve all of the line. If you are fishing a mayfly you want a slow figure-eight retrieve in an upward direction at about a 45-degree angle. I find what also works is if you retrieve a bit of line and stop intermittently. Another method uses short, 2- to 3-inch pulls. This is a good retrieve for dragonfly or damsel nymphs and can be used for leeches or minnow patterns.

If you are fishing a dry fly you want to use a floating line and a straight line cast to feeding trout. If the fish are jumping out of the water and making big splashes they are usually not feeding on the surface. You want to see noses just breaking the surface, small rings or dorsal fins breaking the water. Once you have made your cast to a feeding trout you want to retrieve the slack line. Hold your rod tip low and wait a few seconds to see if the fish is going to take your fly. If nothing happens after a few seconds, give a little pull on the line, just enough so that the fly makes a slight ring on the water, and then wait again. If a fish takes your fly set the hook right away and hold on tight.

Joie Coe poses for a quick photo of his fly-caught rainbow trout. Lisa Andrade photo

A popular cast on moving water when you are using attracter patterns or minnow patters is the swing method. This is done by laying out a straight line cast at about a 45-degree angle downstream from where you are standing. The key to feeling strikes on this cast is to keep your fly line straight between you and your fly. To do this you may want to use a couple of mends in your line. This is done by throwing a little bit of slack line upstream. As the current pulls your line downstream it should straighten out as your fly moves down in front of the holding fish. If you do it correctly and the trout likes your fly it will take your offering. Feeling the strikes takes some getting used to if they are soft, so having almost no slack line between you and the fly is important. This may take a little practice but once you get the hang of it you will catch more fish.

If you are fishing moving water with a dry fly the swing method won't work as well as a dead drift method. With dry flies you don't want any drag on your fly. You want

it to drift downstream over feeding trout so that it appears natural. The dead drift method requires you to put slack line in your cast. This is fairly easy to do on short casts but becomes more difficult on longer casts. If you are fishing nymphs you want to cast more upstream, anywhere from a 90- to 135-degree angle, allowing your nymph to drift downstream naturally in front of feeding trout. This requires accurate placement of your casts and more control of your line.

Payback for a good cast.

I have just touched the surface of fly casting. There are more than 18 different single-hand casts. The main thing to remember with fly-fishing is that you're trying to mimic the natural food source of the trout. You want to try to duplicate the prey animal's size, color, species and movements. When I took my first fly-fishing course the instructor told me fly-fishing took a 20-minute lesson and 20 years of experience. I know exactly what he means now.

No matter what method of fishing you do or how much experience you have, I believe we can all agree that the experience of being out on the water, sharing time with loved ones and friends, is the greatest reward of all.

The frosting on the cake, of course, is landing a beautiful rainbow trout.

A prize rainbow catch.

The center pin reel is a bird's nest waiting to happen.

Think of it. You cast out in a big, sweeping motion and the reel spins at a million miles an hour. The only thing controlling the spin is the light touch of your finger or thumb on the drum of the reel. Monofilament peels swiftly off the reel, delivering your terminal tackle to its destination. It takes practice, lots of practice. And there will be headaches. The smallest of mistakes and the bird's nest of line will blossom instantly into a tangled mess in your hands. But the reward is worth the risk. And that reward is being able to play the steelhead on the single-action reel.

The terminal tackle varies from yarn flies, pink worms, spoons and egg patterns to spinners. The main line and the leader are both attached to a swivel. Usually split shot, pencil lead or other weight variations are fastened to the thicker main line. The weight(s) serves two purposes. First, it provides the torque that enables you to cast your gear. Second, it gets your gear down to the proper depth.

The split shot and gear are suspended from a float, usually a dink float, made of Styrofoam and shaped like a long, narrow cylinder. The main line runs through the dink float. While the float drifts along the river's surface, the main line and terminal gear sit at a preset depth. Some set their depths by wrapping the dink float once with the line, securing it from running through to the bottom. Another method, which is far superior, is attaching a small rubber stopper to your main line that not only runs

Tristan Ruszel hooked and released this 15-pound (7-kg) steelhead doe on the Cowichan River. Gibran White photo

Kevin Pellet used a yarn fly and a DNE float to tempt this prize steelhead from a stream. His drift rig consisted of a custom-built rod and a Raven Matrix XL Reel. Robert Van Pelt photo

smoothly through the eyes of the your rod but snags into the float, suspending your gear at whatever depth you choose.

The best way to fish with a center pin is with a friend. Or in the case I'm about to describe, with a good relative.

Andrew Derton of Powell River was visiting his cousin Brent Marin of Campbell River in the winter of 2009. Andrew wanted to go river fishing, but didn't have any gear. Brent took him to one of his favorite rivers, but with one proviso. Brent's only spare rod and reel setup was a center pin reel with a 10-foot (3-m), 6-inch (15-cm) float rod. Andrew is an avid angler, but had never used a center pin before for river fishing.

For steelheading, don't bother with the expensive tippet in the X range (1X, 2X, 3X), just go get yourself some 10- to 12-pound monofilament.

"I was expecting to have a little fun watching him get used to it," said Brent. And he did. Andrew tried and tried to cast, about ten times, but every time the terminal tackle ended up at Andrew's feet, too close to shore, or behind him on shore. Finally Andrew got the hang of it, sending out one good cast that went about 35 feet (10 m) out and landed in a beautiful slot of water. Brent smiled at first, but that smile soon vanished.

The float had gone down short seconds after hitting the water. A seasoned float fisherman would have struck back immediately, because if it's not a fish, it's bottom, and, well, tackle gets expensive. For that long moment both Brent and his cousin watched the float disappear. And then Andrew struck. It was a good thing that Andrew was an experienced angler, even if not with casting a center pin, because he successfully hooked, played and landed a steelhead that was just over 20 pounds (10

Andrew Derton of Powell River, BC, with a 20-pound (10-kg) steelhead he caught while fishing for the first time with a center pin reel on a north Vancouver Island river.

kg). He caught it on a yarn fly Brent had provided, mainline pound test of 15 pounds (6 kg) and a tippet of 8.

If this story says one thing, it is don't be afraid to experiment with new methods of fishing for steelhead. I prefer fly-fishing above all others, but I have also learned that—in winter especially—it can be challenging and almost impossible if the water's really high.

On a bright sunny day in June of 1992 I ventured out at high noon into the Campbell River. I was still relatively new to the sport and more than one friend had told me not to waste my time fly-fishing when the water is clear and the sun is high and bright. But it was lunch hour and I had four deadlines piling up starting about mid-afternoon, so I didn't have a choice; it was fish during lunch or not all.

I took my 8-weight, 9½-foot Sage rod, a floating line, a 9-foot leader and a steelhead bee to the river that day. It was a classic cast, across and slightly upstream in the Main Island pool. A quick mend with slack line let the fly bob freely on the surface, twisting faintly as it picked up every nuance of the current.

Check your terminal tackle often for wind knots, abrasion, dull hooks, etc., when steelhead fishing. Do this whenever you land a fish, get hung up on a bush or grass or when it's windy.

Just as my line went taut, the fly started to drag and almost skip over the small ripples of the Campbell. That's when I saw the fish roll. A shiny, silver side in a classic head and shoulder rise. I yanked back on my rod, fully intending to cast to where that fish had risen. The fly, however, didn't come back. It and my line and the fish were suddenly across the river. It turned out to be a bright, 9-pound (4-kg) doe.

Another lesson: sometimes fishing suggestions are nothing more than old wives' tales.

A lunch surprise.

In the winter, when the water is high, I love using my float rod, Silex center pin and a spoon, mostly the Ironhead from Gibbs. When I was editor of *BC Outdoors* I happened to get a tour of the Gibbs facility in Vancouver and noticed and remarked upon these spanking, brand-new, gold-plated spoons. I'm not even sure if they were on the market yet, but when I returned to my office on Beatty Street the next day, the marketing department at Gibbs had sent me a box of Ironheads to play with.

Three days later I was home in Campbell River and soon thereafter out on one of my favorite rivers. (Actually they are all my favorites, but some are more favorite than others.) There was a light snow falling. The water was colored nicely and going up or coming down, I didn't know, having not fished it for a week.

The most important thing about using the Ironhead, whether you fish it with a center pin, level-wind or spinning reel, is to fish it thoroughly. I learned that lesson on

Dr. Adipose Huxley with one on the fly in a north Vancouver Island river in full freshet. Yes, flies can work in high water.

that special day. I had been casting out and across the current, keeping my rod high and watching its tip telegraph the wobble and depth of the spoon. But I didn't pay too much attention to it when it first hit the water. I guess I was waiting for the spoon to sink and set up in its drift.

I was about five casts into the pool when the spoon hit the water and a steelhead space-shuttled out of the water with the spoon hanging out of its mouth. I wasn't ready, missed

A Gibbs/Notrac Ironhead.

setting the hook and only caught a pretty picture in my mind.

I did catch a couple on the dead drift after that, feeling and seeing the take of both fish. But I had developed another bad habit. After every drift I would start cranking like mad to retrieve the line and cast again. Perhaps because my wrist was getting sore I decided to slow down the retrieve and reel it slowly through the slacker water closer to shore. It worked that day, taking two more steelhead. And it still does. I believe it should work with some other spoons, but maybe not the deeper-bellied, fatter-bodied models.

Steelhead Hiding – A decaying log, lying diagonally on the beach or with a portion in the river, points toward a steelhead lie. This method is not infallible, but its uncanny accuracy has proven itself too many times to be ignored.

Getting back to fly-fishing, fishing a sinking fly can be very productive. I like to use a medium sink tip and I cut about 5 feet (1.5 m) off it. Then I attach my leader. I find it gives me more control and better feel for the fly, where it is and what's happening to it.

I was using this method on the Campbell River, fishing with an Ugly Pink Fly, when the pink run was in. I went to the Lower Island pool and started in at the head of the pool. I covered all the slacker water that stretched halfway out into the run where the swifter, white-tipped water roared by. Nothing.

I decided I wasn't getting down enough so I returned to the top of the run, cast

Graham Rawlins with a prime steelhead taken while fly-fishing near Tofino last spring. That's his guide, Jay Mohl, holding the rod. Jay's Clayoquot Ventures photo

upstream out and into the rapids and mended the line upstream quickly. Bang. A fish hit, but it wasn't a pink. It was a fresh-run steelhead, a male of about 10 pounds (5 kg) with three of four sea lice on it. It was not more than a day into fresh water.

I landed it in the lower end of the pool and returned to the top. I repeated the cast and hit another steelhead immediately. I landed, returned and cast as before. And another steelhead came to that fly. Three in three casts.

There was only one thing to do. I took out my cellphone and called my friend Dave Hadden. I told him what was happening and that I wouldn't cast again until he came. About twenty minutes later he showed up. I showed him my fly and his eyebrows went up in a quizzical nature. "Really?" he said.

Ugly Pink Fly.

Then he tied on a black fly, I think he called it "The Ace." He started into the pool twenty feet below where I had started in, despite my story. He then worked the entire run down the tail out with nary a take. I had sat and watched and wondered why he didn't take my advice on fly and position. When he came back to me, I asked him that very question. "Well, my friend," he said. "Like all fishermen, you lie. And you lie with the best of them."

Accepting the compliment gracefully, I proceeded to the head of the pool, cast my Ugly Pink Fly into the head of the pool and, whamo, a steelhead. He watched me land it and admired its beauty. Then he started to the head of the run and I asked him if he wanted one of my Ugly Pink flies. There was a humorous twist to his smile as he said, "No thanks, this will do."

He went in at the head of the pool and cast out into the rapids. Then he worked steadily and patiently through the pool again before he came back to where I was sitting. "You must have caught them all," he said. It was an awkward moment that I took seriously. I went to the head of the pool and cast again.

On your home or primary river, keep a log of steelhead caught. List when, where, what time of year, what fly, color; even record the water conditions and the weather. Doing this will provide you with a year-to-year data set that's useful at any given time in the run. This is invaluable for mastering your river of choice.

This time it was the second cast that brought a beautiful steelhead to the beach. Dave watched and there was an odd look in his eyes when he said, "Nice fish." There was another awkward silence. I was going to offer him a fly and the head of the pool again, but when he got up he went to the middle of the pool and started to fish. Not knowing what to do, I returned to the head of the pool where I had had so much success.

And the most awful thing happened. Another steelhead.

This was too much for Dave, who has forgotten more about steelhead fishing than he has taught me. He accepted the Ugly Pink Fly, tied it on and went to the head of the pool and cast into the rapids. And cast, and cast and cast.

I was sitting there on shore waiting for it to happen, but it didn't. He finally came back. Dave is one of the nicest people I have ever met and I think his closest encounter with being rude was when he clipped off the pink fly and handed it back to me. "So," he said, "when you fish for steelhead, do you catch pinks?"

The lesson? The more you understand fishing, the more you don't.

The one method for fishing steelhead I had never tried was rafting a river and back-trolling plugs. I had that wonderful experience provided for me by my good

Brent Marin and Dan Drover (on the right) with a steelhead caught while back-trolling plugs.

friend Dan Drover on the Whatchamacallit River on north Vancouver Island.

I had fished the Whatchamacallit many times but there was so much water I had never seen because I was a Shore Maggot, the affectionate term rafters use for anglers fishing from shore. And it is an affectionate term.

We launched the raft with Dan on the oars and I was immediately glad he was. The river was up and some of the water we went through demanded all his great strength and understanding. I was scared witless. And then we hit the runs.

It was water I had never seen before, or if I had, had never been able to really fish, and water I had always wondered about. Dan had his two spinning rods hooked up with Hot Shot plugs. He drifted through, rowing against the river while the plugs plied the depths.

A fly fisher's dream: big bright steelhead suspended in liquid crystal.

At times we pulled up on shore and took to the bank to throw spoons and flies through the pools before returning to the raft. We saw a lot of beautiful river, but not one steelhead. Dan had been courteous to a guide who was rafting a fly-fishing guest ahead of us. He would stop and wait and give the guide and his angler all the time in the world, and first water. We passed that time with leisurely single-malts.

Then we entered the last run. Dan worked the raft into perfect position, the rod tips quivering as the Hot Shots did their thing. Two beautiful steelhead came out of the last run, one for Brent who had come along and one for me. After Brent and I had landed our fish we told Dan the next fish was his.

"Naw," he said, "I prefer getting you guys into the fish. Besides we're done." We landed at the pull out and headed home shortly after.

I asked Dan later if he would have said the same thing if we had hit fish in the early part of the trip

A Good Knife – A good Swiss knife or a Leatherman tool is one of those vital items all steelheaders should carry with them. I have lost reel nuts and found myself with a broken rod on trips and have blessed these tools for giving me the chance to continue fishing.

instead of the last pool. "Well," he said, "you wouldn't have been touching a rod until my turn was done." He smiled that grinning smile of his and I didn't know if he was serious or not. And didn't care, it was such a great experience.

Lesson? Methodology, in steelhead fishing, is a means to madness.

13 | Frank Dalziel

Cutthroat Trout

Frank Dalziel casting for cutthroat.

One sunny July morning I put on my waders and surveyed the shoreline for the telltale swirls and dimples of coastal cutthroat trout along one of the beach areas I like to fish. Commonly known as sea-run cutthroats, these fish often feed on smaller fish, so I attached a Rolled Muddler fly to my leader. At the edge of the water I stood and watched, hoping to see signs of fish in the calm, early-morning tidal water. At the water's edge I reflected on my experiences with coastal cutthroat trout on Vancouver Island. I caught my first fish when I was very young using a worm in a tiny stream. Later I went on trips with my father to rivers and lowland lakes where we fished from a boat, casting or trolling for larger cutthroat trout using lures and flies. Now I was fishing for beautiful tidal-water cutthroat trout.

A splash to the left caught my attention and I turned in time to see a small swirl and two small fin tips break water. I cast close to the disturbance hoping to hook one of the trout that appeared to be feeding in about 8 inches (20 cm) of water. The line tightened quickly and before I realized what had happened there was a huge swirl close to my fly. Line and backing tore off from my reel. After several good runs and many jumps in the shallow water I knelt and admired a prime, fat 24-inch (60-cm) sea-run cutthroat.

Coastal cutthroats are native trout of the West.

I removed my fly from her jaw and watched her swim away. Those two fins I had seen had been attached to one fish. I continued along the shoreline's sand and gravel bars, near eelgrass beds and large boulders. I watched birds, enjoying the area, and watched for signs of other cutthroats. I saw no more fish that day.

At age seven, Kole Mackinnon hooked this fish on his own rod with a handmade gang-troll and a Cripple K lure with a worm. He played the fish for ten to fifteen minutes and could not hang on any longer, so he passed me the rod to land the fish. He did, however, net his fish, a cutthroat trout 22½ inches (57 cm) long and 7 inches (18 cm) deep. According to my fish calculator it must have been close to 8 pounds (3.6 kg).
Jack Derish photo

Coastal cutthroat trout (*Oncorhynchus clarkii clarki*) are truly the native trout of the West. In British Columbia they occupy all niches and vary in size from tiny but mature 8-inch (20-cm) small-stream residents to large, tackle-busting 15-pound (7-kg) lake dwellers in Pacific drainages. The majority of fish caught in the streams, lakes and tidal water fall between these two extremes, measuring from 10 to 20 inches (25 to 50 cm).

Anadromous (sea-run) coastal cutthroat trout move freely between freshwater and near-shore saltwater habitats along the Pacific coastline. They are an ideal light tackle fish because they often feed in very shallow water. There are times and places where you need to probe deeper water with mid-weight outfits to catch bigger fish using larger lures or flies.

An 8-inch (20-cm) monster.

The other subspecies found in British Columbia is the westslope cutthroat (*Oncorhynchus clarkii lewisi*). Anglers should not mistake one for the other since the distributions of these subspecies is mutually exclusive; westslope cutthroat are found mainly in the far southeastern corner of British Columbia, adjacent to Alberta, though scattered populations exist in central BC. On the other hand, coastal cutthroat trout inhabit Pacific drainages.

In their native area, westslope cutthroat inhabit small streams, rivers and some lakes. Their diet consists mainly of aquatic and terrestrial invertebrates and they are

rarely known to eat fish. The normal maximum size of westslope cutthroats varies from 9 inches (23 cm) in small streams to 16–18 inches (40–45 cm) in larger rivers and lakes. The extreme maximum in larger bodies of water seems to be 24 inches (60 cm) or approximately 5 pounds (2.3 kg). Westslope cutthroat trout are very popular with anglers since their diet makes them an ideal quarry for those using light fly or spinning rods with small flies or lures in shallow waters.

Given the relatively wide distribution of cutthroat trout, British Columbia offers a tremendous variety of opportunities for people of all ages to fish for them. When I was very young my first experience with cutthroat trout was in a tiny stream. I can still remember those "giant" 8-inch (20-cm) fish darting in and out of overhead cover in the two pools my brothers and I fished. I only caught two during many clumsy attempts, but that experience led to a lifelong fascination for cutthroat trout. I graduated to rivers, lakes, estuaries and beaches. In 45 years of fishing for them the toughest part of catching these beautiful nomadic trout has been finding them.

Top: Westslope cutthroat inhabit small streams.

Bottom: Small cutthroat.

Fishing techniques for trout in rivers, lakes and tidal waters are surprisingly similar. No matter what type of gear one uses, locating cutthroats requires knowledge of the fish and its habitat preferences and attention to tides (where applicable), bottom topography, wind and weather, seasons, feed types and run timing. Those who are new to fishing should try to do it with someone with experience. Pay close attention. Learn why your partner is fishing a particular spot—don't just memorize the location.

Lake cutthroat.

A clear understanding of why cutthroat are found in a particular location at any given time will help you to identify fishing spots of your own.

Cutthroat trout have evolved in a region where small streams, rivers and lakes are not always rich in feed, so they move around to find food. They occupy most suitable lakes, streams, or near-shore saltwater areas and use very small headwater streams for spawning and early rearing. Above barrier falls cutthroat fry may remain in small streams until they're mature. When they are large enough and conditions permit, they sometimes move to the richer feeding environments of larger rivers, lakes or tidal waters.

To consistently catch cutthroat trout you need to learn a few things about their food (where it is found, how it behaves), preferred habitats and how to make your fly or lure look like an easy meal. Areas with feed and structure (logs, boulders, pilings, runs, weed beds, etc.) that are adjacent to deeper water are always worth investigating.

Shelter is important for all feeding fish including cutthroat trout, so learning to find them involves finding feed-rich areas close to overhead shelter or deeper water since they are usually opportunistic and aggressive feeders. Generally cutthroat are not overly selective feeders, because infertile coastal and mountain watersheds rarely produce feed in great quantities. A cutthroat will rarely pass up an easy meal, even during a big hatch. However, if you are having trouble catching fish and note that a particular prey item is available in great quantities, try to "match-the-hatch" because cutthroat can become very selective when feeding is good.

A good area with feed is near this weed bed.

Most of the time, westslope and coastal cutthroat trout will forage opportunistically and consume anything that is available. Freshwater prey items include aquatic insects (stone flies, mayflies, caddis flies, chironomids), terrestrial insects (ants, wasps, beetles) and other small invertebrates such as leeches, small crayfish, scuds and earthworms. Westslope cutthroat rarely target fish, but coastal cutthroat eat other fish as soon as they are large enough to do so. So if you're fishing for coastal cutthroat in tidal water, other diet items might include sand worms, salmon eggs and small fish such as fresh and saltwater sticklebacks, all species of salmon fry or smolts, trout fry or smolts, sand lance, herring, small sculpin and pile perch.

Stonefly.

In Pacific drainage rivers, some lakes and tidal water, salmon alevins, fry and smolts are main prey items in the spring and early summer. Later on the coast, insects, other small invertebrates and small resident fish such as stickleback or sculpin

Sticklebacks make up part of a trout's diet.

may become important in the diet until the fall salmon run when salmon eggs and, later, chunks of spawned-out salmon carcasses become available. Farther east where westslope cutthroat trout are found, various stages of insects and small invertebrates are important in their diet on a year-round basis. In those areas, charting terrestrial and aquatic insect hatches in lakes and streams at different elevations is much more critical than knowing the timing of non-existent salmon runs.

Preferred habitats are usually defined by feed, shelter and proximity to "safe" areas. In streams, areas where currents carry feed to lies offering shelter from predators can yield good catches of trout. This shelter might come in the form of undercut banks, boulders, logs, trenches and the edges of drop-offs into pools. The largest trout in any stream pick prime lies which offer easy holding with overhead cover, constant delivery of feed and the safety of deeper water.

A stickleback fly pattern tied sparse.

Drop-off areas in lakes are almost always productive for fishing. These are areas adjacent to both the shallows where most of the feed is found and the deep water that provides safety for the fish. Locate and remember these areas since they will continue to produce fish. In the deeper water of a lake, drop-offs, channels or depressions may not be easy to see because the areas adjacent to shallower water are hard to pick up because of the darkness of the water. Wise anglers in boats or float tubes make use of depth sounders or bathymetric maps to help locate these feeding areas.

In salt water, drop-off areas are not as obvious. Sometimes channels may only be a foot or two deeper than surrounding areas and may be dry during low tides. The observant angler will take the time to find these fish "highways" that cutthroat use on

Releasing a nice healthy cutthroat.

feeding forays into the shallow water adjacent to these channels. Experienced anglers have spent a lot of time, sometimes years, finding these areas so please forgive them if they don't offer explicit directions. Finding fish highways by yourself is part of the fun of angling.

Stream cutthroats, both coastal and westslope, are fond of any aquatic and terrestrial insects that come their way. Especially in smaller streams, most of the larger fish will be in the deeper pools or in runs near undercut banks. They will consume insects whenever these are available in all types of water. Try any of the flies listed in Chapter 8: "Thirty Great Pacific Northwest Fly Patterns." My favorite all-round stream flies are a small Parachute Adams dry fly (size 12 or 14), a very small soft-hackle Spider and small Wooly Buggers (size 10 or 12) in various colors—my

An Olive Wooly Bugger with a marabou tail.

favorites being olive or brown. All wet flies and streamers can be tied with or without a gold bead-head. Small coastal streams may also have salmon runs and if open to fishing, a small salmon egg fly bounced along the bottom will catch cutthroat trout in the pool tail-outs.

In Pacific drainage streams a small lure or streamer fly imitating a salmon fry or other small fish will often be gobbled by greedy cutthroat trout at almost any time of the year. The best time to fish fry flies is in the spring and, since fry migrations mostly occur at night, the best fishing will often be during the low-light hours of morning and evening. During the summer and fall almost any lure will produce cutthroat, as will flies imitating various insects and leeches. In the late fall, after the salmon egg feast when egg flies are so productive, hungry trout may consume "flesh flies" such as tan-colored Wooly Buggers, which imitate flesh from rotting salmon.

Dalziel salmon egg.

Coho fry, common in most coastal drainages, spend at least one year rearing in freshwater and are eaten by cutthroat trout year round. Small flies or lures with a bit of gold and orange or red in them will attract cutthroat trout that are preying on

Above: Limber's Black Wizard.

Left: An open-face spinning reel with a 12-inch (30-cm) cutthroat trout.

Luhr Jensen-Krocodile Brass/Fire strip ⅙ oz.

them. I suggest starting with an Olive or Black Wizard or Wooly Bugger or a small Krocodile Spoon in silver or gold with a red stripe when fishing in areas known as coho nurseries.

Flies can be fished with spinning/casting rods by purchasing a clear float and fishing a fly using a 3- to 6-foot (1- to 2-m) leader behind the clear float that supplies the casting weight. If more depth is required or when trolling flies in a lake, use a few small lead-free shot for weight. This can be an exceptionally effective method of fishing with artificial flies. I used it to catch my first brown trout, on a dry fly (Yellow Humpy) in the Cowichan River on Vancouver Island when I was ten years old. I will never forget it.

Lures or flies should be fished near lake drop-offs, in deeper portions of rivers or creeks or in tidal waters where they imitate fish or other feed of cutthroat trout. Since cutthroat usually do not demand exact imitations, try to choose a fly or lure that is the approximate size and color of the predominant prey fish or insects in the area. A Wooly Bugger, the Olive Green Rolled Muddler or an Olive or Black Wizard in a small size might suggest any type of salmon fry, stickleback or small sand lance, all favorite cutthroat feed. Those fishing with lures might try a very small Krocodile

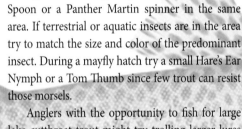

This cutthroat was hooked on a Tomic's Weed Tad plug.

Spoon or a Panther Martin spinner in the same area. If terrestrial or aquatic insects are in the area try to match the size and color of the predominant insect. During a mayfly hatch try a small Hare's Ear Nymph or a Tom Thumb since few trout can resist those morsels.

Anglers with the opportunity to fish for large lake cutthroat trout might try trolling larger lures such as small Tomic Plugs, Apex lures or Wonder Spoons just off the drop-off. The fly fisher might try any of the streamer flies mentioned above but in larger sizes, fished slowly on a sinking line near the bottom. This is specialty fishing often requiring a large boat for safety and specialized fishing techniques and tackle. Large lake cutthroat trout (and other trout) often feed on kokanee and these "lakers," though rarely found in great numbers, can be very large. In fact, the largest coastal cutthroat trout are found in the large lakes.

Shallow or deep presentations may be critical to success when trolling and the correct retrieve or trolling speed may be the key. When trolling lures or flies always work in a "zigzag" pattern and change speeds. This keeps your lures moving up and down in the water column and varies their presentation. Sometimes a particular trolling pattern or direction, like fishing with or against the wind or bringing the lure up in the water column, catches all the fish.

Art Limber's Pink Candy epoxy fly.

In tidal water do not forget that cutthroat trout may also feed on invertebrates such as sand worms and various larvae collectively known as zooplankton. A Pink Candy, a tan Wooly Bugger or a very small Bead-Head Spider fished very slowly or drifted in the tidal current are worth trying when cutthroat are surface-feeding and

Petrea Tiefenbach caught this cutthroat trout on a Wedding Band with a dew worm; it weighted in at 4.5 pounds (2 kg). Chris Boughton photo

don't respond to baitfish flies.

Another method relatively new to most anglers is surface fishing for cutthroat trout in salt water using dry flies or floating sliders. Cast out flies like a small Miyawaki Popper, Michaluk Sedge or your favorite size 6 or 8 foam pattern using a dry line and a 12-foot (3.6-m) leader either dead-drifted or retrieved with a slow hand twist so that a "wake" is created. This is a great way to find fish and the strikes are awesome.

Michaluk Sedge.

"Attractor flies" and lures that seem to imitate nothing on earth will attract the always-hungry cutthroat trout. Sometimes it seems that they will eat anything that appears to be alive. I have no idea if my favorite lure, a FlatFish, looks like something edible or if the wild wobbling action just annoys cutthroat trout, but try trolling one in a lake near a drop-off. You will like the results.

Wild fish are on high alert while in shallow water. Their survival depends on their senses. Careless wading and boat-handling or excessive noise and motion will spook any fish and cutthroat trout are no exception. Approaching cutthroat trout in shallow water covered by ripples or waves is easier than when the water is calm, and they are more often inclined to bite. The trade-off is that they are harder to see in

Worden's Skunk FlatFish F4.

choppy water. Move slowly. Fish feeding in deeper water are often more aggressive and easier to fool, but calm conditions are always difficult. Long lines need to be used if trolling and spin or fly casters need longer leaders and quiet presentations to hook fish under these

Summer fishing can be excellent.

tough conditions.

Trout have seasonal peaks in abundance that vary according to habitat type in streams, rivers, lakes and tidal water. It varies from area to area, year to year and sometimes day to day. "Should have been here yesterday!" is a phrase most seasoned cutthroat fishers have heard. In general there are two peak periods for fresh- and salt-water cutthroat trout: spring and fall. But cutthroat can be caught year round in British Columbia when conditions and regulations allow.

During the spring salmon fry and smolt migrations, feeding cutthroat trout can turn up on any lake, river or beach anywhere at any time. In the salt, shallow estuaries or adjacent bays with virtually no freshwater influx can be hot for short periods while pink or chum fry move out to sea. These small fish are "cutthroat candy." Recently I have noticed that cutthroat, and sometimes coho, will key on the large numbers of hatchery chinook smolts that pass through various bays on Vancouver Island and elsewhere on their way to the ocean. This makes for great sport to those able to find them. You will need slightly larger lures or flies to be consistently successful once you've located the feeding trout.

This large cutthroat was caught on a white muddler in tidal water.

Summer fishing can be excellent, depending on elevation, water temperature and abundance of food. Many of the higher-elevation lakes and streams fish exceptionally well through the summer because the water remains cool. Late summer and early fall are peak times for westslope cutthroats. High-water runoff is a thing of the past and high-elevation fish feed aggressively during this relatively short season of plenty.

Fishing in salt water during this time of year is also excellent; the trick is to find the cutthroat. Some areas always hold fish while others produce only occasionally. Vancouver Island has hundreds of miles of shoreline in fresh and salt water where fish move, hold and feed in areas that see few anglers, so it pays to look around. Gravel points on beaches are great places to look for trout, especially in tidal water since they occasionally show their fins on the surface or move the water while swimming by or feeding. Lakes are harder to read but casting or trolling near points, drop-offs, islands and weed beds is a good start.

Observant anglers watch for bird, insect or small fish movements of any type that could betray the presence of cutthroat trout. When a cutthroat is landed remember when and where, the weather, the successful lure or fly, the time of day and year, the type of feed present (if any) and the height of tide and direction of the current if fishing in tidal waters. Some locations may produce for a day, week or month; others may be consistent on a seasonal basis. Some are sensitive to stages or direction of tides and others may fish well on and off, year round. Keeping an angling log will help to sort out these spots and over time will become a very valuable trip-planning tool.

Bill von Brendel with a beautiful cutthroat trout caught on a small leech.

When coastal cutthroat trout are really aggressive, stripping the fly or working or trolling a lure as fast as possible produces solid strikes. Otherwise your offering may be ignored. Aggressively feeding trout will often nail a fly or lure, yet sometimes a small lure or fly dead-drifted or worked very slowly in the current is the only way to catch fish. Always experiment.

Effective retrieves for fly or lure casting vary, sometimes changing from day to day. Try slow and fast retrieves. You can also try short strips or pulls with pauses (vary the speed) or a "zooplankton retrieve," first described in 1985 in *Fly-fishing for Pacific Salmon* by Ferguson, Johnson and Trotter (Frank Amato Publications). It's a 12-inch (30-cm) strip followed immediately by a quick, short downward flick of the wrist, "just like shaking down a thermometer," followed by a pause, then repeated. It works as well for cutthroat as it does for salmon.

Successful anglers catch fish because they cover lots of water and are constantly alert, observant and persistent. The best way to learn to fish for cutthroat trout is to do so as often as possible, try different retrieves, lures or flies, cast or troll and continue to move around.

Tight lines!

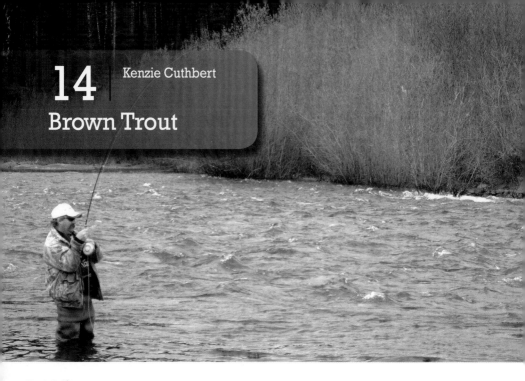

14 | Kenzie Cuthbert

Brown Trout

Kenzie Cuthbert fishing the Cowichan River on Vancouver Island.

Spring was finally here and the temperature of both air and water had finally begun to rise after a long and colder-than-normal winter. The light-green willow leaves were just starting to appear along the river's edge. The fry from the past fall's salmon spawn were emerging from the gravel. The insects could be seen starting to hatch. This is the time of year the brown trout begins to rebuild its body mass after a fall spawn and cold dormant winter.

Best of all, I had the weekend off.

With all that happening along the Cowichan River, I expected great things. On the first day the weather was great but there was nothing overly special in the way of catching fish. They were being difficult. I had tied a new and special fly the night before. I had invented a new eye system for flies that I call "eyes-n-tubes." Until this particular day I hadn't been able to use the flies due to getting the idea patented. I tied about a half a dozen of my "new" flies and put one on my leader. Day two started just like day one, with not much happening. A few hours into the drift I caught a nice rainbow on the new pattern. There was hope. I managed a few more hits before lunch, but still had nothing of great quality to show for it.

A simple block of closed cell foam around your neck will hold your flies—and if you should fall, all your other gear will be safe and dry on shore.

After lunch I enticed a few nice rainbows to rise for dry fly imitations, which is always exciting. I continued onto the next run, little knowing that it would change the day, and maybe my life. There, between overhanging branches along the shore, was some nice, slow-moving, deep water that looked promising, complete with a few fallen trees. I managed to get a roll cast out about 25 feet (8 m). I allowed the fly to sink close to the bottom before stripping it back 12 inches (30 cm) at a time. I had only stripped a few times and it stopped. It felt a bit like bottom. There was a short pause before the fish bolted out between the trees and jumped. I expected a steelhead but was pleasantly surprised to see it was the elusive, much-sought-after big brown. With some assistance from one of my friends I managed to work the fish back to where it could be landed. My new fly had worked, proving itself to everyone watching us net the brown. We took a few nice photos and sent him on his way. These trout are awesome and the big ones are not fooled easily. Anglers, whether using hi-tech fly or gear equipment, must carefully choose their imitations and waters to be fished. Many smaller browns in the 10- to 16-inch (25- to 40-cm) class can and will be caught with less attention to detail.

The author holds a brown trout caught on Kenzie's Eyes-n-Tube Muddler.

Reading the Water

Lanes

Lanes are what we call speed zones or slots of the water moving down the river. Generally you will have a fast-moving section of rapid water with slower-moving water beside it. The slower section or lane beside the rapid water is where you will most often find the brown trout. In early mornings and evenings they can be found in the tail-outs of runs and pools as well. I always look for water that moves at the same speed a person walks. The water easiest to fly fish is the inside of a long gradual corner. A back eddy can also have the right speed and depth but is usually harder to fish.

Rebecca Segal fishing a seam.

Spin fishers do not require as much room for casting, which will usually allow them to fish more overgrown areas.

Fly-Fishing for Large Brown Trout in the Early Stages of Spring

Lines

Putting the fly into the brown trout's feeding lane is crucial in early spring. The water is generally colder, which makes the fish a bit sluggish. Sinking

A healthy brown trout taken on the fly.

tip or multi-tip, loop-to-loop lines are my preferred method for getting the fly down to the fish. The sinking rate of your tip will depend on the type of water being fished. For instance, deep and fast waters will require a heavier tip. The length of the sink tip is also important and can affect the way you fish a section of water. It is difficult to effectively fish a long sink tip in a narrow river. Experiment with different lengths of sink tips to figure out which one is most effective.

Rods

The weight of rod will be determined by the fly line or sink tips you use. In early spring, the best rods I've found will generally be 7- or 8-weight Sages with Islander reels, depending on the river flows and levels. As we move into the later spring we can usually expect lower water flows and more aggressive fish. For these conditions we will use either 5- or 6-weight rods with Islander reels; 100 plus yards (92 m) of backing is a necessity if fishing from shore.

A Sage rod.

Suggested Lines

RIO DC sink tip Type 6 sinking sip WF7F/S6 15-foot (5-m) sink tip. I would use this line in higher flows on the Cowichan River. RIO also makes the same line with a 10-foot (3-m) sink tip, which I would use in lower flows.

RIO Anadromous Advantage is another line we use. It has a multi-tip system that allows you to quickly change the sink tips for different water conditions.

Tippet

The tippet choice is your next step and is also important. Water clarity can be a major factor in selecting the length and pound test of tippet to be used. The clearer the water, the lighter the test and the longer the tippet. If you are targeting the larger brown trout and want better odds, I would suggest nothing less than 6-pound tippet. The larger browns have been known to head straight for structure once hooked. Over time as you start to fool and hook them you may notice that they have an escape route pre-planned and ready if they make the mistake of eating something with too much iron in it.

Top: RIO Anadromous Advantage line.

Our preferred tippet material is RIO Fluoroflex Plus.

Bottom: RIO Fluoroflex Plus tippet.

Flies

There are many flies to choose from. Remember, big browns like to eat big prey. When choosing the fly pattern don't be afraid to use large flies in the 2- to 4-inch (5-

Andrew McGuire with a brown trout from the Cowichan River.

to 10-cm) range. We have had many 12-inch (30-cm) rainbow trout on the line and a massive brown trout trying to steal the rainbow during the fight. Flies can be weighted or unweighted, which will also affect the sinking tip needed to put your fly at the right depth. The large weighted flies can be much more difficult to cast, but are very effective.

Fly Patterns

These are a few of our favorites: Muddler Minnows or Bunny Leeches in a range of different colors and materials; Matukas tied in olive; Zonkers in both black and olive with either silver or gold bodies; Sculpins, which can be tied in numerous different colors and styles; and Kenzie's Eyes-n-Tubes Olive Muddler (shown on page 177).

Casting

Deciding where to cast is the next step in getting your fly into the trout's feeding lane. Start with a short cast at 90 degrees and swing the fly to the shore. If you aren't getting the fly down deep enough try a few different methods to get it to sink deeper. First try to throw a few quick upstream mends into the line once the cast has landed. If this does not work, try a cast slightly upstream with the added mends. If you are still having trouble getting your fly down try changing to a heavier sink tip. Repeat the above steps to try to get the fly into the desired water. The more time spent on the water fishing this way, the easier it should become to choose the right sink tip and either weighted or unweighted fly before starting to fish.

It is important to fish in the right area of the water at the right depth. Early in the spring big fish like browns are generally found near the bottom of the river.

Top to bottom: Zonker with a silver body. Rolled Muddler Minnow. Bead-Head Black Bunny Leech.

Above: Larry Stefanyk releasing a big brown.

Right: A brown laying in a net, ready to be released.

Fly-fishing for Large Brown Trout in the Late Stages of Spring

As we move through spring and the water temperatures warm up, lighter sinking lines such as 5- and 6-weight type 3 and 10-foot (3-m) sink tips or intermediate clear tips will do. For flies I would suggest the same patterns unweighted, because the fish will become more aggressive and move longer distances for the fly. We have caught many large browns just inches below the surface in pursuit of a swung fly.

Gear Fishing for Brown Trout

There are numerous ways to catch browns on gear. It is very common for late-run winter steelhead fishers to encounter browns. Both species can be found in the same type of water, which I referred to previously as lanes.

Equipment

Center pins, bait casters and spinning reels are used extensively by gear anglers after browns. All three of these reels are generally put onto 9- to 12-foot (3- to 4-m) rods and can be used in a variety of ways to present imitation baits to the fish. The float system is very effective in fishing the lanes of the river and is the most commonly used gear. This system consists of a float, which is a large strike indicator that has a line passing through it. The line is then attached to a lead weight. From the weight we run our leader, which is about 24 inches (60 cm) long. At the end of our leader we can use a variety of different lures that imitate the food that fish are looking for.

How to Fish the Float System

The float-to-weight distance is set to slightly more than the depth of the water. The rig (float, weight and lure) is cast into the desired lane of water and drifted down the river with nearly no drag or resistance from the angler. When the float is pulled under, you strike.

Brecks Mister Twister Night Crawler— Bubblegum.

Lures

The lures of choice for the float system are pink rubber worms; small rubber eggs in pink and orange colors; Gooey Bobs in pink and orange; Corkies in orange, red and light pink colors; Spin-N-Gloes in orange, red, chartreuse, and flesh colors; and light Colorado-style spinners in both silver and brass.

Late Spring

Moving into the warmer months, spinning reels become the more common choice of gear anglers. Spin casting to structure in the river such as logs, boulders and underwater drop-offs can be very effective. Another method is to cast and swing the lures through the current as you would a fly.

Gibbs Croc hammered brass fire strip.

Lures of Choice

There are numerous brands of spinners that have a weighted body that allows them to sink while spinning. These can work very well presented in the right waters. Another option is a spoon. These also come in numerous styles and colors. I have found the Gibbs Croc spoons in brass/fire orange to be the most effective. There are other similar lures out there that imitate bait fish that should also work well. It comes down to trying them and finding the one that works best for you.

Kenzie's Eyes-n-Tubes Muddler

Hook: Daiichi 2220 size 4 Streamer hook.
Thread: 6/0 light pink.
Tail: Light-brown mallard (short approx ¼ inch).
Eyes: One set of Barbell style Eyes-N-Tubes 5.5 grains X 2 eyes.
Body: Gold tinsel or wrapping.
Under wing: Lavalace Angel Hair in green.
Wing and head: Olive deer hair.

Trout hooked with Kenzie's Eyes-n-Tubes Muddler.

15 | Bill Luscombe
Brook Trout

Edith Lake holds rainbows and brook trout.

I had been working my dragonfly nymph back and forth along the bottom of the lake for about twenty minutes with nary a tug and was becoming a bit suspect of the fishing prospects for the rest of the day. Just when I was about to give up I felt the familiar slow-but-solid thud of life at the other end of my line. I set the hook hard and tightened up, only to have the fish force me into relinquishing line at several feet per second. Luckily the run was short and we settled into a tug-of-war for the next five minutes: me trying to gain line, it trying to break free of the "insect" that now held it hostage.

After the first run the fish did a series of rolls, then banged the leader with its tail a number of times. The hook held and I gained some line. It then used its sheer weight and power to take more line from the reel and followed this with more violent twists and rolls, reminding me of the wonderful tussles coho salmon give you. As time wore on it became tired, as did my arm. Finally it allowed me to raise its head out of the water and I skated it toward my belly boat into the open net. My partner Ian had been watching nearby and after taking a few photos we estimated its size at about 3 pounds (1.5 kg). We released it.

A 3-pound (1.5-kg) brook trout from Rose Lake.

No, it wasn't a rainbow. It was a brook trout and we weren't fishing in the Laurentians, northern Manitoba or the Nipigon area of Ontario. We were fishing in Black Lake near Kamloops, British Columbia. Surprised? You shouldn't be. British Columbia now has some of the finest brook trout fishing to be found anywhere in the world.

The brook trout, also known as the speckled trout or squaretail, is one of God's most beautiful contributions to this earth. They take my breath away every time I see one. It doesn't put up the fight that the rainbow does, but it makes up for it in tenacity, endurance and bulk. The brook trout fights like a chinook salmon, preferring to stay deep, rolling and making short, strong runs, whereas rainbow trout like long exhausting runs followed by aerial acrobatics. Inch for inch the brook trout will also outweigh a rainbow by as much as one-and-a-half times depending on the overall length of the fish. Besides being a great sport fish, I also believe that they are the best-tasting freshwater game fish an angler can come by.

Trolling Lakes – When trolling for trout at depths of 40 to 60 feet (12 to 18 m), it is important to choose colors that will be visible to cruising fish. Fluorescent orange, pink and chartreuse are the most visible at any depth. Natural colors, such as blue, green and black, are also good. As a rule of thumb, use fluorescent colors on overcast days and naturals on bright, clear days.

The brook trout is not actually a trout at all, but a char related to lake trout, bull trout and Dolly Varden. It is also referred to as the eastern brook trout, an old title given to it when it was first transplanted west. Brook trout occur naturally in the east from Newfoundland to the western side of Hudson Bay; south in the Atlantic, Great Lakes, and Mississippi River basins to Minnesota and northern Georgia in the United States. As people started seriously populating western Canada they brought this fish with them. Records with the BC Ministry of Environment (MOE) indicate introductions of brook trout in a number of streams in BC as early as 1908 (mostly on Vancouver Island) and discussions with biologists revealed that there were earlier introductions. But no one is left alive to tell where the fish were placed or when. The ministry started actively managing the species back in the 1930s and opened a rearing facility at, of all places, Spectacle Lake on Vancouver Island, which was used for decades as the provincial source for all brook trout stocked throughout BC. Later on Spectacle Lake was closed down in favor of Aylmer Lake in the interior

Trolling for brook trout.

and Aylmer is still the central source for brook trout stock in the province. Over the last decade the MOE has stopped stocking brook trout on the coast, preferring to stock rainbows and cutthroat trout in an attempt to reintroduce native species to the area. However, brookies are stocked across most of the rest of the province on an annual basis.

If you just landed a fish after a long fight, replace the tippet. Don't believe that it's okay if it "feels" right. What is a couple of feet of tippet and a few seconds not fishing worth if you break off the next one?

Many of the lakes that now support brook trout also support rainbows, but it has been my experience that neither species reaches exceptional proportions when the two live together. On the other hand numerous lakes are populated strictly with brook trout and some have produced exceptionally large fish in excess of 6 pounds (2.7 kg).

Normally in BC illegally introduced species are eradicated, if possible, before they can spread and become a pest or, worse, compete directly with our native species. In this case, however, the MOE told me that because of their special characteristics brook trout are actually being managed and utilized as an enhancement to the sport fishing opportunities in the province.

Because brook trout are char they spawn in the fall. This gives them a major advantage as a sport fish. BC's native true trout spawn in the spring and anyone who fishes for trout knows what it is like to hit a lake in the middle of the spawn. But if you visit a lake or stream that harbors brook trout you can catch nice fat silver fish when the rainbows are

Releasing a Rose Lake brookie.

all dark, skinny and egg-bound. In addition, brook trout are hardier than true trout and although they prefer water temperatures colder than rainbow and cutthroat, they tolerate higher temperatures and lower oxygen levels. When the rainbows and cutthroat start sulking on the bottom due to warmer water or low oxygen levels, the brook trout will often continue to feed. And because of their tolerance of lower oxygen levels, brook trout can often survive a "winterkill" situation that kills true trout. So you can see just how valuable a management tool this fish is to the MOE and what a bonus it is for us sport fishers. It also has the potential to open up more bodies of water and thus take some of the fishing pressure off the other trout lakes.

A Green Thorax Montana pattern has worked its magic.

Even better, fisheries management staff are now triploiding brook trout. Triploidy renders the fish sterile; they don't spawn and thus spend all their time eating and growing. So even fall fishing for brookies can produce great, clean, fat fish in lakes where triploids have been stocked. A quick visit to the Freshwater Fisheries Society of BC website at www.gofishbc.com/fishstocking.htm will lead you to the locations where fertile and triploid brook trout have been stocked in your area.

And speaking of the brook trout as a sport fish, they are also tough fighters and delicious eating. These char feed on all the standard trout fare and as such can be fished pretty much as you would fish for a rainbow or cutthroat. They rise to hatches and feed on the same staples of scuds, chironomids and leeches. They do, however, fight differently and exhibit some habits different from the true trout. Brook trout have a different morphology than trout; they are, after all, a char and not a trout. They are a much stockier fish. Their bodies are generally deeper and wider than trout and thus are significantly heavier per inch of length. I have found that a brook trout over 14 inches (35 cm) in length will be roughly one-and-a-half times the weight of a rainbow trout of the same length. They have a habit of sounding when they are hooked and love to run for the cover of logs and weeds. This habit, along with their naturally heavier bulk, makes them formidable opponents on light or moderate trout gear. As I have said they remind me of salmon and I like to refer to them as bulldogs. They don't make the long, exciting runs that rainbows do but they will give you a longer and more determined tussle because they conserve energy and if you hook a big one over weeds or logs you're in for big trouble. Their first run is a burst of energy straight for the cover and if you aren't ready they'll break you off in the weeds before you can say "Whoa!"

Shiny Lures Pay – Dull lures get dull results. Polish all your lures, making sure to thoroughly rinse off all traces of the cleaner afterward. That extra sparkle adds to your catch.

A Panther Martin black with green dots spinner.

Fishing for brookies in BC is much the same as fishing for them anywhere else in the country. They like small lures such as the Panther Martin and will come to a gang troll as well, but my preferred method is with a fly. When a hatch is on, brook trout rise nearly as readily as rainbows and will take a well-presented dry fly with enthusiasm. The best success I have had is fishing a black leech pattern, dragonfly nymph or damselfly nymph near the bottom when no hatches are occurring. In fact I have had more success with this method during a midge hatch than I have had actually matching the midge hatch. I have found over the years that brook trout don't like to rise as much as true trout do and prefer to stay in their hiding holes. They also seem to prefer deeper water than trout, although that is just my personal experience. A slow and deep retrieve seems to be most effective and these char tend to mouth the fly instead of hitting it hard like rainbows. Combine this soft take with their bony mouths and you will find that you have to be ready to set the hook when you think you have snagged bottom and must ensure that your hook is razor sharp or you'll end up losing a lot more than you catch.

I have a favorite fly that I use for brook trout. I still have not figured out exactly why they like it so much, but I have caught more brook trout on this pattern than any other. It even out-fishes the black Woolly Bugger—my second-favorite—on most occasions. The pattern is called the DDD. I found it in an old fly pattern book from Washington State decades ago. I thought it would be good for the stained coastal waters but discovered that it

Luscombe's Black Wooly Bugger.

was a great fly everywhere, much loved by trout and char alike. For all you fly-tiers, here is the pattern:

The DDD (Dave's Delectable Dragonfly)

Hook: Mustad 9671 #12 or #14.

Thread: Black or green monocord.

Tail: Pheasant tail fibers.

Abdomen: 4 strands of peacock herl.

Rib: None.

Thorax: Olive Chenille.

Shellback: Pheasant tail fibers.

Beard: None.

Swimmerets: Pheasant tail fibers.

Tying Steps

1. Wrap on tying thread and tie in the tail of 4–5 strands of pheasant tail, about shank length long.
2. Secure to the butt 4 stands of peacock herl. Spin to twist them together and wrap to a point midway between the hook point and the eye of the hook. Tie off and cut.
3. Tie in a small bunch of pheasant tail fibers.
4. Tie in the olive chenille and wrap it to just behind the eye. Tie off and cut, leaving enough room to tie in the swimmerets and whip finish.
5. Pull the pheasant tail fibers over the back, tie off and cut off excess.
6. Tie in 4 strands of pheasant tail at the head so that they trail back along the left side of the fly, about shank length. Repeat for the right side.
7. Tie off and whip finish the head.

The DDD was originally designed as a dragonfly nymph, but it is too slender to be such, though it makes a great generic nymph pattern as well as a pretty good damselfly nymph imitation. Tie a few up and try them; it's one of my favorites.

Two happy fishermen with a catch of brook trout.

Brookies are easy to identify because of their generally darker skin color adorned with small, light-colored spots.

You should remember that brook trout tend to school, sometimes in very large numbers. They also tend to not move far from where you find them. Rainbows seem to be cruisers, but brookies stay put and simply mill around a given area. So if you are prospecting a new lake and luck into a fish, take note of where you picked it up and at what depth. If there is a major break in the bottom topography, or downed trees, etc., chances are that the school is holding in and around the break. Work the area over at different depths and you will more than likely pick up more fish from the same spot.

Trigger Strikes while Trolling: When you're trolling with plugs, spinners, spoons or flies, drop your rod tip back once in a while rather than maintaining a steady pull. Dropping back causes the lure to tumble momentarily, triggering strikes from any fish that may be following.

In addition to being a great fish to pursue with rod and reel, this char appears to be the fish of choice for ice fishers. Since brookies like to school and are fairly aggressive winter eaters that are fooled into biting quite easily, this can, unfortunately, be a real issue. When the ice fishers find the brook trout they can take many fish over a short period of time, and in many lakes the MOE has been hard pressed to keep the populations up because of this winter overfishing. In some areas the situation has become so problematic that ice fishing bans have been put in place.

Brook trout are a beautiful fish and easily identifiable. As with all char they have a generally darker skin color adorned with small, light-colored spots, whereas true trout have bright skins with dark or black spots. Their sides exhibit characteristic

A nicely colored brook trout.

magenta spots with blue halos and their fins are a dusky orange trimmed along the leading edges with bands of black and white. Their back and dorsal fins are not spotted but are detailed with vermiculations. Vermiculations are worm-like patterns of light green over a darker green background that provide perfect camouflage for the fish when viewed from above. The brook trout's tail is relatively short and the end is square with no forking at all—hence the name "squaretail." Its belly is white and edged with rust toward the sides. The males have very large mouths with hard jaws full of teeth. When fishing for these char it's a good idea to keep this in mind. You must use very sharp hooks and set the hook well when you get a strike. I have bent the tip of many hooks when fishing for brook trout because of their bony mouths.

An interesting thing that I have noticed as I have pursued this fish across the southern half of the province is that they tend to change their overall shade to suit their environment. That's not to say they change quickly like a chameleon, but over time their color tones appear to take on the shade best suited to their surroundings. The fish I have caught in Spectacle Lake on Vancouver Island all exhibit a dark shade that blends in with the tea-colored water and mud bottom of the

Wonderful table fare.

lake. The same applies to the brookies I have caught in little Rose Lake and Red Lake near Kamloops. Other brookies that I have caught in lakes such as Black Lake (very near Rose) have shown much less color and a lot more silver. Black Lake has a white marl bottom and very clear water, so the silver shade would naturally provide better camouflage in these conditions. I don't know if anyone has scientifically investigated this, but if you travel around in pursuit of this fish you will see what I mean.

The brook trout is well known as a meat fish and makes wonderful table fare. It is a plump, meaty fish with bright orange flesh and it fries, bakes or smokes up superbly. The meat is oilier than true trout and produces profuse drippings when smoked, but it is delicious.

British Columbia is blessed with a wide array of fresh- and saltwater game fish. I have had the pleasure and privilege of angling for most of them during my lifetime. While most of these fish are native to the province, some have been introduced from elsewhere. Some of the introductions have had detrimental effects on our fisheries, but brook

Bill Luscombe with a fly-caught brookie.

trout are an exception. They have been a wonderful addition to our sport fishing opportunities and if you take the time to pursue them consider yourself warned. Once you catch one you may be smitten too.

Dolly Varden

Nobody should be tasked with writing a precise piece about fishing for Dolly Varden. That's because there isn't a lot of precise information about the fish. For instance, I was amazed to discover that Alaska had considered the Dolly Varden such a threat to young salmon fry that it offered a 2.5-cent per head bounty on the fish.

Check your regulations to find out which lakes hold Dollies.

According to BC's environment ministry, Dolly Varden "are found in fresh and salt water from just south of the Canadian border to at least the Seward Peninsula in Alaska. Their distribution does not extend far inland, although they are found in the very headwaters of the Fraser, Liard and Peace River systems. They extend farthest inland in the Skeena and Fraser River drainage systems. They are not found in the Columbia River system. Freshwater residents may remain in streams or move into lakes.

"They spend time in the ocean as well as in rivers and streams; they do not seem to move out into the open ocean, but remain close to river mouths and the shore. Resident fish can be found in very steep, small streams (with slopes well above 20 percent). They move upstream again to take advantage of seasonal feeding opportunities. They may migrate up a stream that leads to a lake to overwinter and in the spring go back to sea. This back-and-forth migration continues for a few years until the waterway increases in sedimentation, reduces cover and raises water temperature."

Dolly Varden in shallow water.

So where to find Dollies? Just about anywhere. Not that they are widely spread at all. In fact they are blue-listed, meaning they are a species of concern in all watersheds.

I have been fortunate to find Dollies in lakes, rivers and tidal waters. My best fishing, however, has been on rivers, often ones leading to lakes. The most success I have had is in the upper tidal reaches of the system. Where the last bit of tidal inflow raises the river level, that is a good place to find Dollies.

Color-coded Flies: When tying nymphs, streamers or wet flies with weighted bodies, use a specific color of thread to form the head. For example, red denotes heavily weighted; yellow, lightweighted and black, unweighted.

Because they are blue-listed by the ministry, and for ethical reasons, I prefer to not draw a specific map to their locations. I will, however, tell you that most of the locations remain somewhat secret because the fish has had a bad rap, that it's not a good fighter, and that it's regarded as similar to the pink salmon before fly fishermen found otherwise.

I have, for the past twenty years, made special excursions to fish Dollies on an annual basis. What I found on one particular river was astonishing.

On that river Ken and I left camp and fished downstream toward the ocean for hours and miles. We tossed flies and spinners and spoons. Nothing. We were early, we were late, the run's fished out—all those things went through our minds. Until we came to that section of the river, the upper tidal influence just below where the brackish water of the estuary took over and the fishing was always just awful.

The Doc working in his outdoor office.

It was, as they say, the end of the road. We had traveled a long distance at great expense of time and money to show up at a river that was bereft of the Dolly run. We had spent the entire morning fishing down to this spot and touched nary a fish. A driftwood log to sit on, a quick bite to eat and the soothing trickle of single malt down our throats did little to alleviate our disappointment. We had a long way to go home and few alternatives for fishing on the way.

We noticed that the log on which we were sitting would, in the hours of the incoming tide, be under water. The river, even as we watched, was inching up. The shallow bar in front of us lost its noise and velocity. The small rapids there smoothed over as the ocean's influence raised the water level. And then we saw the first fish.

We looked at each other and then back to the river. Another.

Ken was up first, stripping line off his reel while he was still ten yards from the river. I was behind him, took an elbow or two, and then both our flies were in the water.

"Wham ... wham." Double-header. They were bright Dollies, both about 3 pounds (1.3 kg).

The next hour was unbelievable. That old "fish on every cast" saying came true.

Most of the Dollies were in that 3-pound (1.3 kg) range, but others were heavier. And get this—they came out of the water and went on long runs we couldn't believe. *These were Dollies, weren't they? Dollies don't jump. Dollies don't go on long runs.*

We were using 6-weight fly rods with medium sink tips and 9-foot (2.7-m) leaders. Any black pattern worked well but after catching so many, Ken switched to what I can only call a Mad Muddler. It had glass eyes with little black beads rolling around and a fat green body somewhat like a muddler but more like a mouse pattern.

Current Provides Action – Trout lie below undercut banks in streams. Try a FlatFish without a sinker; just open the bail on your spinning reel and let the current carry it past the bank, then crank to stop the line from coming off and retrieve s-l-o-w-l-y, letting the current provide the action.

I laughed so hard when he put it on. I cried so long when the fishing slowed down and the only thing that interested these Dollies was the Mad Muddler. He didn't have another to lend me, or so he said.

I eventually used that Mad Muddler pattern on lakes. Although I haven't caught a Dolly, I have had some nice-sized cutthroats and rainbows on it. The only problem is fly-casting the frickin' thing; one mistake and it's a concussion.

We also found that the Dollies would take a green spinning lure and sometimes even an Ironhead from Gibbs.

Gibbs Ironhead green scale.

And we realized that the Dollies we were catching were three, four and five years old. Thinking that someone would put a "bounty" on their heads was ridiculous. Sure, they eat salmon fry, but they also eat species that prey on the fry and the salmon eggs. I would humbly suggest that Dollies have much more success with the latter, and that salmon runs are better off because of it.

17 | Ron Thompson

Ice Fishing

Ice fishermen look forward to the first good cold snap of the season, anxious to take advantage of some of the best fishing for rainbow and brook trout.

Plunging temperatures and flying snow mean the end of the fishing season for most BC anglers. For others, however, the fun is just beginning. December's cold usually signals the start of the interior's ice-fishing season.

In fact some of the best fishing for rainbow and brook trout comes before Christmas, when oxygen levels and water temperatures beneath the ice are still high enough that fish are actively feeding. Ice fishermen anxiously wait for the first good cold snap of the season, waiting for the ice to freeze thick enough to support a person's weight. An ice thickness of 6 inches (15 cm) is advised for ice fishing alone, 12 inches (30 cm) is recommended for groups and 18 inches (45 cm) is the minimum if you plan on taking a vehicle out onto the frozen lake surface.

Ice fishing can be as simple or as complex as you want. Equipment can range from a spool of line and a hook to hi-tech systems including depth finders, electronic strike indicators and power ice augers. But at its core, ice fishing is about cutting a hole in the ice, dropping in bait and waiting for the fish to bite. Winter fishing action can be fast and furious or painfully slow; ice fishing is often more cyclical than summer fishing. Trout will feed aggressively for a short period, then turn off for no explainable reason. Looking down into the water through the ice provides a perspective on the trout's world that summer fishing does not, especially if you lie on the ice and watch through the hole as the trout circles the bait and then—hopefully—strikes.

A mess of brook trout caught at Red Lake outside of Kamloops, BC, in December.

Equipment

Ice-fishing equipment need not cost much money. A spool of line, some split shot, a couple of bobbers and a few hooks is all you really need. Many people just manipulate the line with their fingers as they watch through the hole, then haul up the fish by hand when it strikes. A rod and reel will provide more feel for a fish's take and more control over the fight—particularly with bigger fish as rods also allow for quicker hook sets, which are important on days when fish are picky and not aggressively taking baits, lures or flies. The rods are typically short—28 inches (70 cm) maximum—because you want to stay close to the hole. A small spinning or mooching reel loaded with 6- to 8-pound test monofilament line completes the package. Bait hooks in size 6 to 10 with a little split shot help get hooks down to the bottom fast.

An ultra-light open-face spinning reel and rod combo.

A key piece of gear is an ice auger. While an axe will cut a hole, it will not do it as quickly or cleanly as the ice auger. Hand augers can be purchased for around fifty to seventy dollars depending on the size. Remember that 8-inch (20-cm) holes are easier to fish through than 6-inch (15-cm) holes. Power augers make the job of cutting through ice a breeze, and can be biceps savers when the ice is really hard and thick or when you need to drill lots of holes.

There is a wide variety of accessories ice anglers will likely acquire with time, from ice skimmers to shelters and heaters. As with most recreational activities, your budget is the only thing limiting the gear.

A skimmer is a large metal spoon with holes in it. It's used to remove new ice as it forms and to clear slush left over from making the hole.

In selecting your clothes for ice fishing it is important to stay warm and comfortable, no matter what type of weather you encounter. This means dress in layers. The layer closest to your skin is crucial to keeping you dry. Any type of perspiration on this layer will eventually make you cold and can lead to serious conditions such as hypothermia or even frostbite. Clothing made of polypropylene will do this nicely. Cotton can also be worn but it may get wet and stay wet.

Top: Using a hand ice auger to drill a hole.

Above left to right: A gas-powered ice auger. A skimmer is a large metal spoon with holes in it.

The warmth layer is the next layer you need to concentrate on. Fleece is popular and so is wool; both will keep you warm and dry even if you become slightly damp.

Your outer layer can be a windbreaker. Down jackets are nice since they often have a wind-breaking shell on the outside. If you choose to wear wool or fleece as a warmth layer, be sure to top it off with a rip-stop nylon windbreaker shell. Out on the lake the wind can cut through even the warmest wool sweater or jacket. Wool is a good choice for hats and mittens so long as they have protective fabric on the inside or outside to act as a barrier to moisture and wind. A one-piece insulated coverall is ideal for this sport, especially if it has a hood that can be left open or pulled tight around the face and neck.

Canada is home to the greatest number of people who participate in the wonderful sport of "hard-water fishing."

Your feet will take the most abuse from winter weather since they are in constant contact with the ice and snow. Purchase the best waterproof and well-insulated winter boots you can afford. Leave your boots loosely tied until you arrive at your fishing site. If you begin to get warm along the way, make sure you unzip your jacket to let out some of the heat or even take off a layer. A good idea is to carry an extra pair of dry felt boot liners, moisture-wicking socks and mitten liners. A facemask or neck warmer is essential in windy weather. Also be sure your hat has earflaps that cover your ears.

Baits

A wide range of baits, lures and flies will catch trout under the ice.

The right clothing will make your day.

There is commercial bait available like Power Honey Berkley PowerBait Worms. Shrimp, the kind you buy in little cans at the grocery store, are one of the favorite baits. Just thread a whole shrimp onto a jig hook and dance it lightly above the bottom. Traditional baits like maggots, earthworms and mealworms also do a fine job, and spoons, jigs and spinners can be effective too. Sometimes a spoon or jig tipped with a piece of worm, maggot, shrimp or even cheese can be deadly.

For fly anglers, traditional open-water patterns like shrimp, leeches and nymphs will catch fish. The only problem is trying to a cast a fly into the hole. The retrieve can be tricky too.

In most lakes it's possible to see to the bottom clearly, even in depths exceeding 10 feet (3 m). You will be able to see sedge pupae and other insects crawling across the bottom and fish are easy to spot. It's even possible to watch a fish take the bait. In some cases,

Left to right: Mealworms make great bait. Power Honey Berkley PowerBait Worms.

On the ice.

especially when fishing in shallow water, trout will take baits less than 3 feet (1 m) below the angler, almost close enough to touch.

Techniques

The big key to ice fishing? Find the fish. It's always good to start your day fishing in shallow water—10 feet (3 m) or less—over top of structure like weed beds or rocky points. This puts baits and lures within 12 inches (30 cm) of the bottom. Then move them up in the water column until you find the fish. That might mean drilling a number of holes across a wide area. Sometimes trout don't move much in winter, while at other times they will cruise an area as if on patrol. When looking down into the hole you have drilled through the ice, you will see fish regularly if you are over a prime spot. Twenty minutes without seeing a fish is a good hint the area is devoid of trout, so move on. Moving a short distance often makes a big difference when it comes to catching fish. You may even need to go right into the shallows, over water less than 3 feet (1 m) deep. Sometimes you catch fish just inches below the bottom of the hole.

Anglers move their jig in an up-and-down jigging motion and fish become accustomed to this presentation. Try holding the line between your index finger and thumb, then roll or twist the line between your fingers. This will cause the jig to spin in the water while remaining at the same depth.

If you don't want to lie on the ice and stare into the hole, fishing with a bobber is a good way to go. Use the smallest one possible, as smaller bobbers offer less resistance to the fish when it bites. Hang the bait below the bobber at the appropriate depth and wait for the fish to nibble.

Another method is to bring a 5-gallon (20-L) pail loaded with all your gear. Unload your gear, turn the pail upside down, put your cushion on the pail and you are set. Anglers with no ice tent put a blanket over their body, making sure to cover the hole too so they

A 5-gallon (20-L) pail will carry your gear, and makes a great stool turned upside down.

An ice-fishing tent is like a five-star hotel to an ice fisherman.

can see the fish more clearly. The nice thing about an ice tent is that it gets you out of the elements. You also get comfortable seating, and a two-man tent will give you company as well. Some anglers use stoves and heaters to keep warm. Others set up small burners outside on the ice to warm their hands or their whole bodies while they fish. Use caution with any heat source.

Where to Go

British Columbia is filled with great opportunities for ice fishing, but not all lakes are open to winter fishing—pay close attention to the fishing regulations. Some of the area's most popular summer lakes have winter closures, usually from December 1 to April 30.

West Pubnico, a small fishing village on the south shore of Nova Scotia, gets it name from the Mi'kmaq word *Pombcoup*, meaning "a hole that has been cut in the ice for fishing."

All the usual fishing regulations apply to ice fishing, including catch limits and gear restrictions. Lakes not identified in the regulations as being closed for the winter can be ice-fished, as long as you can get to them. Snow often makes travel in the backcountry difficult and many lakes are inaccessible to vehicle traffic.

Around Kamloops, lakes Edith, Tulip, Rose, Horseshoe, Heffley, Pinantan, Paul, Knouff, Red and Walloper are among the most popular for ice fishing.

Special Considerations

Ice fishing is safe winter fun but there are special risks people need to prepare for before heading out. It is a stationary sport and the cold can feel much worse if you don't move at all. There is also often little shelter on a lake, making people vulnerable to wind chill. Warm clothes are a must—a good hat and gloves and heavy winter boots can make all the difference when spending a day on the ice.

Show caution about ice thickness, especially in the early season; 6 inches (15 cm) is the minimum needed to venture out. Breaking through the ice may not be fatal but it can be awfully close. Many area lakes are also aerated to help keep fish alive through the winter. The aerators pour a stream of bubbles into the water to provide oxygen and stop the water around the fish from freezing. People should stay well away from working aerators and should never climb protective fences to fish in the open water next to them.

By allowing the jig to bounce off the bottom, a small cloud of bottom debris and sound is created that will attract fish from a distance. At times it can be productive to allow the jig to hit the bottom and then lay at rest there.

You don't need to kill every fish you catch, it's possible to release fish safely back into the hole in the ice to be caught another day.

Late-winter warm spells can destroy the texture of the ice, which, while still of the required thickness, will not adequately support weight. This is called "rotten ice" or "soft ice" and is exceedingly dangerous. Many cars, trucks, SUVs and snowmobiles have fallen through the ice so be careful in late winter and early spring.

An ice-fishing rod.

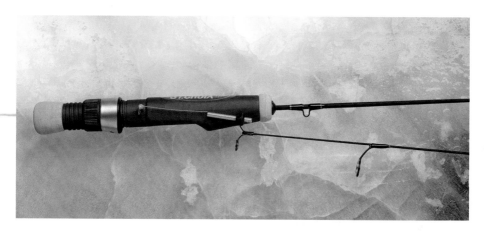

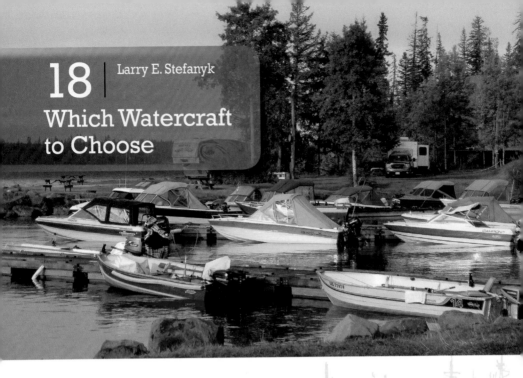

18 | Larry E. Stefanyk

Which Watercraft
to Choose

What boat is the best choice for your fishing requirements?

British Columbia has a wealth of lakes ranging in size from tiny mountain tarns to large bodies of water. Unfortunately, boat rentals are getting hard to find if the lake doesn't have fishing resorts on its shores that rent out boats. This means that anglers must provide their own means of flotation or cast from shore. What best to choose? Well, while no one boat will serve all purposes, a few manage to come fairly close.

For big lakes it's not a stretch to simply employ relatively large, seaworthy boats like those used for fly-fishing on salt water. One of the most common for offshore is the 17-foot (5.2-m) Boston Whaler Montauk, or one of various clones of these popular cathedral-hull vessels that have evolved over the years. They are functional, safe, stable, maneuverable and large enough to be comfortable yet transportable enough for one person to easily launch or haul out. Depending on their configuration, with a center or side console or steering from the stern seat, they might be powered with outboard motors ranging from 40 to 100 or more horsepower, and may have

A 17-foot (5.2-m) Boston Whaler.

something in the 10–15 hp range as an auxiliary motor.

Another point in favor of this shallow-draft style of boat is that it can be launched in as little as 6 to 8 inches (15 to 20 cm) of water, which is often the case at small, unpaved boat ramps. This is assuming, of course, that the tow vehicle has four-wheel drive.

A lightweight aluminum boat is ideal for family fishing excursions.

While boats of this size easily carry three or four people, for the sake of safety from flying hooks only two should cast at any given time. The stability provided by the wide cathedral hull means that fly fishers can usually stand comfortably while casting, retrieving and fighting fish.

It is probable that 12- to 14-foot (3.6- to 4.3-m) aluminum boats make up the largest component of our inshore saltwater fleet, and they do the same on lakes. Being light in weight, these boats are easy to tow and can usually be launched at the crudest of ramps. They can also be rowed on lakes that do not allow motors.

Two anglers should be the maximum and whether or not one or both stands up will depend entirely on variables as wide-ranging as the boat's hull shape and stability to an individual angler's age, agility and sense of balance. Some 14-foot boats are quite stable, while others are anything but. With 12-footers, remaining seated is usually the safest option.

Cartoppers usually fall in the 10- to 12-foot (3.0- to 3.6-m) range. As their name implies, these boats are light enough to carry on a roof rack or in the back of a pickup with the tailgate down. Most will easily handle two people but due to space limitations anglers must work in concert. A plus in favor of cartoppers is that they can be carried or dragged short distances for launching when no ramp is available.

Punts designed specifically for one person—common throughout the BC Interior,

Mark Your Anchor Rope – I use a waterproof black felt marker to indicate depths on my anchor rope. I mark it every 10 feet (3 m) using one band for 10 feet, two bands for 20 feet (6 m), three bands for 30 feet (9 m), etc. When I reach 50 feet (15 m), I use a wide band; 60 feet (18 m) is one wide and one narrow band, and so on. This way I know what depth I'm at when trout fishing.

Ralph Shaw's punt fits in his truck box and holds all his gear.

Cariboo and Chilcotin—are appearing more frequently. Constructed from aluminum, fiberglass or plywood, they range in lengths from 8 to 10 feet (2.4 to 3 m). The width and depth vary but punts are usually at least 4 feet (1.2 m) across at the widest point,

almost always have a flat bottom and contain an abundance of flotation material. These lightweight craft are easy to row and are amazingly fast when powered by even a small electric motor.

Possibly the most famous fly-fishing punt in BC was owned by the late Jack Shaw of Kamloops, a fly-fishing pioneer and best-selling author. The amount of equipment that he packed into his 9½-footer (2.7-m) was astonishing, but once afloat he never had any reason to go ashore until his long day's fishing was done. Ralph Shaw (no relation), Jack's close friend and fishing companion for several decades, had a similar punt when he moved from Kamloops to Courtenay in the early 1980s. I use the past tense because he has since modified it by shortening it to just under 8 feet (2.4 m) so it will fit inside the box of his pickup truck.

Shaw's punt showing the wheel on the front of his fishing machine.

He then mounted a single wheel on the bow and removable handles on the stern that allow him to move the punt around like a large wheelbarrow. Once the punt is in the water the wheel flips up and out of the way and the handles are removed from the stern and stored until needed again. And like his friend and mentor's famous punt, Ralph's is usually loaded to the gunwales with fishing gear.

Canoes remain popular with some anglers. Depending upon their length, design and the material used in their construction, these range from featherweight aluminum shells capable of carrying one person to hefty fiberglass or wooden freighters that easily handle four people and are best propelled with an outboard motor. One of

Canoes comes in many different materials and colors.

the most popular with anglers is the venerable 14-foot (4.3-m) Sportspal, which is fashioned from lightweight aircraft-grade aluminum, carpeted throughout with buoyant Ethafoam and has a large Ethafoam sponson on each side for added flotation and stability. It's easily carried—it weighs about 37 pounds (17 kg)—and will support three passengers.

Inflatable boats, pontoon boats and float tubes are commonly found bobbing about on lakes. The latter are often the solution to the "private property" signs posted around urban lakes, which limit access to public footpaths. Rafts and pontoon boats are also useful for fishing in rivers that are simply too deep to wade. While some anglers might grumble about "rubber hatches" cluttering up the rivers, in the hands of an angler who is skilled at rowing and reading the current, rafts and pontoon boats are actually quieter and less disturbing than a wading person and have little, if any, disruptive effect on spawning fish and their redds or on the peace and quiet of anglers on shore.

Fifty years ago "inflatable" meant an oval- or egg-shaped craft that was usually of war-surplus vintage. From these basic, clumsy, uncomfortable vessels have evolved some of the most versatile fishing platforms available. They offer portability, light weight, speed, safety and stability, plus the added attraction of requiring little long-term storage space.

Inflatables are great to fish out of.

When it comes to size and shape, inflatables come in an amazing range of categories, from 20-foot (6-m), rigid-hulled hybrids used for rescue and fisheries enforcement work on the open ocean to circular or U-shaped float tubes propelled by swim fins or flippers.

The carrying capacity of an inflatable is about two to three times that of a similar-sized traditional boat. Depending on the construction and size of the air chambers, a 12-footer (3.6-m) can support from 1,200 to 1,700 pounds (550 to 800 kg). Aluminum cartoppers of equivalent length are rated at 350 to 600 pounds (160 to 270 kg).

A common misconception is that an inflatable will sink if punctured. In this unlikely event there is still plenty of flotation because all modern inflatables have several individual chambers. Unlike vehicle tires, they rely on air volume rather than high pressure—usually about 1½ to 2 pounds per square inch (10 to 14 kPa). Thus a punctured chamber will deflate slowly rather than blow out like a tire, and the rapid application of a simple duct-tape patch will usually stem the flow of leaking air until the hole can be permanently repaired.

A family selection of inflatables.

Inflatables do have an annoying habit of expanding and contracting due to temperature and elevation changes. A boat pumped to proper rigidity at high noon on a hot day will sag noticeably in the cool night air, and vice versa. A boat pumped up at a low elevation will also be drum tight if taken to a lake at much higher altitude.

Use a gasoline motor only on large lakes. Cut the motor and use your oars to row quietly and slowly as you approach the shoal or drop-off you are going to fish. Maintain a distance of at least 150 to 200 feet (45 to 60 m) from other anglers already anchored. This should be especially noted when in a tube because your depth perception is distorted by your proximity to the surface. As you move into position never, ever come between another angler and the shoreline.

Inflatables of interest to anglers come in five basic configurations: dinghy, kayak, sport boat, pontoon boat and float tube. Dinghies are either oval- or U-shaped and lack extended stabilizers at the stern. Rather than rigid floorboards they depend on tubular-shaped air chambers to provide moderate rigidity and range in lengths from lightweight 8-footers (2.4 m) to sturdy 20-foot (6-m) river rafts. They are a good choice for use in rivers where you're likely to encounter rough water, swift currents and rocks. Combining low air pressure with material of high tensile strength, an inflatable absorbs collisions with rocks, even those with sharp edges. Should the craft swamp, the air chambers provide more than enough buoyancy to support the passengers. If an occupant is thrown overboard, it is far easier to crawl back over the side of an inflatable than that of a standard boat.

Because of their hull configuration and lack of a keel, dinghies have poor handling qualities in wind and waves. Their most dangerous trait is a tendency for the bow to lift while heading into waves against an oncoming wind. Under these circumstances, a sudden surge of motor power might cause a dinghy to rear up and flip over backward.

Today's kayaks can be decked out for fishing.

Kayaks are of similar construction to dinghies, but narrower and longer—usually about 11 to 12 feet (3.3 to 3.6 m). Propelled by a double-bladed paddle, they are faster and easier to control than rowed dinghies. But the occupant is confined to sitting. If used for fishing they must be properly set up to secure the rod(s) in outside holders.

Lightweight "back packers" suitable for use on protected waters and in some cases slow-moving, obstacle-free streams, are usually of the small dinghy or kayak configuration. Because of its strength and flexibility, unreinforced PVC is the most popular material used. Generally, the larger the boat the thicker the PVC. Some 8-footers (2.4-m) weigh as little as 15 pounds (7 kg). Although quite capable of supporting two people, they are cramped because the side and floor air chambers take up much of the interior. It may be worth opting for a slightly longer boat in the 9 to 10 feet (3 m) range; weight increases accordingly—20 to 30 pounds (10 to 14 kg)—but so does capacity, leg room and comfort.

Fishing from a float tube can be very rewarding.

Sport boats are the least portable of the inflatables, much more expensive and, because of their size, configuration and assembled components, usually have to be trailered. They also range up to 20 feet (6 m) long and generally incorporate rigid floorboards, a spray dodger, a motor bracket, seats and a steering console. The main air chambers on both sides extend back beyond the transom, creating stubby, cone-shaped tails. These provide increased support for heavy outboard motors and improve the fore-and-aft stability. These boats are the most comfortable of the inflatables and standing to cast or fight fish should prove no problem.

Your boat should carry at least one anchor, preferably two (bow and stern), because that setup keeps the boat from swinging in the wind. This gives you much better control of your fly line so that you, not the wind, can control your important retrieve.

When it comes to float tubes and pontoon boats, Manitoba trout guru Bob Sheedy goes back to the early days of their introduction. In his excellent book *Lake Fly Fishing Strategies*, he offers a wealth of in-depth information on how to choose and use float tubes, along with the best waders and swim fins to go with them. Following are some paraphrased excerpts from what Bob advises in much greater detail in his book, which is available at www.mwflyfishing.net.

A 5-pound (2.3-kg) rainbow caught at first light in 3 feet (1 m) of water. Tom Johnanneson photo

Float tubes are available in two basic configurations: circular and U-shaped. The former is most economical and generally uses a 20- or 22-inch (50- or 55-cm) truck inner tube for the air chamber, while a U-tube usually has a seamless bladder. The latter is easiest to enter and exit and travels through the water with less drag.

Characteristics and features that either style should have in common:

- A heavy, sun-resistant nylon cover manufactured with double reinforced stitching. The zipper should be of a heavy-duty composite material that is "self-repairing." If it pops due to expansion of the air chamber, simply bleed off a bit of air, then fully open and close the zipper to reseal it.
- Large, preferably compartmentalized pockets for storing lunches, fly boxes, cameras, raincoats and so forth.
- A large apron that can hold up to 80 feet (24 m) of sinking line without tangling. Preferably it should incorporate a ruler along the front edge for measuring fish.
- D-rings for backpacking and attaching accessories.
- Side handles for picking up the tube while walking into or out of the water.
- A fairly high, comfortable backrest to deflect waves and spray.
- A second internal tube for safety. This is a "must." Most setups use a motorcycle tube in the backrest for this. No backup tube, no sale.
- Some seamless padding on the seat.
- Avoid bright colors except on the back, a large patch of Day-Glo orange or red for visibility, with a phosphorescent and reflective strip sewn onto it in an "X" configuration for low light conditions.
- Avoid "add-ons" like extra Velcro patches, line cutters, tippet dispensers, drink holders and so forth. They are notorious line snaggers.

Wearing a life jacket just makes sense.

Pontoon boats provide comfortable mobility while retaining most of the stealth characteristics of a float tube (assuming that you row quietly). Most have ample cargo space in pockets or modular clip-on racks and large stripping aprons that accommodate any amount of line. These are "triple-threat" outfits in that they can be rowed, propelled with swim fins or powered by an electric motor. Often all three are used interchangeably during a day of fishing.

Unlike a float tube, a pontoon boat can't be tossed inside your car when it's assembled and inflated; in fact, some won't even fit into the back of a short-box pickup truck unless the tailgate is down. Nor do they backpack easily while assembled and inflated and definitely not when there is an electric motor and full-sized, deep-cycle battery involved.

Long pontoons provide the best flotation and stability, but they don't turn as fast or as easily as short ones, which is essential when working in fast water or shallows. For larger lakes where oars or a motor are used more often than swim fins, opt for long floats; otherwise consider the more maneuverable blunt, banana-shaped pontoons.

This great boat is what I fish out of today.

Avoid foot brace configurations that form a solid bar in favor of two-piece braces that fold out of the way when not in use.

Get a solid, padded seat and be certain that it also has padded armrests on both sides.

Another option is the Porta-Bote, which is constructed out of a space-age engineered resin hull and hinges. The 10-ft-8-inch (3.3-m) model weighs 67 pounds (30.5 kg)—less than half the weight of a comparable aluminum or fiberglass boat.

And the big advantage is that it folds up to be only 4 inches (10 cm) thick, so that when the season is over you can hang it on your garage ceiling or wall. I purchased one a couple of years ago and I have enjoyed the fact that it fits on the side of my camper and is great for trout fishing.

My Porta-Bote loaded on the truck.

While no single fishing platform will serve every situation and freshwater condition, the inflatable family probably comes closest, with a float tube by far the most economical and versatile. On even the smallest of urban lakes or remote mountain tarns an angler can fly fish easily from a float tube and then do precisely the same thing on the largest of lakes simply by driving to a specific area and fishing close to shore. But when it comes to overall comfort it's hard to beat those large, stable boats that must be trailered. It's all about what best serves your purpose and meets your needs—and, of course, what you can afford.

19
Knots

Larry E. Stefanyk

Fishermen should be familiar with basic knots used in rigging.

Learning to tie basic fishing knots is easy. Here is a complete list of knots and instructions for both casting a lure or fly-fishing.

There are many different kinds of fisherman's knots. There are basic knots used in rigging that you should be familiar with. These knots will cover just about every situation you will encounter where a specific knot is needed. Remember that your knots are typically the weakest connection between you and the fish. Many beginning anglers lose fish due to poorly tied knots. Please practise tying these knots at home before you go fishing. Learning to tie knots is something you need do right, not fast. Speed will come with time.

THE BASIC CONNECTION

1 Arbor Knot

2 Nail Knot

3 Nail Knot

4 Double Surgeons Knot

5 Connecting Knot:
• Lefty Kreh Loop Knot
• Improved Clinch Knot
• Palomar Knot

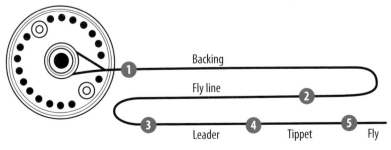

Backing

Fly line

Leader

Tippet

Fly

Arbor Knot

This knot is used to connect your backing or line to the reel. For fly-fishing, backing is used to provide capacity to your reel. Most fly lines are around 90 feet (27 m) long and a large fish would certainly make off with that quite quickly. Most backing comes in 20- or 30-pound (9- or 14-kg) strength and is made from Dacron. Before you start putting line on your reel for fly-fishing, find out how much backing you'll need by reading your reel instructions; some companies print tables based on the fly line. Some fly lines are longer than others and some will reduce the capacity of a reel because of their large diameters in the belly. As a rule of thumb, less backing is used on reels that have double taper (DT) fly lines than those with Weight-forward (WF) Lines. This is because a double taper has a more even diameter in the belly than a WF. DT line is much thicker throughout and therefore takes up more room on your reel.

Nail Knot—to backing

Next you will connect your fly line to your backing. This requires a secure knot. Since the materials are different (Dacron to plastic), the most common knot here is the nail knot. It's a relatively small knot that slides easily through your guides.

Nail Knot—to fly line

This knot connects your leader to your fly line and is most important because your leader is designed to turn your fly over when casting. The transition from fly line to monofilament is paramount. The nail knot provides a clean and effective connection that gives the leader proper transition from the fly line, which is important for casting accuracy. Heavier pound test at the knot location is paramount.

Double Surgeon's Knot—leader to tippet

Used to connect your tippet to your leader, this knot is suitable when connecting two similar diameters of monofilament. The tippet is the section of monofilament fishing line that attaches your fly to your leader. Leaders are typically knotless, tapered and pre-made. By adding a tippet section you can extend the life of your leader by simply replacing a worn section or changing the tippet diameter for a smaller or larger fly.

Connecting Knot—lure or fly to fishing line or tippet

This knot is for connecting your fly to your tippet or lure to your line. It is critical to ensure you have a strong, correctly tied knot, or you will certainly lose flies, lures and—worst of all—fish.

There are many choices for attaching your lure or fly to the line. The most important is consistency. Learn a few different knots and practise until perfect. I have covered a few knots: Lefty Kreh Loop Knot, Improved Clinch Knot and the Palomar knot.

Few knots are 100 percent of the line's rated strength but if you moisten all knots with a little saliva before drawing them tight, tighten them slowly and test every knot by pulling on it hard, you will reduce the chance of losing that fish of a lifetime. Be sure to replace leaders, tippets and lines when they show signs of wear or abrasions.

Instructions for Tying Knots:

1. Arbor Knot
How to tie:

Step 1: Pass the line around the reel spool.

Step 2: With the free end, tie an overhand knot around the standing section, leaving a long tag end.

Step 3: Tighten and trim the tag end close to the knot.

Step 4: Tie a second overhand knot to prevent the end sliding through the first knot.

Step 5: Trim the end.

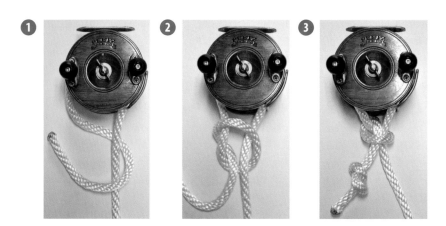

Alternative:

I recommend winding the loop twice around the arbor before making the first overhand knot. This increases the friction, which may be useful on some of the more polished reels.

Advantages:

The arbor knot is simple, easily learned and effective.

2. Nail Knot

The nail knot was originally named because a nail was inserted as a guide when threading the line. It is easier to use a small straw if you can. It's an important fishing knot used to join two lines of different diameters and allows for line diameters to diminish down to the fly, i.e., it is useful for attaching your backing to the fly line, and your fly line to the leader.

A neat little tool for tying nail knots.

How to tie:

The drawing shows the smaller line being threaded through the loops using a straw.

Step 1: Hold the tube and the two lines together.

Step 2: Wrap the smaller line under and around the tube and the larger line.

Step 3: Make six complete turns around the straw and the main line (three in the diagram for demonstration.)

Step 4: Pass the line through the tube.

Step 5: Tighten the knot neatly around the tube.

Step 6: Withdraw the tube and re-tighten the knot, then add a little saliva to the knot and gently pull it tight.

Step 7: Trim the ends.

Alternative:

The line can be threaded beside a nail (hence its name) or pulled through with a needle.

Advantages:

The nail knot makes a smooth compact knot that will readily pass through the guides.

3. Double Surgeon's Knot

The double surgeon's knot is used to join two lines of moderately unequal size, leader to tippet. It is an easy knot to learn and tie and allows you, with the same leader, to select the right size tippet to suit the size of your fly.

How to tie:

The double surgeon's knot can only be tied with a tippet because the entire length of the tippet has to be passed through the overhand knot twice.

Step 1: Place the leader and tippet side by side.

Step 2: Overlap enough to tie the overhand knot.

Step 3: Pull the long end of the tippet through and then pass both ends through a second time.

Step 4: Add a little saliva to the knot and gently pull it tight.

Step 5: After forming the knot, carefully set it by pulling on all four ends.

Step 6: Trim the ends.

Alternative:

As an option, the two lines can be passed through the overhand knot a third time to form the triple surgeon's knot.

Advantages:

The double or triple surgeon's knots are excellent knots to join two lines of moderately unequal size.

4. Lefty Kreh Loop Knot

Lefty Kreh is one of the best-known names in fly-fishing today, both for his fly casting and his fishing expertise.

When tying flies onto their tippet, most fishermen use a "new improved clinch knot." This results in a fixed connection and the fly is restricted to moving to the same line as the tippet. This probably works fine, but think of the advantages of having a loop connection to your fly—the fly is free to move the swivel and will have a lot more subtle movement during pauses and twitches if it is not fixed tightly to a regular knot. You may think this is a small detail, but I can guarantee that delicate lures and flies will not swim properly if they are knotted too tightly.

How to tie:

Step 1: Form a basic overhand knot in the leader and then take the tag end through the eye of the hook.

Step 2: Take the tag end through the knot on the main line.

Step 3: Move the overhand knot close to the eye to size your loop and then take three twists around the main line with the tag end.

Step 5: Feed the tag end through the little triangle between the twists and the overhand knot.

Step 6: Add a little saliva to the knot and gently pull it tight, keeping an eye on the size of your loop.

Step 7: Trim the end.

Advantages:

This knot allows the lure to move naturally. It also retains most of the line.

5. Improved Clinch Knot

The clinch knot provides one good method of securing fishing line to a hook, lure or swivel. The "improved" version includes an extra tuck under the final turn, shown in step 4. It is commonly used to fasten the tippet to the fly.

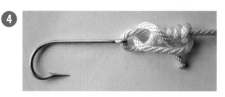

How to tie:

Step 1: Pass the end of the line through the eye of the hook.

Step 2: Wrap it around the standing end five complete turns.

Step 3: Pass the end back through the loop beside the eye.

Step 4: Then pass the end under the final turn.

Step 5: Add a little saliva to the knot and gently pull it tight.

Step 6: Trim the end.

It is important to wind the loops as a neat spiral around the standing line. Hold the loops under your fingers as you wind the line on.

Advantages:

The improved clinch knot is regarded as a fisherman's reliable standby.

6. Palomar Knot

The Palomar knot is a simple knot for attaching a line to a hook, or a fly to a leader or tippet. It is regarded as one of the strongest and most reliable fishing knots and is recommended for use with braided lines.

How to tie:

Step 1: Form a loop in the end of the line.

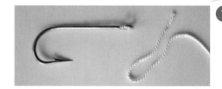

Step 2: Pass the loop through the eye of the hook.

Step 3: With the loop, tie an overhand knot.

Step 4: Pass the loop over the hook.

Step 5: Pull the two ends to snug down the loop.

Step 6: Add a little saliva to the knot and gently pull tight.

Step 7: Trim the end.

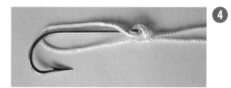

Advantages:

Some fishermen recommend that the loop be pulled off the hook and down against the rest of the knot. This leaves the hook free to rotate in the knot. With a little practice the Palomar knot can be tied in the dark.

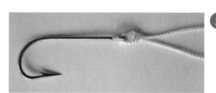

Disadvantages:

The loop must pass through the eye of the hook, which can be awkward on smaller hooks and depends on making the loop large enough.

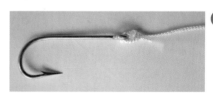

20 Larry E. Stefanyk

Catch and Release
Do It Properly

F ish are released for various reasons: they are out of season, below the minimum size limit, above the maximum length, are not a desirable food fish, or simply because you practise limiting your catch instead of catching your limit, thereby ensuring that the fishing will remain good in your favorite waters. While voluntarily releasing a portion of your allowable catch is fine and noble, it must be done properly in order that the fish isn't damaged any more than the puncture wound resulting from the hook. Fortunately, much of this process involves nothing more than common sense and being prepared ahead of time.

Net released trout.

Start with the tools of the trade. The first is a landing net that has a small, knotless neoprene mesh, not the old knotted nylon type that damages a fish by scraping protective slime from its body, tearing the membrane between the fin rays, dislodging scales or damaging the eyes. Body slime is the only protection a fish has against water-borne diseases, and eye damage often leads to blindness. Either can sound the death knell for your "released" fish.

Have needle-nose pliers, a hemostat or a release tool handy where it can be found quickly and picked up without fumbling. Keeping your pliers in a belt holster, for example, or your hemostat clipped to a pocket flap is perfect.

Right: Always have a pair of needle-nose pliers handy to release fish.

Use line that is strong enough to do the job; leave the 1- and 2-pound test for those

Caught and released, and never taken out of the water.

who really should know better. Stress is a major killer of fish. It releases lactic acid reserves into the system that creates shock and exhaustion. Over-playing a fish on line that is too light leads to stress.

If fishing with bait use a circle hook, which will greatly reduce the chance of hooking a fish anywhere but in the jaw. If it's hooked deeply, cut the leader. In most cases the fish's stomach acids will quickly dissolve the hook.

If using spoons or plugs with treble hooks, consider switching to a single, barbless hook (its gap should measure the same distance as from point to point on two of the treble's hooks). If this alters a plug's action, experiment with running a narrow strip of lead golf tape down the bottom of the body.

If you are not going to photograph a fish, don't remove it from the water. Simply remove the hook as quickly as possible and then point the fish into the current or support its belly on your cupped hand until it can swim away under its own power.

If you want a picture, have the photographer get prepared ahead of time, then lift the fish from the water just long enough to get the job done. Never— ever—lift a fish by its gill cover; you risk damaging the gills. Instead, cup one hand under a large fish's belly and grip its tail with the other hand, with the thumb on top so your hand doesn't cover its tail.

It's permissible to grip a bass by the lower jaw.

With small fish that are hooked in the lip, grip the lure or fly and lift while supporting the fish—even a small one—under its belly. After the picture is taken, return the fish to the water and twist the hook free.

It's permissible to grip a bass by the lower jaw, but DO NOT bend this down like you see in some pictures. Yes, this immobilizes the fish, but it also injures its jaw.

Again, lift the fish horizontally while supporting its belly.

Catch-and-release fishing is all about enjoying the sport, for us, for our grandchildren and beyond. Releasing fish is the best tool we have for preserving quality fisheries. Granted, there are times when a species of game fish overpopulates a river or lake, but this doesn't happen very often. If you want good sport tomorrow, release your fish today.

Just because a fish swims away after it leaves your hand, don't assume it's healthy. A fish that is carelessly handled then released, may die later the same day, or may be so weakened or injured that it dies a week or month later. It takes care—and caring—to properly catch and release a fish so it stays healthy. Here are a few guidelines.

- Use barbless hooks. An easily removed hook reduces the amount of fish handling.
- Use the strongest tippet you can get away with. Fragile tippets are not "sporting." They are fish murderers. The longer you have to play a fish, the more exhausted it becomes and the less likely it is that it will recover.
- Play fish quickly. If a fish is becoming exhausted from being played too long, clamp the line to the rod and point the rod at the fish. Let it break off.
- Watch the water temperature. When the water is above 70°F (21°C), coldwater fish like trout and steelhead are under stress and should be played quickly. If it's over 75°F (24°C), don't fish for coldwater species.
- Before handling a live fish, wet your hands. This helps prevent the removal of the fish's protective slime. There is some discussion of using dry hands so you do not squeeze the trout as much while trying to hold it. I do not know any fishermen who have dry hands when it comes time to handle fish.
- Back the hook out carefully, preferably with a suitable tool such as forceps, pliers or one of those nifty new catch-and-release tools.

Keep the fish in the water. If you want to take a photo of it out of the water, get everything set up, then lift the fish and snap the photo quickly.

To revive a tired fish, grasp it in front of the tail and move it gently in the water.

- Keep the fish in the water. If you want to take a photo of it out of water, get everything set up, then lift the fish and snap the photo quickly. Then immediately put the fish back in the water. Keep the out-of-water time under 15 seconds.
- Don't squeeze the fish.
- Don't put your fingers in its gills or on its eyes.
- Don't let the fish flop around on rocks or in the bottom of a boat.
- If the fish is hooked any deeper than the lips, clip off the hook and let it go. Quickly.
- Don't grab the fish by the tail then lift it vertically from the water.
- Avoid using a net. Fish get tangled in them and can damage their gills, eyes and slime coating.

To revive a tired fish, grasp it in front of the tail and move it gently in the water. Remember fish gills only take in oxygen from water that comes in from the mouth. Pulling the fish back and forth basically says "breathe, don't breathe, breathe, don't breathe" and will diminish the survival rate.

Too many anglers, with a fish obviously exhausted, frantically move it back and forth in an effort to keep the fish alive. Little do they know that they are killing it. Keep the fish head pointing upstream and moving through the current. Pulling it backward will effectively stress the fish. Don't let go the first time the fish tries to swim away. Let go the second time. In a river, block the current with your upstream leg and revive your fish in the quiet water behind it.

- If a fish rolls over on its side or back, it's exhausted. Take special care of it.
- Don't dump a fish into fast water. It can start to tumble and not be able to get in a position so it can breathe. Its anatomy is not designed to withstand bumps into rocks, which could prove fatal.

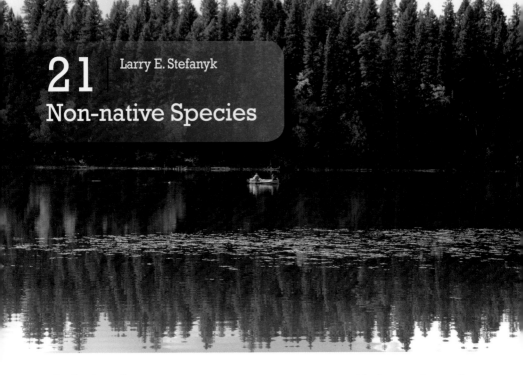

21
Larry E. Stefanyk

Non-native Species

Illegally introduced fish species impacts our native fish stocks irreversibly.

The Ministry of Environment (MOE) is responsible for providing quality fishing opportunties as well as protecting native fish species. Unfortunately, the growing number of waters with illegally introduced fish species poses a huge threat to our native fish stocks and the benefits we derive from them.

Recently reported introductions of fish such as bass, pike and yellow perch are almost certainly due to deliberate and illegal activities of individuals intent on creating new fisheries. While these species may support fisheries in some locales, the unauthorized spread of these species in British Columbia will come at the expense of our native fisheries. The impact will be irreversible.

Ministry Response

The MOE is getting tough with illegal fish introduction in order to protect our native resources. Policy is now in place to enable removal or control of such species where they pose high risks. In support of this policy, a new management approach has been developed that emphasizes zero-tolerance for new illegal introduction of fish species such as bass, yellow perch, black crappie, walleye and pike.

Black crappie.

People caught moving or releasing live fish into lakes or streams will be prosecuted. (This, of course, does not apply to catch-and-release fishing, when releasing fish directly back into the water at the point of capture. The point being: kill them, don't

Smallmouth bass.

put them back.) If newly introduced fish species are discovered, the fishing may be closed on that water to provide a strong disincentive for future introductions and to prevent future spread. At a minimum, a strictly enforced fishing closure for the introduced species will be imposed on the lake or stream.

The MOE recognizes that in some cases fisheries for introduced species have been long established. These fisheries may be managed to maintain fishing opportunities where they pose minimal threat to native resources. However, if a water is identified as being the source of fish for illegal introduction, it may be closed to fishing for that species.

This new mangement approach will be phased in across the province over the next few years. In 2009, the Kootenay region was piloting new regulations aimed at addressing the issue of illegal introduction of non-native fish species.

Notice to Anglers in Region 4 – Kootenay

It is now illegal to fish for bass, perch, pike or walleye in the Kootenay Region, with the exception of certain waters with exciting fisheries, as listed in the Water-Specific Tables. This is part of BC's new, zero-tolerance approach to illegal fish introduction.

Northern pike. Ian Colin James photo

You Can Help!

Protecting our native aquatic systems and the fisheries they support is a high priority and a responsibility that we all share. Report any suspicious activity related to the illegal transfer of live fish to the Conservation Officer Service (1-877-952-7277).

Walleye.

It is ILLEGAL to release alien species or any other live fish into BC's lakes or streams, an offense which holds a **penalty of up to a $100,000 for first-time offenders, and/or a prison term of up to 12 months for a second offense**. In addition, a REWARD **of up to $20,000** is available to anyone providing information leading to the successful prosecution of individuals responsible for illegal activities under the provincial Wildlife Act, or the illegal transfer of alien fish species into BC waters. This reward is ongoing and is supplied by the **BC Wildlife Federation, in co-operation with the Ministry of Environment**.

Yellow Perch

This non-native species has been introduced illegally into Elk, Langford and

Yellow perch.

Shawnigan lakes on Vancouver Island. The stocks appear to be thriving despite competition from established native trout and bass populations. Yellow perch are highly adaptive and females produce thousands of eggs for every inch of total length. Biologists are concerned about the serious impact this species may have on our native wild fish populations. They invite anglers to enjoy fishing for this species (catch limit, 20 per day) but remind you that moving live yellow perch—or any other species for that matter—can do irreparable harm to native fish populations and is an offense punishable by a fine. If yellow perch are found in other lakes, please report to regional fisheries staff in Nanaimo (telephone 1-250-751-3100).

For Reference: Appendix 1

Select Lakes of the Pacific Northwest
By Larry E. Stefanyk

A: British Columbia

Region 1: Vancouver Island

South Island

Elk Lake
Waypoint: 48° 32′ 00″ N, 123° 24′ 00″ W
Location: 8 miles (13 km) north of Victoria
Elevation: 720 ft (220 m)
Surface area: 610 ac (247 ha)
Max. depth: 63 ft (19 m)
Stocking data: Rainbow and cutthroat trout
Directions: Located in Elk Beaver Lake Regional Park, next to Pat Bay Highway 17 north of Victoria. Several exits from highway to eastern shores of lake.
Facilities: Picnic area and two boat launches plus fishing pier.
Fish found: Rainbow and cutthroat trout and smallmouth bass
Regulations: Regional regulations

![fish] Indicates stocked lake

Cowichan

Cowichan Lake
Waypoint: 48° 52′ 00″ N, 124° 16′ 00″ W
Location: Town of Lake Cowichan
Elevation: 538 ft (164 m)
Surface area: 15,325 ac (6,201 ha)
Max. depth: 499 ft (152 m)
Stocking data: None
Directions: Highway 18 west of Duncan on Cowichan Valley Highway to the town of Lake Cowichan. From town both paved and gravel forestry roads circle the lake.
Facilities: Six recreational sites, resorts and campgrounds.
Fish found: Rainbow, cutthroat and brown trout, Dolly Varden and kokanee
Special regulations: 2 cutthroat limit per day and none can be longer then 20 inches (50 cm). Single barbless hook requirement and no bait fishing allowed between November 15 and April 15. Speed restriction on parts (8 km/h) plus overall 10 km/h speed restriction within 200 ft (60 m) of shore.

Central Island

Spider Lake

Waypoint: 49° 20′00″N, 124° 37′00″W
Location: Access from Qualicum Beach is via Highway 19 to Horne Lake Road and Spider Lake Road.
Elevation: 459 ft (140 m)
Surface area: 109 ac (44 ha)
Max. depth: 43 ft (13 m)
Stocking data: Rainbow and steelhead trout
Directions: Located 10 miles (16 km) west of Qualicum Beach, 5 miles (8 km) west of Highway 19 on Horne Lake Road and Spider Lake Road (both gravel). Follow the signs to Horne Lake Caves off the highway.
Facilities: Spider Lake Provincial Park: Day-use, cartop boat launch
Fish found: Rainbow and steelhead trout, smallmouth bass—excellent bass lake
Regulations: Regional regulations

Pacific Rim

Sproat Lake

Waypoint: 49° 16′00″N, 125° 00′00″W
Location: 10 miles (16 km) west of the town of Port Alberni
Elevation: 105 ft (32 m)
Surface area: 9,324 ac (3,775 ha)
Max. depth: 640 ft (195 m)
Stocking data: Steelhead, rainbow and cutthroat trout
Directions: There is easy access off Highway 4, which runs for 7 miles (11 km) along the lake's northern shore.
Facilities: Boat launches, campsites, Sproat Lake Provincial Park, Fossil and Taylor Arm are day-use plus private campgrounds.
Fish found: Rainbow, steelhead and cutthroat trout plus salmon
Regulations: Regional regulations

North Central

Comox Lake

Waypoint: 49° 37′00″N, 125° 10′00″W
Location: 6 miles (10 km) southwest of Courtenay
Elevation: 440 ft (134 m)
Surface area: 5,187 ac (2,100 ha)
Max. depth: 358 ft (109 m)
Stocking data: None
Directions: Access to the east end of the lake is via the road to Cumberland, west off Highway 19, 10 miles (6 km) south of Courtenay. Access to the north shore is via Comox Lake Road.

Facilities: Boat launch near Cumberland, campsites, picnic sites

Fish found: Rainbow and cutthroat trout, Dolly Varden, kokanee

Special regulations: No trout/char over 20 inches (50 cm) in size, November 1–April 30. Single barbless hook requirement and bait ban between November 1 and April 30.

Brewster Lake

Waypoint: 50° 06′00″N, 125° 34′00″W

Location: Campbell River

Elevation: 620 ft (189 m)

Surface area: 1,020 ac (413 ha)

Max. depth: 81 ft (24.5 m)

Stocking data: Cutthroat and rainbow trout

Directions: Proceed 10 miles (16 km) along highway 19 toward Sayward, then turn onto Menzies Main and follow it for 10 miles (16 km) to Brewster Lake, or via the Brewster Main 22.3 miles (36 km) by way of heading toward Gold River, turning off Camp Road past Elk Falls Provincial Park from Campbell River.

Facilities: Cartop boat launch plus a number of forestry campsites

Fish found: Rainbow and cutthroat trout, Dolly Varden

Regulations: Regional regulations

North Island

Alice Lake

Waypoint: 50° 28′00″N, 127° 25′00″W

Location: 5 miles (8 km) northeast of Port Alice, part of the Marble River basin. Off Highway 19 north of Port McNeill.

Elevation: 180 ft (55 m)

Surface area: 2,678 ac (1,084 ha)

Max. depth: 234 ft (71 m)

Stocking data: None

Directions: Accessed off the Port Alice Road, which passes on the west side of Alice Lake.

Facilities: Boat launch, campsite— Marble River Recreation Site (33 units), Link River Regional Park (42 units), Pinch Creek Recreation Site (3 units) and Alice Lake Recreation Site (10 units)

Fish found: Rainbow and cutthroat trout, Dolly Varden

Special regulations: Ban. No trout over 20 inches (50 cm) in size. Single barbless hook requirement and no bait.

Region 2: The Lower Mainland

Rice Lake

Waypoint: 49° 21′ 24.0″ N, 123° 0′ 49.2″ W
Location: North Vancouver, exit 22 north, 3.7 miles (6 km) northeast.
Elevation: 659 ft (201 m)
Surface area: 17.8 ac (7.2 h)
Max. depth: 16 ft (5 m)
Stocking data: Rainbow trout
Directions: North Vancouver, in the Lower Seymour Conservation Reserve. Take exit #22A from Hwy #1, turn left at the intersection onto Lillooet Road and follow to parking area. Follow short trail to the lake. For wheelchair access, see gate operator.
Facilities: Pier, pit-toilets, day-use picnic area
Fish found: Rainbow trout
Regulations: Regional regulations

Browning Lake

Waypoint: 49° 38′ 39.9″ N, 123° 12′ 27″ W
Location: 9 miles (15 km) south of Squamish
Elevation: 449 ft (137 m)
Surface area: 6.4 ac (2.6 ha)
Max. depth: 33 ft (10 m)
Stocking data: Rainbow trout
Directions: Located 9 miles (15 km) in Murrin Lake Provincial Park right next to the Sea to Sky Highway 99
Facilities: Paid parking in paved lot, day-use picnic area, pit-toilets
Fish found: Rainbow trout
Regulations: No powered boats

Mike Lake

Waypoint: 49° 16′ 27.7″ N, 122° 32′ 22.8″ W
Location: 3.7 miles (6 km) northeast of Maple Ridge
Elevation: 804 ft (245 m)
Surface area: 10 ac (4 ha)
Max. depth: 16 ft (5 m)
Stocking data: Rainbow trout
Directions: North of Maple Ridge in Golden Ears Provincial Park. From Maple Ridge, follow Dewdney Trunk Road, turn north on 232 Street, east (right) on Fern Crescent and follow road into park. Turn left on the gravel Mike Lake Road.
Facilities: Wharf, day-use area and cartop boat launch at the lake. Golden Ears Provincial Park has three different camping areas at Alouette, Gold and North Beach with a total of 334 campsites. Full facilities—sani-stations, showers and toilets.
Fish found: Rainbow trout
Regulations: No powered boats

Klein Lake

Waypoint: 49° 43′47″N, 123° 58′8″W

Location: 2.8 miles (4.5 km) southeast of Earls Cove

Elevation: 466 ft (142 m)

Surface area: 35 ac (14 ha)

Max. depth: 138 ft (42 m)

Stocking data: Cutthroat trout

Directions: Northern end of the Sechelt Peninsula on the Sunshine Coast, southeast of Earls Cove. Turn east off Sunshine Coast Highway 101 just before Earls Cove and follow the Egmont Road to the west end of North Lake, to North Lake Forest Service Road. Turn right (south) onto the road, then right again onto Klein Lake road at the south end of North Lake, Klein Lake is on your right.

Facilities: None

Fish found: Cutthroat trout

Regulations: Electric motors only

Harrison Lake

Waypoint: 49° 32′00″N, 121° 49′00″W

Location: North of Harrison Hot Springs

Elevation: 36 ft (11 m)

Surface area: 53,820 ac (21,780 ha)

Max. depth: 915 ft (279 m)

Stocking data: None

Directions: From Highway 1, follow Highway 9 north to Agassiz. Continue west to Hot Springs Road, which branches north from Highway 7. This road leads almost directly to a boat launch and marina at the east end of Esplanade Avenue.

Facilities: There are a number of recreation sites on the shores of the lake, including boat launches, plus facilities in the resort town of Harrison Hot Springs.

Fish found: Cutthroat and rainbow trout, Dolly Varden, kokanee and whitefish

Regulations: Speed restriction 10 km/h at south end, as buoyed and signed

Alouette Lake

Waypoint: 49° 20′7″N, 122° 24′34″W

Location: 8 miles (13 km) northeast of Maple Ridge

Elevation: 410 ft (125 m)

Surface area: 4,061 ac (1,643 ha)

Max. depth: 522 ft (159 m)

Stocking data: Rainbow and cutthroat trout

Directions: North of Maple Ridge in Golden Ears Provincial Park. From Maple Ridge, follow Dewdney Trunk Road to 132 Avenue and then finally along Fern Crescent to the lake. Road is paved and all vehicles can access the lake.

Facilities: Golden Ears Provincial Park—west side of the lake. Picnic area and boat launch at the south end of lake.

Fish found: Rainbow, cutthroat and lake trout

Regulations: Speed restriction 8 km/h at south end of lake, south of a line drawn from the BC Park boat launch ramp on the east side of the lake.

Region 3: The Thompson / Nicola

Heffley Lake
Waypoint: 50° 49′52″N, 120° 3′24″W
Location: Northeast of Kamloops
Elevation: 3,097 ft (944 m)
Surface area: 549 ac (222 ha)
Max. depth: 79.7 ft (24.3 m)
Stocking data: Rainbow trout
Directions: 18 miles (30 km) northeast of Kamloops,
    travel north on Highway 5 to the community of
    Heffley Creek. Signs point to Sun Peaks ski resort,
    follow road east for 12 miles (20 km) to the lake.
Facilities: Heffley Lake Recreation Site, 30 units with
    boat launch.
Fish found: Rainbow trout
Regulations: No towing speed restriction (15 hp)

Paul Lake
Waypoint: 50° 44′26″N, 120° 6′49″W
Location: East of Kamloops
Elevation: 2,523 ft (769 m)

Surface area: 964 ac (390 ha)
Max. depth: 239 ft (73 m)
Stocking data: Rainbow trout
Directions: From Kamloops, follow Highway 5 north
    out of city, then turn east at the Husky station 11
    miles (18 km) out of town onto the Paul Road to
    Paul Lake Provincial Park.
Facilities: Paul Lake Provincial Park, full-service
    campground as well as day-use plus hand launch
    for cartoppers.
Fish found: Rainbow trout
Regulations: Regional regulations

Lac Le Jeune Lake
Waypoint: 50° 28′50″N, 120° 28′11″W
Location: South of Kamloops
Elevation: 4,186 ft (1,276 m)
Surface area: 489 ac (198 ha)
Max. depth: 90.9 ft (27.7 m)
Stocking data: Rainbow trout
Directions: 13 miles (21 km) south of Kamloops via
    Coquihalla Highway and Exit 336 to the Lac Le
    Jeune Road.

Facilities: Lac Le Jeune Provincial Park—north side of the lake, offers full service, 144-unit campsite, boat launch and fishing wharf
Fish found: Rainbow trout
Regulations: Speed restriction (20 km/h)

Pinantan Lake

Waypoint: 50° 43′ 22″ N, 120° 1′ 18″ W
Location: Northeast of Kamloops
Elevation: 2,831 ft (863 m)
Surface area: 168 ac (68 ha)
Max. depth: 60.7 ft (18.5 m)
Stocking data: Rainbow and cutthroat trout
Directions: North of Kamloops on Yellowhead Highway (#5), turn right on Paul Lake Road to the lake.
Facilities: Paul Lake Provincial Park and resort on northwest shore. Public boat launch at the west end of lake.
Fish found: Rainbow and cutthroat trout
Regulations: Electric motor only

Red Lake

Waypoint: 50° 53′ 34″ N, 120° 47′ 27″ W
Location: East of Cache Creek
Elevation: 3,117 ft (950 m)
Surface area: 269 ac (109 ha)
Max. depth: 34 ft (10 m)
Stocking data: Brook and rainbow trout
Directions: 27 miles (44 km) east of Cache Creek. From Trans-Canada Highway (#1) follow Deadman–Vidette road north to Criss Creek. The Johnson/Criss Creek Forest Road branches east and loops and twists over to the Copper Creek Road via the Seven Lakes Road. Take the Copper Creek Road north to the lake. GPS is a definite asset.
Facilities: Cartop boat launch with an undeveloped campsite. Nearest campsite Saul Lake east of Red Lake or Steelhead Provincial Park.
Fish found: Brook and rainbow trout
Regulations: Engine power restriction (10 hp)

Kamloops Lake

Waypoint: 50° 44′ 00″ N, 120° 39′ 00″ W
Location: West of Kamloops
Elevation: 1,125 ft (343 m)
Surface area: 13,800 ac (5,585 ha)
Max. depth: 495 ft (150 m)
Directions: Trans Canada Highway (#1) runs along the south shore providing access, north shore less accessible with few direct access points.
Facilities: Boat launches at Savona and Kamloops. Steelhead Provincial Park provides facilities for the angler, with a boat launch and wharf.
Fish found: Rainbow trout, Dolly Varden and kokanee
Regulations: Regional regulations

Region 4: The Kootenays

Rosebud Lake
Waypoint: 51° 00′00″N, 116° 46′00″W
Location: 10.5 miles (17 km) south of Salmo
Elevation: 2,654 ft (809 m)
Surface area: 33 ac (13.4 ha)
Max. depth: 59 ft (18 m)
Stocking data: Rainbow trout
Directions: Lake is 37 miles (60 km) west of Creston
and 18 miles (30 km) southeast of Salmo. If
traveling east on Highway 3, 8.8 miles (14.3 km)
past Salmo, take Highway 6 toward the US/Canada
border for 5.5 miles (9 km), then turn left on
Rosebud Lake Road for another 3.7 miles (6 km).
Facilities: Cartop boat launch and small wilderness
campsite.
Fish found: Rainbow trout
Regulations: Trout daily quota = 2; no power boats

Summit Lake
Waypoint: 50° 09′00″N, 117° 38′00″W
Location: 10 miles (16 km) southeast of Nakusp
Elevation: 2,506 ft (764 m)
Surface area: 370.4 ac (149.9 ha)
Max. depth: 55 ft (17 m)
Stocking data: Rainbow trout
Directions: 10 miles (16 km) southeast of Nakusp on
Highway 6 or 16 miles (26 km) southwest of New
Denver.
Facilities: Summit Lake Provincial Campgrounds—35
sites and two boat launches.
Fish found: Rainbow trout
Regulations: Regional regulations

Cherry Lake
Waypoint: 49° 10′00″N, 115° 32′00″W
Location: 20 miles (32 km) southeast of Cranbrook
Elevation: 4,025 ft (1,227 m)
Surface area: 94.8 ac (38.4 ha)
Max. depth: 42.6 ft (13 m)
Stocking data: Rainbow trout
Directions: Getting to Cherry Lake can be an
adventure. Take Kikomen Newgate Road from
Highway 3/93 over Lake Koocanusa to Craven

Creek Forest Service Road. Follow road past Bloom
Creek Forest Service Road for 2.4 miles (4 km) until
you reach turnoff to lake. Road can be rough.
Facilities: Cherry Lake Forestry Recreational Site a
small cleared area with room for a few tents and a
small cartop boat launch.
Fish found: Rainbow and cutthroat trout
Regulations: Regional regulations

North Star Lake
Waypoint: 49° 20′00″N, 115° 15′00″W
Location: 8 miles (13 km) west of Elko
Elevation: 2,778 ft (847 m)
Surface area: 51.8 ac (21 ha)
Max. depth: 32.8 ft (10 m)
Stocking data: Rainbow trout
Directions: Follow Highway 3/93 to Jaffray and then
south along the Jaffray–Baynes Lake Road for 3
miles (5 km) until you reach the branch road east
to North Star Lake.
Facilities: North Star Recreational Site—9 sites and
cartop boat launch
Fish found: Rainbow trout
Regulations: Regional regulations

Quartz (Rockbluff) Lake
Waypoint: 49° 53′00″N, 115° 38′00″W
Location: 29 miles (47 km) north of Cranbrook
Elevation: 3,100 ft (945 m)
Surface area: 45.7 ac (18.5 ha)
Max. depth: 84 ft (25.6 m)
Stocking data: Rainbow trout
Directions: Access from Highway 92/93, 29 miles
(47 km) from Cranbrook; well-marked signs at
the turnoff lead 7.4 miles (12 km) into the park.
Continue past Premier Lake and main campground
to Rockbluff Lake.
Facilities: Premier Lake Provincial Park (57 sites on
Premier Lake)
Fish found: Rainbow trout
Regulations: Regional regulations

Peckhams Lake
Waypoint: 49° 32′00″N, 115° 29′00″W
Location: 13.5 miles (22 km) east of Cranbrook

Elevation: 2,739 ft (835 m)

Surface area: 33.3 ac (13.5 ha)

Max. depth: 30.8 ft (9.4 m)

Stocking data: Rainbow trout

Directions: Follow Highway 3/93 to Fort Steele and turn east onto Wardner–Fort Steele Road. Travel 10 miles (16 km) and after passing the junction with Fenwick Road, you will arrive at Peckhams Lake.

Facilities: Norbury Lake Provincial Park, 46 sites. Boat launch

Fish found: Rainbow trout

Regulations: No power boats

Region 5: The Cariboo

Hathaway Lake

Waypoint: 51° 39′ 28″ N, 120° 50′ 6″ W

Location: 20.5 miles (33 km) east of 100 Mile House

Elevation: 3,674 ft (1,120 m)

Surface area: 375 ac (152 ha)

Max. depth: 147 ft (45 m)

Stocking data: Rainbow trout

Directions: From Highway 24 at Interlakes Corner, turn north onto Horse Lake Road straight onto Mahood Lake Road and follow to lake.

Facilities: Boat launch along western shore with picnic site.

Fish found: Rainbow and lake trout

Regulations: Regional regulations

Ten Mile Lake
Waypoint: 53° 5′ 4″ N, 122° 27′ 18″ W
Location: North of Quesnel
Elevation: 2,320 ft (707 m)
Surface area: 600 ac (243 ha)
Max. depth: 26 ft (8 m)
Stocking data: Kokanee and rainbow trout
Directions: 6.7 miles (11 km) north of Quesnel, access off Highway 97. Take Ten Mile Lake Camp road to the lake.
Facilities: Ten Mile Lake Provincial Park, 144 units, boat launch, sani-station and picnic area.
Fish found: Rainbow trout, kokanee and mountain whitefish.
Regulations: Regional regulations

Dugan Lake
Waypoint: 52° 10′ 11.8″ N, 121° 54′ 14.3″ W
Location: East of Williams Lake
Elevation: 3,095 ft (922 m)
Surface area: 238 ac (96.3 ha)
Max. depth: 46 ft (14 m)
Stocking data: Rainbow and brook trout
Directions: 9.3 miles (15 km) east of Williams Lake on Highway 97 then turning on to Horsefly Road, finally turning on to Dugan Lake access.
Facilities: Dugan Lake Recreation Site with boat launch
Fish found: Rainbow and brook trout
Regulations: Regional regulations

Quesnel Lake
Waypoint: 52° 31′ 32″ N, 121° 0′ 44″ W
Location: Northeast of Williams Lake
Elevation: 2,391 ft (729 m)
Surface area: 67,173 ac (27,196 ha)
Max. depth: 518 ft (158 m)
Directions: 42 miles (68 km) northeast of Williams Lake, take Highway 97 turning on to Horsefly–Likely Road.
Facilities: Cedar Point Provincial Park on Quesnel Lake and Horsefly Lake Provincial Park on Horsefly Lake plus a number of recreational sites around the lake.

Fish found: Rainbow and bull trout, salmon and kokanee
Regulations: Bait ban, single barbless hook. Trout/char daily quota = 2 (none under 12 inches/30 cm); only 1 lake trout; release all rainbow trout over 20 inches (50 cm) and release all bull trout.
NOTE: See *Fishing Regulations Synopsis* for other water-specific regulations.

Milburn Lake
Waypoint: 53° 1′ 22″ N, 122° 40′ 50.2″ W
Location: 9.3 miles (15 km) West of Quesnel
Elevation: 2,687 ft (819 m)
Surface area: 84 ac (34 ha)
Max. depth: 8.5 ft (2.6 m)
Stocking data: Rainbow and brook trout
Directions: From Quesnel, cross the Fraser River to west Quesnel, turn right on Elliot Street and then left on to North Fraser Drive which turns into Blackwater Road. Follow Blackwater Road to Nazko Road and turn right (north) on Milburn Lake Road.
Facilities: Small private camping facility with cartop boat launch.
Fish found: Rainbow and brook trout
Regulations: Regional regulations

Charlotte Lake
Waypoint: 52° 11′ 53″ N, 125° 19′ 18″ W
Location: West of Williams Lake
Elevation: 3,852 ft (1,174 m)
Surface area: 16,300 ac (6,596 ha)
Max. depth: 331 ft (101 m)
Directions: 180 miles (300 km) west of Williams Lake off Highway 20.
Facilities: Charlotte Lake Recreation Site with boat launch.
Fish found: Rainbow trout
Regulations: Regional regulations

Region 6: The Skeena

Lakelse Lake
Waypoint: 54° 22′48″N, 128° 33′37″W
Location: South of Terrace
Elevation: 249 ft (76 m)
Surface area: 3,608 ac (1,460 ha)
Max. depth: 104 ft (32 m)
Directions: approximately 12 miles (20 km) south of Terrace and 24 miles (40 km) north of Kitimat, west off Highway 37.
Facilities: Furlong Bay Campsite—158 units in Lakelse Lake Provincial Park with paved boat launch.
Fish found: Wild cutthroat
Regulations: Regional regulations

Ross Lake
Waypoint: 55° 15′34″N, 127° 31′7.7″W
Location: East of Hazelton
Elevation: 1,324 ft (404 m)
Surface area: 82 ac (33 ha)
Max. depth: 27 ft (8.2 m)
Stocking data: Rainbow and brook trout
Directions: From New Hazelton head east (toward Smithers) on Yellowhead Highway (#16) for 1.2 miles (2 km), then turn left on Ross Lake Road for 2.4 miles (4 km).
Facilities: Rose Lake Provincial Park with boat launch
Fish found: Rainbow and brook trout
Regulations: Electric motors only

Tyhee Lake
Waypoint: 54° 42′54″N, 127° 2′12″W
Location: Southeast of Smithers
Elevation: 1,713 ft (522 m)
Surface area: 914 ac (370 ha)
Max. depth: 73 ft (22 m)
Stocking data: Rainbow trout
Directions: Turn off Yellowhead Highway (#16) onto Tyhee Lake Road in Telkwa and follow to Provincial Park.
Facilities: Tyhee Lake Provincial Park—concrete boat launch
Fish found: Rainbow and cutthroat trout, whitefish and burbot
Regulations: Regional regulations

Kathlyn Lake
Waypoint: 54° 49′27.3″N, 127° 12′23.2″W
Location: 3 miles (5 km) north of Smithers
Elevation: 1,673 ft (510 m)
Surface area: 420 ac (170 ha)
Max. depth: 15 ft (6 m)
Directions: Drive northwest on the Yellowhead
Highway (#16) from Smithers, then turn left on
Lake Kathlyn road.
Facilities: Kathlyn Lake Beach Park—cartop boat
launch
Fish found: Wild cutthroat trout
Regulations: No power boats

Round Lake
Waypoint: 54° 39′29.3″N, 126° 55′18.6″W
Location: 6.8 miles (11 km) southeast of Telkwa
Elevation: 1,919 ft (585 m)
Surface area: 450 ac (182 ha)
Max. depth: 67 ft (20 m)
Stocking data: Cutthroat trout
Directions: Drive southeast from Telkwa on
Yellowhead Highway (#16) and turn left (north)
onto Round Lake East Road.

Facilities: Community hall on the northwest corner of
the lake has a dock, boat launch and picnic area.
Fish found: Cutthroat trout
Regulations: Regional regulations

Tchesinkut Lake
Waypoint: 54° 5′39″N, 125° 37′48″W
Location: South of Burns Lake
Elevation: 2,437 ft (743 m)
Surface area: 8,359 ac (3,382 ha)
Max. depth: 489 ft (149 m)
Directions: Along Highway 35 between Burns Lake
and Francois Lake. To get to recreation site turn
east onto the Tchesinkut Lake/Agate Forest
Service Road.
Facilities: Agate Bay Recreation site, there is a boat
launch at Beaver Point Resort, with cabins and
40-unit campground.
Fish found: Lake and rainbow trout and kokanee
Regulations: Release lake trout all year EXCEPT during
months of February and July (when regional
quotas apply); single barbless hook

Region 7A: Omineca

Hart Lake
Waypoint: 54° 28′ 7.2″ N, 122° 39′ 13″ W
Location: Northeast of Prince George
Elevation: 2,345 ft (715 m)
Surface area: 128 ac (52 ha)
Max. depth: 29 ft (8.7 m)
Stocking data: Rainbow trout
Directions: 43 miles (69 km) northwest of Prince
    George in Crooked River Provincial Park on
    Highway 97; 100 m (300 ft) walk to the lake.
Facilities: Hand launch for small boats. Campground
    on Bear Lake about 1 mile (1.6 km) away.
Fish found: Rainbow trout
Regulations: No fishing November 1–April 30.
    Rainbow trout daily quota = 1 (none over 16
    inches/40 cm), bait ban and single barbless hook.

Eena Lake
Waypoint: 54° 3′ 3″ N, 123° 1′ 18″ W
Location: Northwest of Prince George
Elevation: 2,500 ft (762 m)
Surface area: 134 ac (54 ha)
Max. depth: 75 ft (23 m)
Stocking data: Rainbow trout
Directions: 17.4 miles (28 km) northwest of Prince
    George. Take Hart Highway (#97) north for about
    9 miles (15 km) to Chief Lake Road. After traveling
    7 miles (12 km), turn right, following Chief Lake
    Road to Eena Lake Road. From Eena Lake Road turn
    left onto Woods Road and right onto Qinn Road,
    then follow to the boat launch at the lake.
Facilities: Gravel boat launch at northeast side of lake.
Fish found: Rainbow trout
Regulations: Electric motors only

Hobson Lake
Waypoint: 53° 34′ 50″ N, 124° 43′ 51.9″ W
Location: 41.5 miles (67 km) southwest of
    Vanderhoof
Elevation: 2,972 ft (906 m)
Surface area: 179 ac (72 ha)
Max. depth: 23 ft (7 m)
Stocking data: Rainbow trout
Directions: Drive south from Vanderhoof on Kenney
    Dam Road, then east on 500 Road. The unmarked
    turnoff to the lake is 5 miles (8 km). This one-lane,
    1.8-mile (3-km) access road can be difficult to
    navigate in wet weather, and is best tackled in fair
    weather.
Facilities: Hobson Lake Recreation Site—small site
    with cartop boat launch.
Fish found: Rainbow trout
Regulations: No fishing November 1–April 30.
    Rainbow trout released, bait ban and single
    barbless hook

Nulki Lake
Waypoint: 53° 54′ 35″ N, 124° 8′ 15″ W
Location: Southwest of Vanderhoof
Elevation: 2,359 ft (719 m)
Surface area: 4,092 ac (1,656 ha)
Max. depth: 14 ft (4 m)
Stocking data: Rainbow trout
Directions: 18 km (11 mi) from Vanderhoof, drive
    south on Kenny Dam Road for about 14 km (8.6
    mi). Pass through Stoney Creek Reserve and
    continue for another 3–4 km (1.8–2.4 mi) (still
    on Keny Dam Road) to the Saik'uz Park and
    Campground. Turn left into the campground.
Facilities: Full facilities including a good boat launch,
    camping, cabins, potlatch house/community hall.
Fish found: Rainbow trout
Regulations: Regional regulations

Tachick Lake
Waypoint: 53° 57′ 22″ N, 124° 11′ 27″ W
Location: Southwest of Vanderhoof
Elevation: 2,336 ft (712 m)
Surface area: 5,456 ac (2,208 ha)
Max depth: 25 ft (7.6 m)
Stocking data: Rainbow trout
Directions: 9 miles (15 km) southwest of Vanderhoof,
   accessed from Yellowhead Highway (#16) off
   Kenny Dam Road to both lakes.
Facilities: Saik'uz Park camping and cabin rentals
   with boat launch
Fish found: Rainbow trout
Regulations: No fishing west of a line between signs
   on Nulki lakeshore near the mouth of Corkscrew
   Creek from April 1–May 31 to protect spawning
   trout.

Kathie & Eskers Park Lakes
Waypoint: 54° 4′ 20.7″ N, 123° 10′ 17.9″ W
Location: Five lakes in Eskers Provincial Park
   northwest of Prince George
Elevation: 2,490 ft (759 m)
Surface area: 110 ac (45 ha)
Max depth: 56 ft (17 m)
Stocking data: Rainbow trout
Directions: Located 20 miles (32 km) northwest of
   Prince George, west on Highway 97 onto Chief
   Lake Road. Continue west for 17 miles (27 km)
   to the west end of Ness Lake and turn north onto
   Ness Lake Road North. Follow this road for 600
   yards (550 m) to the park entrance. Access to
   Kathie Lake is by foot along a developed trail.
Facilities: Eskers Provincial Park day-use
Fish found: Rainbow and brook trout
Regulations: Regional regulations

Region 7B: The Peace

Quality Lake
Waypoint: 55° 5′ 55″ N, 120° 53′ 37″ W
Location: 4.3 miles (7 km) east of Tumbler Ridge
Elevation: 3,464 ft (1,056 m)
Surface area: 49 ac (20 ha)
Max. depth: 20 ft (6.2 m)
Stocking data: Rainbow trout
Directions: From Tumbler Ridge, head north on the
   Heritage Highway (#52) for 3 miles (5 km), then
   turn south (right) onto Bearhole Lake Forest Road
   and follow it 4.3 miles (7 km) to lake.
Facilities: None; campsite at Timber Ridge
Fish found: Rainbow trout
Regulations: Regional regulations

Charlie Lake
Waypoint: 56° 20′ 0″ N, 120° 59′ 16″ W
Location: North of Fort St. John
Elevation: 2,276 ft (694 m)
Surface area: 4,415 ac (1,787 ha)
Max. depth: 49 ft (15 m)
Stocking data: Rainbow and brook trout
Directions: 6.8 miles (11 km) north of Fort St. John at
   the junction of the Alaska Highway and
   Highway 29.
Facilities: Charlie Lake and Beatton Provincial Parks
   are both open year round and have boat launches.
   Camping and boat launch at Rotary RV Park and a
   fourth boat launch on the west shore, across from
   the Mile 54 turnoff.
Fish found: Rainbow and brook trout, northern pike,
   burbot, walleye and perch
Regulations: Walleye daily and possession quota= 3;
   northern pike daily and possession quota = 3

Inga Lake
Waypoint: 56° 36′ 54″ N, 121° 38′ 23″ W
Location: North of Fort St. John
Elevation: 2,729 ft (832 m)
Surface area: 140 ac (57 ha)
Max. depth: 14 ft (4.3 m)
Stocking data: Rainbow trout

Directions: 45.3 miles (73 km) north of Fort St. John on Alaska Highway off 170 Road, 1.8 miles (3 km) to recreation site.

Facilities: Inga Lake Recreation Site—boat launch

Fish found: Rainbow trout

Regulations: Engine power restriction (10 hp).

Sundance Lakes

Waypoint: 55° 50′3″N, 121° 43′2″W

Location: East of Chetwynd

Elevation: 2,335 ft (720 m)

Surface area: 24 ac (9.9 ha)

Max. depth: 16 ft (5 m)

Stocking data: Rainbow trout—only the west lake, on the south side of the highway, is stocked.

Directions: 9 miles (15 km) east of Chetwynd alongside Highway 97.

Facilities: None

Fish found: Rainbow and brook trout

Regulations: Regional regulations

Swan Lake

Waypoint: 55° 31′3″N, 120° 0′55″W

Location: Southeast Dawson Creek

Elevation: 2,382 ft (726 m)

Surface area: 1,483 ac (600 ha)

Max. depth: 10 ft (3 m)

Stocking data: None

Directions: From Dawson Creek travel south towards Alberta on Highway 2 for 22 miles (35 km) then follow signs to Swan Lake Provincial Park.

Facilities: Swan Lake Provincial Park, 42 units with boat launch.

Fish found: Walleye, northern pike and perch

Regulations: Walleye release

Boulder Lake

Waypoint: 55° 20′14″N, 121° 38′47″W

Location: 25 miles (40 km) south of Chetwynd

Elevation: 4,091 ft (1,247 m)

Surface area: 37 ac (15 ha)

Max. depth: 54 ft (17 m)

Stocking data: Rainbow trout

Directions: Access from Chetwynd via Highway 29 for 20 miles (33 km), then turn right and travel 4 miles (6.5 km) on the gravel Dome Petroleum Road. Take the right fork in the road and travel 7 miles (11 km) to the H2S sour gas pipeline. Extreme right and travel down pipeline another 300 m to the old Forest Service Recreation site. Short hike to lake.

Facilities: None. The nearest formal camping is at Gwillim Lake, south of the turnoff to this lake on Highway 29.

Fish found: Rainbow trout

Regulations: No powered boats

Region 8: The Okanagan

Echo Lake

Waypoint: 118° 42′00″W, 50° 12′00″N
Location: 31 miles (50 km) east of Vernon
Elevation: 2,755 ft (840 m)
Surface area: 173 ac (70 ha)
Max. depth: 164 ft (50 m)
Stocking data: Rainbow trout
Directions: Located 31 miles (50 km) east of Vernon, take Highway 6 to Lumby. Turn right onto Creighton Valley Road and follow road for 13.6 miles (22 km) to the lake.
Facilities: Echo Lake Provincial Park
Fish found: Rainbow and lake trout
Regulations: Regional regulations

Hidden Lake

Waypoint: 50° 34′00″N, 118° 49′00″W
Location: East of Enderby
Elevation: 2,099 ft (640 m)
Surface area: 328 ac (133 ha)
Max. depth: 151 ft (46 m)
Stocking data: Rainbow trout
Directions: 15 miles (24 km) east of Enderby off Highway 97A, proceed for 5.5 miles (9 km), then turn south on Hidden Shuswap Road. This road will take you to a fork, take the left fork and proceed to lake.
Facilities: 46 campsite units in three separate Foresty Recreation sites. All have boat launches.
Fish found: Rainbow trout
Regulations: No towing

Mabel Lake

Waypoint: 50° 35′00″N, 118° 44′00″W
Location: 19 miles (30 km) east of Enderby
Elevation: 1,296 ft (395 m)
Surface area: 14,795 ac (5,990 ha)
Max. depth: 655.6 ft (200 m)
Stocking data: None
Directions: Located northeast of the city of Vernon. From Vernon travel north on Highway 97A to the community of Enderby. Turn east (right) and follow the road about 23 miles (37 km) to King

Fisher on Mabel Lake. Another route to the lake is from Vernon east to Lumby and then, from Lumby travel northeast to Shuswap Falls. At Shuswap Falls, turn north and follow the road to Mabel. This way will give you access to the east side of the lake, and its beautiful provincial park.
Facilities: Mabel Lake Provincial Park
Fish found: Rainbow and lake trout, Dolly Varden, whitefish and kokanee
Regulations: Dolly Varden daily quota = 1 (none under 20 inches/50 cm), single barbless hook, also check regional regulations

Kalamalka Lake

Waypoint: 119° 32′37″N, 50° 17′16″W
Location: Between Oyama and Vernon
Elevation: 1,283 ft (391 m)
Surface area: 8,073 ac (3,267 ha)
Max. depth: 485 ft (148 m)
Stocking data: In 1978; 30,000 lake trout
Directions: Along Highway 97 between Oyama and Vernon, Kekuli Bay Provincial Park is located 6.8 miles (11 km) south of Vernon.
Facilities: Kekuli Bay Provincial Park—concrete double land boat launch, Kaloya Regional Park, Coldstream Creek
Fish found: Rainbow and Lake trout, northern pike, whitefish and kokanee
Regulations: Kokanee daily quota = 2. Speed restriction or "No vessels" (as buoyed and signed), various locations

Jewel Lake

Waypoint: 49° 10′00″N, 118° 36′00″W
Location: 6 miles (10 km) northeast of Greenwood
Elevation: 3,724 ft (1,135 m)
Surface area: 185 ac (75 ha)
Max. depth: 78 ft (24 m)
Stocking data: Rainbow and brook trout
Directions: Between Grand Forks and Greenwood, turn north off Highway 3 and drive 7.4 miles (12 km) to the provincial park.
Facilities: Jewel Lake Provincial Park—cartop boat launch
Fish found: Rainbow and brook trout

Regulations: Engine power restriction 10 hp and
  speed restriction of 8 km/h

Yellow Lake

Waypoint: 119° 45′00″W, 49° 20′00″N
Location: 15.5 miles (25 km) southwest of Penticton
Elevation: 2,500 ft (762 m)
Surface area: 80 ac (32.5 ha)
Max. depth: 118 ft (36 m)
Stocking data: Rainbow and brook trout
Directions: The lake is 15.5 miles (25 km) from
  Penticton. Follow Highway 97 south past Kaleden
  and turn west onto Highway 3A, lake is on left side
  of highway.
Facilities: None
Fish found: Rainbow and brook trout
Regulations: Engine power restriction 10 hp

B. Washington State

West Side

Williams Lake

Waypoint: 47° 32′85″N , 117° 68′27″W
Location: 12 miles (19 km) southwest of Cheney
Elevation: 2,057 ft (627 m)
Surface area: 3 miles (5 km) long
Max. depth: Unknown
Stocking data: Rainbow trout
Directions: From I-90 Westbound, take exit 270
  (Cheney/Four Lakes). This puts you on Highway
  904, which goes through Cheney. Drive through
  the town of Cheney and make a left onto Cheney
  Plaza Road across from the Mitchell's Harvest
  Foods grocery store. Go about 12 miles (19 km)
  and make a right onto Williams Lake Road.
  Located 12 miles (19 km) southwest of Cheney via
  Mullinex Road.
Facilities: Public access on the northwest shore and
  several resorts
Fish found: Rainbow and cutthroat trout
Regulations: Statewide minimum size/daily limit

Louise Lake

Waypoint: 46° 77′01″N, 121° 71′76″W
Location: A reservoir in Whatcom Country
Elevation: 364 ft (111 m)
Surface area: 39 ac (15.7 ha)
Max. depth: Unknown
Stocking data: None
Directions: Located 1.5 miles (2.5 km) southeast of
  Stillicum.
Facilities: Shore fishing
Fish found: Rainbow trout, largemouth and rock bass,
  perch and brown bullhead
Regulations: Statewide minimum size/daily limit

Silver Lake

Waypoint: 48° 58′05″N, 122° 04′24″W
Location: In Whatcom Country
Elevation: 794 ft (242 m)
Surface area: 173 ac (70 ha)
Max. depth: Unknown
Stocking data: Rainbow trout
Directions: 3 miles (5 km) north of Maple Falls
Fish found: Rainbow, cutthroat, brook trout and
  crappie
Facilities: Boat launch
Regulations: Statewide minimum size/daily limit

Wapato Lake

Waypoint: 47° 55′29″N, 120° 10′40″W
Location: Lake is a dam in Chelan Country
Elevation: 1,240 ft (378 m)
Surface area: 28 ac (11.3 ha)
Max. depth: Unknown
Stocking data: Rainbow trout
Directions: This small juveniles-only lake is located in
  Wapato Park in southeast Tacoma; bank access is
  through the park.
Facilities: Boat launch, dock
Fish found: Rainbow trout and brown bullhead
  catfish
Regulations: Statewide minimum size/daily limit.
  Catch and release. Selective gear rules.

Tarboo Lake

Waypoint: 47° 51′07″W, 122° 51′07″W

Location: In Jefferson Country

Elevation: 627 ft (191 m)

Surface area: 24 ac (9.7 ha)

Max. depth: Unknown

Stocking data: Rainbow trout

Directions: Tarboo Lake is at the end of Tarboo Lake Road, which is 2.5 miles (4 km) south on Chimacum Center Road, off Highway 104. There are 13 lakes in a 10-mile (16-km) radius here in Jefferson County.

Fish found: Rainbow and cutthroat

Facilities: Boat launch

Regulations: Statewide minimum size/daily limit; up to 2 over 14 inches (35 cm) may be retained. Internal combustion motors prohibited.

East Side

Badger Lake

Waypoint: 47° 21′01″N, 117° 37′50″W

Location: In Spokane Country

Elevation: 2,178 ft (664 m)

Surface area: 244 ac (98.7 ha)

Max. depth: Unknown

Stocking data: Rainbow trout

Directions: A mayfly hatch later in the season usually provides great dry fly-fishing. Located 12 miles (19 km) south of Cheney on the Cheney–Plaza Road, Badger has resorts and public access (where launching might be limited to cartopped boats due to low water). Disabled accessibility level 1.

Fish found: Rainbow trout

Facilities: Boat launch

Regulations: Statewide minimum size/daily limit

Appendix 2

Fishing Checklists

The following checklists will help to make your fishing excursions both safe and enjoyable:

If you do not need the item, leave the box empty.

If you require more than one item write in how many after the box.

As you pick your items, mark.

As you load, mark.

Your load is double-checked and you are ready to go.

Gear Fishing

☐ __Weights
☐ __Bait
☐ __ Bobbers/floats

Miscellaneous:

☐ __ Map
☐ __ Compass
☐ __ Insect repellent
☐ __ Binoculars
☐ __ Knife
☐ __ Multi tool
☐ __ Disposable lighter
☐ __ Waterproof matches
☐ __ Camera
☐ __ Log/diary/pen/pencil in plastic bag
☐ __ Freshwater fishing license
☐ __ Plastic bag
☐ __ Flashlight/lantern
☐ __ Fluids
☐ __ Nutrition
☐ __ Waders
☐ __ Wading belt
☐ __ Wading boots
☐ __ Wading boot guards
☐ __ Wading staff

Safety and comfort:

☐ __ Hat
☐ __ Vest
☐ __ Rain gear
☐ __ Polarized sunglasses/sunglasses
☐ __ Protective case for sunglasses
☐ __ Sunscreen
☐ __ Lip balm
☐ __ Band Aids
☐ __ Small bottle of Aspirin, Advil or Tylenol
☐ __ Antacid
☐ __ Small towel
☐ __ Toilet paper in zip-lock bag

Fly Fishing

☐ __Saltwater fishing license
☐ __Freshwater fishing license
☐ __ Kit bag/tackle box
☐ __ Two rods (8.5 to 9.5 foot / 2.5 to 3 m)
☐ __ Two reels (simple drag system)
☐ __ Spare reel spools
☐ __ Floating lines
☐ __ Sinking lines
☐ __ Clear intermediate:
☐ __ Type 2
☐ __ Type 6
☐ __ Sink tip

Leaders and Tippet:
☐ __ Butt material for leaders
☐ __ Tapered leader:
☐ __ 9 feet (3 m): 3x
☐ __ 9 feet (3 m): 4x
☐ __ 9 feet (3 m): 5x
☐ __ 15 feet (5 m): 3x
☐ __ 15 feet (5 m): 4x
☐ __ 15 feet (5 m): 5x
☐ __Tippet
☐ __Flurocarbon:
☐ __ 3x
☐ __ 4x
☐ __ 5x

Fly Boxes (small, organized by food groups):
☐ __ Chironomid
☐ __ Caddis and mayflies
☐ __ Leeches
☐ __ Dragon and damsels
☐ __ Scuds: boatman and backswimmers
☐ __ Dry flies
☐ __ Salmon

Accessories
☐ __ Thermometer on a string
☐ __ Nippers (2), one on a retractor
☐ __ Hemostats or forceps

Indicators:
☐ __ Corkies
☐ __ Yarn
☐ __ Split shot
☐ __ Barrel swivels:
☐ __   #12
☐ __   #16
☐ __ Floatant
☐ __ Creel/burlap
☐ __ Scale
☐ __ Measuring tape/ruler
☐ __ Dip net
☐ __ Net
☐ __ Hook file/stone
☐ __ Needle-nose pliers
☐ __ Finger guard
☐ __ Line cleaner

Miscellaneous:
☐ __ Map
☐ __ Compass
☐ __ Insect repellent
☐ __ Binoculars
☐ __ Knife
☐ __ Multi tool
☐ __ Disposable lighter
☐ __Waterproof matches
☐ __ Camera
☐ __ Log/diary/pen/pencil in
     plastic bag
☐ __ Plastic bag
☐ __ Flashlight/lantern
☐ __ Fluids
☐ __ Nutrition
☐ __ Waders
☐ __ Wading belt
☐ __ Wading boots
☐ __ Wading boot guards
☐ __ Wading staff

Safety and comfort:
☐ __ Hat
☐ __ Vest
☐ __ Rain gear
☐ __ Polarized sunglasses/
     sunglasses
☐ __ Protective case for
     sunglasses
☐ __ Sunscreen
☐ __ Lip balm
☐ __ Band Aids
☐ __ Small bottle of Aspirin,
     Advil or Tylenol
☐ __ Antacid
☐ __ Small towel
☐ __ Toilet paper in zip-lock bag

Ice Fishing

- ☐ __ Fishing license
- ☐ __ Fishing rod (2)
- ☐ __ Reel: spinning reel
- ☐ __ Tip-ups
- ☐ __ Line: 4-8-lb test
- ☐ __ Bait
- ☐ __ 5-gallon (20-L) bucket
- ☐ __ Needle-nose pliers
- ☐ __ Fingernail clippers
- ☐ __ Ice scoop

- ☐ __ Jigs, spoons or hooks
- ☐ __ Ice auger
- ☐ __ Sled
- ☐ __ Hook sharpener
- ☐ __ Small shovel
- ☐ __ Ice picks
- ☐ __ Fishfinder
- ☐ __ Spud bar
- ☐ __ Ice cleats

Miscellaneous:
- ☐ __ Map
- ☐ __ Compass
- ☐ __ Insect repellent
- ☐ __ Binoculars
- ☐ __ Knife
- ☐ __ Multi tool
- ☐ __ Disposable lighter
- ☐ __ Waterproof matches
- ☐ __ Camera
- ☐ __ Log/diary/pen/pencil in plastic bag
- ☐ __ Plastic bag
- ☐ __ Flashlight/lantern
- ☐ __ Fluids
- ☐ __ Nutrition
- ☐ __ Waders
- ☐ __ Wading belt
- ☐ __ Wading boots
- ☐ __ Wading boot guards
- ☐ __ Wading staff

Safety and comfort:
- ☐ __ Ice-fishing shelter
- ☐ __ Heater
- ☐ __ Hand/foot warmers
- ☐ __ Hat
- ☐ __ Vest
- ☐ __ Rain gear
- ☐ __ Polarized sunglasses/sunglasses
- ☐ __ Protective case for sunglasses
- ☐ __ Sunscreen
- ☐ __ Lip balm
- ☐ __ Band Aids
- ☐ __ Small bottle of Aspirin, Advil or Tylenol
- ☐ __ Antacid
- ☐ __ Small towel
- ☐ __ Toilet paper in zip-lock bag

To download a printer-friendly version of these checklists, go to
http://www.harbourpublishing.com/title/UltimateTroutFishing

Index